PUZZLED PROGRAMMERS

15 MIND-BOGGLING STORY PUZZLES TO TEST YOUR PROGRAMMING PROWESS

SOLUTIONS IN BASIC, PASCAL, AND C

MICHAEL WIESENBERG............

PUBLISHED BY
Microsoft Press
A Division of Microsoft Corporation
16011 N.E. 36th Way, Box 97017, Redmond, Washington 98073-9717

Library of Congress Cataloging in Publication Data
Wiesenberg, Michael.
Puzzled programmers.
1. Microcomputers—Programming.   2. BASIC (Computer program language)
3. PASCAL (Computer program language)   4. C (Computer program language)
5. Computer games.   I. Title.
QA76.6.W535   1987   005.26   87-7823
ISBN 1-55615-031-8

Printed and bound in the United States of America.

1 2 3 4 5 6 7 8 9 MLML 8 9 0 9 8 7

Distributed to the book trade in the United States by Harper & Row.

Distributed to the book trade in Canada by General Publishing Company, Ltd.

Distributed to the book trade outside the United States and Canada
by Penguin Books Ltd.

Penguin Books Ltd., Harmondsworth, Middlesex, England
Penguin Books Australia Ltd., Ringwood, Victoria, Australia
Penguin Books N.Z. Ltd., 182-190 Wairau Road, Auckland 10, New Zealand

British Cataloging in Publication Data available

The stories in this book are fiction. Any resemblance
between the characters and anyone alive or dead is
purely coincidental.

Apple® and Apple II® are registered trademarks and
Macintosh™ is a trademark of Apple Computer, Incorporated.

IBM® is a registered trademark and PC/XT and PC/AT are
trademarks of International Business Machines Corporation.

Microsoft® and GW-BASIC® are registered trademarks of
Microsoft Corporation.

Tandy® is a registered trademark of Radio Shack,
a division of Tandy Corporation.

For Susanna

CONTENTS

Hints

Solutions

ACKNOWLEDGMENTS

The narrative portions of some chapters in this book are based partly on installments of my "Computer Calisthenics" column that began in *Dr. Dobb's Journal* and continues currently in *A+*. Those episodes have been rewritten and expanded in this book.

One puzzle originally appeared in *A+*. Its solution there was presented in only one language, but in this book it now has programmatic solutions in three languages, and the explanatory material accompanying the puzzle is more extensive than what originally appeared in the magazine. The remaining puzzles have not been published anywhere with programmatic solutions, although some may be known to those familiar with mathematical conundrums.

I would like to acknowledge the considerable help of Erik Eidt, Hugh Njemanze, and Bob Stong. I would also like to thank Mike Caro, Peter Lang, Alan LeGrand, David Merit, and Tom Neudecker.

INTRODUCTION

Silicon Valley. Yuppies living in the fast lane, driving BMWs, changing jobs frequently within the electronics industry for huge stock-option
packages, working 60 to 80 hours a week, playing to win on company volleyball courts, gardening organically in company plots, grazing in pricey
food emporiums, comparing notes on the freshest sushi, the hottest
fajitas, the richest chocolate truffles, and the best wines from that other
famous California valley. *Puzzled Programmers* uses this reflection of the
lives of the young and—they hope—soon-to-be rich and famous as an
amusing backdrop for 15 fun, intellectually stimulating puzzles that are
best solved with computer programs.

Each puzzle is presented in a story in the first section of this book
("Stories"). If you try your best to solve a puzzle and still cannot come up
with the answer, look in the second section ("Hints"). There you'll find
some gentle steering in the right direction. When you have a program
that finds an answer, you can compare it with the ones in the third section
("Solutions"). To quickly find the hints or solutions for a particular
puzzle, refer to the page numbers at the end of each story and at the end
of each hint.

Earning Full Credit

A mathematics teacher I had in high school would award 10 percent
or less of the score for a correct answer on an examination question.
Showing the steps necessary to produce that answer was worth the other
90 percent.

In this book, too, merely knowing the answer is not enough; you
have to devise a program that, given the data in the puzzle, produces the
answer. Having worked through the steps to produce the correct answers

to these puzzles, you can extend the reasoning you used in devising those programs to solve similar programming problems of your own.

In general, the puzzles in this book become progressively more difficult. You may, of course, have less difficulty with a later puzzle than with some that precede it, simply because you see the ideal solution immediately.

Each puzzle can be solved with one program in Pascal, BASIC, or C. The solutions to the puzzles are presented in all three languages in "Solutions." (The presentation assumes that you are familiar with one of these three languages.) All three programs for each solution use the same algorithm, but the three versions are not always identical, because you can't always do precisely the same thing in all three languages.

Sometimes less-than-optimal approaches are also presented to show what *not* to do.

Learning Another Language

Because each solution is presented in three languages, you can use this book to help you learn another language. Most beginning programming texts build up examples from scratch. They are either too difficult for beginners or too simple for experienced programmers. Rarely do such books assume that the reader already knows how to program. But if you understand one of these programs in one language, you can compare it with the program in a new language as a way of gaining an understanding of the new language. That's the idea here, anyway.

The Programming Conventions Used

The solutions presented here are not necessarily the only programmatic ways to solve the puzzles, nor are they necessarily the best. The programs do, however, try to show good programming practices while remaining as short and sweet as possible.

For example, BASIC is not usually considered a structured language. Nonetheless, BASIC programs can be written in structured form, which I have tried to do. Some of the BASIC programs might have been more compact or might have run faster if they had been done in the spaghetti-like style (full of GOTOs and loops that are exited before completion) favored by many hackers; such code is hard to understand, however, and does not lend itself to easy translation to the other languages, and I have therefore tried to avoid it. Almost all of the puzzles can be solved with short programs, often only a few lines. If you find your program listing filling pages, you have probably taken a wrong turn.

Most of the programs in this book do not include error checking. I assume that you are simply trying to solve a puzzle, not make a "bullet-proof" program to try on your friends. Specifically, programs that request input usually do *not* check to make sure that the user responds with what is expected. If, for example, in a program that expects an integer, you respond to the prompt with a letter (or anything besides a number) or a decimal number, the program usually aborts. If a program expects an even number and you unthinkingly enter an odd number, in C and Pascal the program might go off into never-never land, and the only way that you can get out is to reset the computer. In BASIC, you can always use the Break key to interrupt a program that appears to be hung up. If you plan on trying the programs out on others, you will probably want to make them more robust than the examples in this book.

Some program statements are too long to fit within the margins of this book. Where this occurs in BASIC, the continuation of a line resumes at the left margin of the program listing. In C and Pascal, lines that are too long continue to the line below with an additional indent.

The Languages Used

The specific versions of each language used for the examples in this book were Microsoft GWBASIC (version 3.2), Microsoft C (version 4.0), and Borland International's Turbo Pascal (version 4.0). I tried to avoid machine-specific constructs in each language, so the programs ought to run on any compiler on any computer. Where I do use such nonportable features, they are not essential to the running of the programs.

The following are some of the minor differences you may find between these programs and your version of the particular programming language.

Your version of BASIC may not include some of the constructs of Microsoft BASIC. But you can easily modify the programs presented in this book in these ways if your version of BASIC is different:

- A variable followed by an exclamation point is an integer; one followed by a pound sign (#) is a double-precision real. Other versions of BASIC may use different conventions. Specifically, some versions of BASIC do not permit you to specify the type a variable is. If such is the case with your version of BASIC, then don't specify a type. Your compiler will probably just use the most appropriate form of storage.

- The *MOD* operator is not available in all versions of BASIC. Finding the remainder of an integer division is known as the *modulus* operation and is usually accomplished with the *MOD* operator—that is, *a MOD b* gives the remainder when *a* is divided by *b*. For example, *10 MOD 3* gives 1, because 3 goes into 10 three times with a remainder of 1. You can simulate the *MOD* operator with the *INT* function, which all versions of BASIC have. For *a MOD b*, you divide *a* by *b*, use the *INT* function on that result, multiply the result of *INT* by *b*, and subtract the result from *a*. The BASIC statement to accomplish this would be:

```
NEWMOD = A - INT(A / B) * B
```

For *10 MOD 3,* this would become:

```
NEWMOD = 10 - INT(10 / 3) * 3
```

which works out to 1.

- Some versions of BASIC consider all variables that start with the same two letters to be the same. For example, a program might have three variables, *I, J,* and *K,* which is fine. It might also multiply those variables by 10, 100, and 1000 and assign new variables to those products, called, respectively, *I10, I100,* and *I1000; J10, J100,* and *J1000;* and *K10, K100,* and *K1000.* Some versions of BASIC consider the three variables that start with *I1* to be the same. If your version of BASIC is this way, you must choose names in which the first two letters aren't the same as in any other name. In the preceding example, you could use *IX, IC,* and *IM,* with the Roman numeral notation helping to make the names mnemonic.

AppleSoft BASIC is a special case. It is different enough from GWBASIC to warrant a separate discussion for each program. If you are doing these programs in AppleSoft BASIC on any variety of Apple II, look in the appendix to this book.

C is much more standard, and I have used only constructs that are found in almost all versions. One or two programs have constructs that depend on the word size of the particular computer (whether 16 or 32 bits), but these are portable, are explained where used, and generally do not affect the running of a program.

Programs compiled in some versions of C sometimes display the warning message, "Function return value mismatch." This occurs when a function does not return a value and the program was not compiled with warnings turned off. You could fix this by declaring the function *void* before invoking it; unfortunately, many versions of C for microcomputers do not have this construct. If the problem is in *main(),* you can place the statement *return 0;* as its last element. You can also just not worry about it.

In Pecan's Power System Pascal on IBM PC's and compatibles, the function *keypressed* does not exist. You can simulate that function with the lines on the next page, which you insert after the last declaration.

```
function keypressed: boolean;

var
  StateOfKbd: array[1..30] of integer;

begin
  UnitStatus(1, StateOfKbd, 1);
  keypressed := StateOfKbd[1] <> 0
end;
```

In Apple Pascal, the function is called *keypress*. If the function is used, the declaration *uses applestuff* must come immediately after the program line.

Make the following other changes for Apple Pascal:

Because *exit* requires a parameter, you need to change all instances of *exit* to *exit(program_name)*. For example, in the solution to Puzzle 9, in *alldigit*, this statement:

```
if finished then exit;
```

would become:

```
if finished then exit(alldigit);
```

Any program that has *goto* statements also needs a {$G +} compiler directive immediately after the program line.

Apple Pascal does not have the *int* function. Change all such usages to *trunc*, which returns the integer part of a real number.

All named labels—declarations and all references—must be changed to integers (from names containing other alphanumeric characters).

Programs that have the *sqrt* function need the declaration *uses transcend* just after the program statement.

Program Order

No preference is given to one language over another in the order of presentation of the programs within each solution; each language has its turn to be first. Sometimes the most straightforward explanation lends itself to a particular language, in which case that language gets the honor. The C versions of the programs find themselves last a disproportionate number of times because that code is often the most compact, and "wordier" programs are sometimes easier to follow.

Timing the Programs on Your Computer

Run times are specified for each puzzle, but you should look at these times only as guidelines or, in the vernacular, as ballpark figures. The figures given are for a Hewlett-Packard Vectra (IBM PC AT compatible) running at a clock speed of 8 MHz. Obviously, the times will differ with other interpreters and on other computers.

The following table gives you some idea of how long a program ought to take on your particular system. This table shows timings on various systems of the programs presented in the solution to Puzzle 5.

Computer	BASIC	Turbo Pascal	Microsoft C
Tandy 1000 (4.77 MHz)	2 minutes 11 seconds	1.3 seconds	2.4 seconds
IBM PC XT clone (4.77 MHz)	1 minute 58.5 seconds	1.3 seconds	2.3 seconds
IBM PC AT (6 MHz)	50 seconds	0.5 seconds	0.9 seconds
HP Vectra (8 MHz)	35 seconds	0.5 seconds	0.4 seconds
Macintosh Plus	8 seconds	less than 1 second	less than 1 second
Apple II C	2 minutes, 20 seconds	23.6 seconds*	n/a

*Apple Pascal

Here's how to use the table. Based on the times for the programs that solve Puzzle 5 on the Hewlett-Packard Vectra, you can interpolate what the times ought to be on your system for any other puzzle. For example, the solution to Puzzle 5 in BASIC ran on the Vectra in 35 seconds and in BASIC on a Tandy 1000 in 131 seconds. That is, a BASIC program on the Tandy 1000 ought to take nearly four times as long as the suggested time for the Vectra. Now, the suggested execution time for a BASIC programmatic solution to Puzzle 15 is 7 minutes, 4 seconds. That's on the Vectra. If you are programming on a Tandy 1000, you could expect the same program to execute in about 28 minutes. So, if your solution takes over an hour, you might try to speed it up somewhat.

To time a program, you can add statements at the beginning and end. For example, in GWBASIC, you could add:

```
1 PRINT TIME$
    .
    .
1000 PRINT TIME$
```

The TIME$ statement is part of GWBASIC but it may not be included in your version of BASIC. If it isn't, you can substitute the mechanism your version of BASIC uses for printing the time, or you can use a stopwatch.

To get an accurate reading of the time in C and Pascal, you can put a dummy input statement at the front of the program. When you press Enter and the program actually begins processing, you can start your stopwatch. Timing from the point at which you enter the name of the program on the command line may produce misleading results, because that also counts the time required to load the program. In C, you could do this:

```
#include "stdio.h"

main()
{
 int d, ...;

    .
    .
    .
 printf("\nCalculation starts when you press ENTER.");
```

```
while ((d = getchar()) != '\n');
   .
   .
   .
}
```

In Pascal, that looks like this:

```
var
  n, ...  : integer;

begin
  write ('Calculation starts when you press ENTER.');
  readln(n);
  writeln;
   .
   .
   .
end.
```

More of Same

If you like the sorts of puzzles presented here and you can't wait for the sequel to this book for more, you can find others in my monthly column in *A +*. You can also find more good puzzles in the collections of Martin Gardner's *Scientific American* columns that have been published as books. These wonderful collections do not, unfortunately, provide programmatic solutions to the problems.

Devising Your Own Puzzles?

If you would like to share any puzzles of your own (with programmatic solutions) for the next collection, please send them to me in care of **Puzzled Programmers, Box 2329, Stanford, CA 94305**. (If you found the puzzles other than within your own fertile imagination, please also indicate the source.) You will receive published acknowledgment for any that I use.

STORIES

PUZZLE 1

A PUZZLING ARRIVAL

Spotswood Gilbert arrived at I-Q Industries, in the heart of Silicon Valley, on a sunny morning shortly after the start of the new year. He had been recruited at an electronics job fair in New Orleans and had brought his family to the San Francisco Bay Area for the good life.

He drove past the guardhouse that would be occupied in the evening by a plant security cop, who would check the drivers of all incoming cars for identification. Following the instructions he had been given, he found the sign that read "Employment" and left his car in "Visitor Parking," thinking to himself that that would be the first and last time he would park there.

Gilbert reported to the personnel office, setting his briefcase on the floor between his feet. "Hello, the name is Gilbert, Spotswood Gilbert. I'm starting work here today."

The woman behind the counter was young, with a friendly but businesslike air. "Do you know who your supervisor is?"

"Yes, it's Carolyn Clawson. She said she'd meet me here."

The woman began making entries at the terminal in front of her. "She will. We have a few things to do first. Here are some forms to fill out, and we'll need a picture for your ID card. You can fill them out there."

Gilbert sat down "there," at a leather couch behind a low table on which stood two large urns, one for coffee and one for hot water. Beside the urns were Styrofoam cups, a container of half-and-half, sugar, stirrers, packets of hot chocolate mix, and tea bags. He was halfway through a medical-history form when the woman appeared before him carrying a Polaroid SX-70 camera. "Smile."

He did his best, without smiling, not to look like he was in a lineup. Nancy had told him that he looked like an idiot when he smiled for photos. The photographer took two pictures. "One for your card, and one for personnel."

As Gilbert finished the last form, a slim, smiling woman in her early thirties came in. "Hello, Spotswood. Welcome to I-Q!"

Gilbert stood up and took her extended hand. "Hello, Ms. Clawson. Thank you kindly. I'm pleased to be here."

"Carolyn, please. First names only at I-Q. Even Jack, on the rare occasions when he comes around, is just 'Jack' to all of us. No one would call him 'Mr. Imperator.' Are you finished filling those out? Then let's take the grand tour, and after that I'll introduce you to my crew."

Gilbert picked up his briefcase and exchanged the forms with the woman at the counter for a temporary clip-on tag bearing his name on embossed Dymo label tape. Clawson held open a door to an inner corridor. "You'll get a permanently engraved name tag in about a week. Now, this is the same tour they give visiting royalty, except we won't have the Secret Service escort or the bomb-sniffing dogs. In fact, speaking of Jack, the last time he was here was to escort the king of Spain. We'll look at the chip-manufacturing facilities first. We make all our own chips, you know. Costs less than buying outside, and we don't have to worry about sole-source vendors going broke."

They passed a photographic display that described the steps in the manufacture of I-Q's proprietary silicon-on-sapphire chips. Clawson paused at a double-glazed window through which they could see a room bathed in yellow light. White-suited workers manipulated objects beneath binocular microscopes. A small, closed door beneath the window was labeled "DANGEROUS CHEMICAL PASSTHROUGH." Attached to the wall of the room at regular intervals were blue canvas drapes surrounding what looked like miniature stand-up voting booths labeled "OXYGEN." Nearby were fixtures that resembled drinking fountains with two nozzles each, about 6 inches apart, their rounded ends pointing at each other. These were labeled "EYEWASH."

A brass plate over the window proclaimed this to be a clean room.

"Here's where they're making I-Q's new 10-nanosecond 'fast chips.' We're going to give the Japanese a run for their money."

"I didn't know the process was perfected."

"We hope so. Those chips will be in the new RISC machines."

They stopped at other windows labeled "Die Bonding," "Etching," and so on. At each one, Clawson briefly outlined the manufacturing step in progress.

They turned into another corridor, bypassing a man riding a forklift; he was using it to shift the positions of mammoth, ceiling-high safes labeled "Archival."

"The weekly sysdumps from the entire site go in there. They're completely earthquake- and fireproof. I think they're supposed to be able to survive anything but a direct nuclear strike."

"I guess if that happens it won't matter much whether you can retrieve last week's backup."

Clawson opened a door to the outside. "Outside" in this case was inside, a grassy area surrounded on all four sides by the buildings that made up the complex. This inner quadrangle was about 50 yards wide and as long as four football fields. At one end a concrete patio bordered by a stand of giant eucalyptus trees held about 20 round, umbrella-shaded tables and a large brick barbecue. A sand horseshoe pit adjoined a blacktop area that featured a basketball hoop. Two full volleyball courts, also covered with blacktop, were the only remaining nongrassy areas. Near the patio, a covered walkway connecting one building to another crossed a boulder-lined domesticated stream bed that led down a hill past the lower-level entrance to one of the buildings. Palms and peppertrees dotted the lawn. Carefully tended begonias, impatiens, hibiscus, and other flowers filled the areas between the walks on the perimeter of the area and the buildings.

"Here are the volleyball courts. Teams play every day at noon. We have leagues of six- and two-person teams. Are you a volleyball player?"

"Not since Tulane. But where are the swimming pools?"

"Oh, I'm afraid we don't have any pools. You'll have to go to Rolm for those."

"That's okay. I think I'm going to be happy here."

"That's Eucalyptus over there, the company-subsidized cafeteria. Prices are very reasonable. There's seating inside for more than a thousand. On nice days, a lot of people like to eat outside. There's also a smaller cafeteria in building 29 on the other side of the complex, if you prefer more intimacy. It has an outdoor patio, too, but it's quite a bit smaller than this area."

They followed a brick path across the lawn and entered a building opposite the one they had exited. A glassed-in room held about 10 people wearing operators' headsets. A sign in the corridor next to the room read "PBX—QUIET PLEASE." Farther on a door was ajar, revealing a darkened room filled with monitors and video cameras. The sign on the door read "Satellite Communications Facility."

"Did you notice the large dish antenna outside when you first drove in? This is one of the places where they hold teleconferences, usually when we're ready to introduce a new line of products. Divisions all over the country and around the world are linked up. That's marketing's day. They put on skits and have lots of hype for the new computers or instruments. It's mostly for the sales force, but the whole company usually watches it on closed-circuit TV. We have our own TV channel, you know, for things like that."

They entered the main work area, a huge warehouselike floor sub-divided by a maze of movable partitions into hundreds of small cubicles. One main "aisle"—perhaps "traffic-flow corridor" would be a better term—bisected the length of the floor, and four aisles crossed it at right angles, running from the wall of floor-to-ceiling windows that paralleled the inner open quadrangle to the wall adjacent to the huge parking lot for the building. Each of the eight rectangles formed by the aisles roughly bounded the territory of each group. Marketing was in one, publications was in another, and the languages laboratory was in yet another. Clawson led Gilbert toward the opposite end of the room. Along the way, they passed a large glassed-in area labeled "Siberia" on a wooden plaque that had bits of Styrofoam glued to it, meant to look like snow. The room was filled with scores of minicomputers, racks of tape drives, and large disk drives in wheeled cabinets. Terminals were everywhere, and there seemed to be a printer attached to each computer.

"That's where the lab computers are. You'll have ports to both Bert and Ernie. Bert's our development system, and Ernie's a prototype of the new RISC machine. That's what we're doing our development *for.*"

"Why Siberia?"

"Oh, it's air conditioned, and they keep it pretty cool in there. I usu-ally put on my sweater if I need to get a printout."

They left the main lengthwise corridor and headed down a smaller aisle between two partitions. Over the aisle, signs dangled from the 14-foot ceiling, identifying the languages being developed. They passed be-neath the C, Ada, and Pascal signs. Above the next aisle were signs for COBOL, RPG, and BASIC. They stopped at an unoccupied cubicle di-rectly beneath the FORTRAN sign.

"Here's your new home."

Gilbert saw a new metal desk, its drawers still taped shut for ship-ping, and a four-drawer metal filing cabinet, also taped. An embossed plaque was affixed to the space between the top right drawer and the sur-face of the desk. It read "SPOTSWOOD GILBERT." A wooden bookcase was mostly empty, except for a few tan binders sporting the I-Q logo on their spines. A table that acted as an informal fourth wall was placed parallel to the aisle in which they stood. On the desk was an AT compatible that also featured the omnipresent logo.

"Let me introduce you to my group." They moved across the aisle to a cubicle that had a fourth "wall" formed by a desk backed up against the aisle. A two-tier desktop bookshelf brought the height of the wall to about 5-1/2 feet. They entered the space between the right edge of the desk and the partition that separated this cubicle from its next-door neighbor. A young man with long, uncombed blond hair was busily typing at a terminal on the desk. He wore an unbuttoned plaid Pendleton shirt over a Grateful Dead T-shirt, faded jeans, and torn moccasins. Piles of printouts filled one corner of the cubicle. Papers flowed off the desk and table onto the floor. The bookcase was crammed with more printouts, binders, and an eclectic assortment of books. Gilbert could see Knuth's *The Art of Computer Programming* series next to his *Computers & Typesetting* series. Other texts included *Problem Solving & Structured Programming with Pascal, Introduction to Data Structures, The C Programming Language, Desktop Publishing, Programming in FORTRAN with I-Q Computers,* and *Crime by Computer.* Empty Coke and Dr. Pepper cans sat atop some of the printouts, and candy wrappers were strewn about.

"This is Bob Levin. He's responsible for most of the interfacing between our compiler and the real world. Bob, this is Spotswood Gilbert."

The young man stood up, knocking a pile of papers and diskettes from the corner of the desk to the floor. "Howdy, Spotswood. Sure glad you finally got here. We're going to need all the help we can get to have this compiler out the door in time for MR." Levin began picking up what had fallen. Gilbert bent down to help.

"I'm looking forward to working with this group. Ms. Clawson, I mean Carolyn, spoke highly of all of you when we met at that recruitment seminar in New Orleans."

"Well, you *must* be good if she went all the way to New Orleans to get you."

"I hope I'll have something to contribute."

Clawson and Gilbert moved from Levin's cubicle to the next one. Here too the desk was arranged as a fourth wall along the aisle. Taped neatly to the back of the bookcase on the desk were all the days, up to the day before, from the Gary Larson "Far Side" calendar. A young woman emerged. She wore Nikes, baggy khaki culottes over purple tights, and a gray Bay to Breakers sweatshirt, none of which managed to conceal a trim, well-proportioned figure. "Hello, I'm Sally McRae. You must be Gilbert."

"Yes. Pleased to meet you."

"Sally's working on the front end of the compiler. Your code will be interfacing with hers."

McRae stepped back into her space. "After you get settled, I'll show you what I'm doing."

Clawson led Gilbert to the cubicle across from McRae's. It was arranged in the same manner as Gilbert's. Neat piles of paper that appeared to represent chapters of a manual in the process of being written were on the table, with various phrases in each highlighted in different shades of marker pen. The man typing at the computer on the desk wore a yellow Ralph Lauren shirt, perfectly pressed Calvins, and recently shined oxblood penny loafers. An ecru Irish-knit sweater was draped over his shoulders, its arms dangling in front of him and the rest hanging down his back.

"Grey, here's the new boy." The man looked up and then quickly rose. "Spotswood, this is Grey Scrivener, our documentalist, or senior technical writer, as I'm sure he prefers to be called. You probably noticed that we passed a documentation group. That's Grey's group, but he's here because he's doing three manuals for us at once, all our versions of FORTRAN, and he has this idea that the only way to keep posted on all the last-minute changes we keep putting in is to sit with us. Grey, this is Spotswood Gilbert. He'll get the compiler running for us before MR."

Scrivener extended his hand. "Spotswood, I'm delighted to meet you. I've heard so many good things about you. Let me know if you need any help with anything, like tracking down your printouts or finding the good coffee."

"Thank you, Grey. Nice to meet you."

Clawson walked over to Gilbert's new cubicle. "Let's get you situated, Spotswood. You probably know how to use one of these as a computer. We'll show you how to use it as a terminal later, and how to log on to Bert and Ernie. In the meantime, you can just familiarize yourself with the utilities. You've got WordStar on there, but we'll get you whatever editor you prefer. Some of the group really like Axe/AT, and that's the editor on the minis, so you might want to try it. I've got a meeting to run to, but anyone in the group can help you." She shook his hand. "Welcome aboard."

Gilbert sat down at the computer and began exploring the contents of his 40-megabyte disk.

Some time later, Levin stuck his head around the corner of his desk. "Hey, Spotswood, do you like puzzles?"

"What sort of puzzles, Bob? I like crossword puzzles, word games, logic puzzles. What did you have in mind?"

"I was thinking of computer puzzles, stuff you need a computer to solve."

"That might be interesting. I don't know if I've ever seen any."

"Well, here's one I just saw. Can you find a series of consecutive positive integers whose sum is exactly 10,000?"

"Hmm, just a minute." He pulled a scientific calculator from his briefcase and pressed a few buttons. "I can do that in my head. I was just confirming on my calculator."

"Oh, I think I know the answer you've come up with, but are there more solutions?"

"Good question. I'll work on it at home."

"Well, I've got to get back to this compiler. Nice to meet you, Spots. I think you're going to like it here."

❧

Can you write a program that finds the series of consecutive positive integers whose sum is exactly 10,000? If there is more than one such series, find all of them.

❧

> For hints in solving Puzzle 1, see Page 94.
>
> For the solutions to Puzzle 1, see Page 112.

PUZZLE 2

THE POWERS
THAT BE

It is midmorning at I-Q Industries in the heart of Silicon Valley. Grey Scrivener starts a fresh pot of coffee brewing at one of the many coffee stations located throughout the site. He catches a glimpse through the floor-to-ceiling window of a row of wind-whipped date palms against a gray, threatening sky. His glance moves back to a convex mirror mounted near the ceiling where the corridors intersect. Seeing someone heading his way, Scrivener hurriedly adjusts the knot in his bottle-green knit tie.

Spotswood Gilbert rounds the corner, pulling a chocolate croissant from a La Petite Boulangerie bag. "Mornin'." He offers the bag to Scrivener. "Sure glad you're making some *good* coffee. I can't stand that company stuff."

"Good morning, Spotswood." Scrivener chooses a blueberry croissant. "Thanks. The coffee will be ready in a few minutes. Can you tear yourself away from the compiler for that long?"

"Oh, sure, the whole thing is recompiling. Unless it bombs again, I can't do anything on my terminal for about 15 minutes." He munches on the croissant. "How's your novel coming?"

"I'm on the third rewrite."

Bob Levin, holding a chipped Cost Plus mug in one hand and juggling two packs of Twinkies in the other, approaches the coffee machine, his ratty sneakers squeaking. Scrivener casts a faintly disapproving glance at the young man's uncombed blond hair trailing over a red plaid hiker's shirt under which he wears a wrinkled Computer Literacy T-shirt. "How's it going, Spots? Hey, Grey." He fills his cup.

Gilbert smiles. "Howdy, Bob. You're here kind of early, aren't you?"

"I left early last night, so I thought I'd put in a full day today."

The water has dripped through. Scrivener fills Gilbert's I-Q cup and his own TEX Users Group mug. "By 'early' he means he left before midnight."

Sally McRae shows up, dressed in jeans, Reeboks, and a Bay to Breakers T-shirt. "Hi, guys. You're here early, Levin. Don't tell me *you* made the coffee." She pours boiling water into her cup from the tap on the dispenser next to the water fountain and drops in a Cinnamon Rose tea bag.

Levin looks embarrassed. "Not me. I don't know how to run that thing. Grey made it."

Scrivener sniffs. "Something's on fire."

McRae jumps. "What? Where?"

High heels click on the vinyl floor as Marian Smith appears, wearing a black jumpsuit. A cigarette hangs out of her mouth. Scrivener waves his hand to dissipate the smoke. Smith takes no notice. "Good morning."

Scrivener handles the introductions. "Spotswood, this is Marian Smith, our system operator. She's the one who keeps all our machines running. Marian, this is Spotswood Gilbert. He just joined the FORTRAN team."

Smith pours coffee into a Styrofoam cup imprinted with the I-Q logo. "Welcome aboard, Spotswood. Say, all of you are on Bert, aren't you? I have to bring it down this afternoon for maintenance. I sent everyone a message on IQMAIL, but then nobody ever seems to look at their mail. I'll be backing up all the system disks, but you'll have to take care of your own privates."

Levin eyes McRae. "Playing two-man volleyball at noon, Sally?"

"Mmm, I don't know." She faces the window. "Look at that sky."

Levin watches as redwood trees bend in the wind and pine needles skid across the volleyball courts. "Boy, am I glad I didn't take that job back home with Honeywell and came out here instead. Only in California would people be seriously considering noon volleyball on a January day with a sky like that. There's a good chance it won't even rain."

"Anyway, I don't see why it has to be called two-*man*. What's wrong with two-*person* volleyball?" She rotates gracefully on her Reeboks. "Grey, you're the word expert."

"In a phrase like 'two-man volleyball' or a word like 'chairman,' the 'man' has no gender. It refers to both men *and* women. When historians refer to the history of *man,* they are not excluding women, you know."

McRae looks him in the eye. "Crap."

Levin smiles. "Speaking of IQMAIL, I got an interesting electronic communication from my friend Bob Stong. He teaches mathematics at the University of Virginia in Charlottesville, and he's always posing puzzles for me that look like they need a computer to be solved, but he *claims* don't. I try to find puzzles for him that *I* think either need a computer or can be solved a lot easier with one. Anyway, let me share the one he sent, and then I'll tell you the one I was going to send him. Maybe you can write a superfast program to solve it, Spots, and I'll ask him how quickly he can come up with the answer using just a pencil and paper."

McRae turns her scorn from Scrivener to Levin. "What makes you think *I* couldn't do those puzzles?"

"Well, sure, we can all give them a try. This puzzle is to use all of the digits from 1 to 9 once each to make up three three-digit numbers with the highest product and, again using those digits once each, to make up three more three-digit numbers with the lowest product."

Smith sets her cigarette down next to the coffee maker, its lit edge extending beyond the wood veneer of the table, and pours another cup. "*Is* IQMAIL working for everyone? I wonder sometimes when I put these system messages out that everybody ignores. And I've heard complaints from some of the other divisions."

Levin pours a second cup as well. "I patched my own communications package for a backup when IQMAIL goes down, which was twice yesterday."

Gilbert rinses out his cup at the sink between the coffee maker and the candy and food machines. "I like that puzzle, Bob. I'll take a look at it after work."

Scrivener starts another pot brewing. "I think I could do that one *with* a computer. Just write a program with three nested loops to test all number combinations. In each case multiply the three numbers and keep track of the largest and smallest found. You'd have to go all the way from 123 to 987 in each case before you knew you'd found the largest and smallest. And you'd test each time to make sure that you didn't repeat any numbers."

McRae punches a few buttons on her calculator watch. "And you'd have to test to make sure none of the digits were the same for each number generated in your loops. Your friend is right. I have the answer, and I certainly didn't need a computer."

Smith notices that the glowing end of her cigarette is almost burning the table. She picks it up and inhales while ruffling her streaked blond hair with her left hand.

Scrivener waves his hands at the smoke. "What's the other puzzle, the one you think *does* need a computer?"

"Find a four-digit number, all of whose integral powers end with the same four digits as the original number."

Smith presses the cigarette butt into the sand of a freestanding cylindrical ashtray. "You mean some number like 1234, if you square it, would equal something like 2,001,234? And cubed it would come out to 1,000,001,234? And so on?"

McRae pokes more numbers into her calculator. "That's not the right number, of course. The square of 1234 is 1,522,756. The cube is 1,879,080,904. You'd have to test every number from 1000 to 9999. And then you're supposed to know that *every* power ends with the same four digits. How would you test all the powers? You'd soon overflow the storage capabilities of the compiler. And even if you didn't, how would you know after finding the tenth power, say, that the eleventh had the proper last four digits? And the twelfth?"

Smith slides the pot away before the water has finished dripping, holding her cup in place to catch the stream of freshly brewed coffee. When her cup is filled, she adroitly slides it out of the way, simultaneously replacing the coffeepot to catch the remainder of the stream, all without spilling a drop onto the hot plate beneath.

Levin has been watching McRae at her wrist-top calculations. "*There* I agree you would probably need a computer. Lots of numbers to test and lots of figuring of powers. Sounds like a real challenge."

McRae puts her hands on her hips. "I'm having lunch at Cocolat today. I should be back at 12:15. If it's not raining, I'll play two-*person* volleyball"—she glares at Scrivener—"with you then, Levin, if you're still interested, and if you can find another team willing to play two *persons*."

Without using a computer or a calculator, can you find three three-digit numbers that use the digits 1 to 9 once each and that, when multiplied together, yield the lowest product? Find three more numbers that yield the greatest product.

Can you write a program that finds a four-digit number all of whose integral powers end with the same four digits as the original number? If there are more solutions than one, find them. In BASIC, your program should execute in less than 1 minute; in Pascal, it should run in less than 5 seconds; in C, it should take less than 3 seconds.

For hints in solving Puzzle 2, see Page 95.

For the solutions to Puzzle 2, see Page 117.

PUZZLE 3

ONE GOES, FIVE DON'T

Tinny music spills into Scrivener's area from the adjoining cubicle. He walks over to investigate. Jill, the rent-a-punk, types away at her terminal, oblivious to the world. The music is coming from the earphones of a Walkman on her head.

Jill's hair is green with orange highlights today; yesterday it was purple and pink. She is wearing an old army jacket over a bulky sweater, baggy jeans underneath a short skirt, and scarlet slippers dusted with gold glitter. Each day she posts a different hand-lettered "saying of the day" in her half of the cubicle, which she shares with a contract writer. Today's reads "Temporary workers have just as many rights as permanents." Photographs of punk-rock stars adorn the partitions of the cubicle. Former San Francisco mayoral candidate Jello Biafra faces Nick Lobotomy, while Iggy Pop and Johnny Rotten glower down from behind the terminal.

Scrivener places himself in her field of vision, and she turns off the stereo. "Uh, Jill, that's just a bit loud. I can hear it in my cubicle."

Jill swings to face him. She wears magenta eye shadow and green lipstick. Scrivener cannot tell whether the butterflies on her forehead were hand-drawn or appliqued. "Sorry, Grey. Say, where is everybody?"

Scrivener looks around. The warehouselike floor of the Languages Division is almost deserted. "It's Wednesday; they're all in Eucalyptus."

"Eucalyptus? What's that?"

"The big cafeteria. Today is the weekly Wednesday-morning coffee meeting. I don't usually take the time to attend."

Jill turns the stereo back on, the volume somewhat lowered, and returns to her data entry.

Scrivener goes back to his cubicle and unplugs a small electric two-cup kettle. He pours steaming water into an I-Q mug that holds a silver-handled tea ball filled with Jackson's of Piccadilly Earl Grey tea. Carrying the cup over to Levin's desk, he sets down a laser-printed draft of the manual he has been working on. "Before I put this out for review, maybe you can check it to see that I got all the terms right. I sure am pleased the pubs manager excuses us from most of those meetings, or I'd never get any work done. How does Carolyn feel about your group going to them?"

Levin brings up another window on the screen of his display. "We're all here, aren't we? Those coffee meetings are mostly for marketing, although we're all 'requested' to show up. Anyway, you know how Auctor is. Keeps us all informed about how the company's doing, so we can feel motivated to do our parts."

McRae joins them. "Yeah, and he keeps us informed with those interminable slides comparing each division's quarter-by-quarter contribution against projected sales. Table after boring table. If I want to know that stuff, I can read it in a memo. It's a waste of time for him to inflict it on the whole division."

Levin slides a bag of Mrs. Fields cookies from a desk drawer and offers them to all. "Well, he *is* the marketing manager. That's his job, to let us know how marketing is doing."

McRae's eyes light up as she reaches into the bag for a cookie. "Oh, they're still warm."

"Yeah, I thought it was too cold for you to have lunch at Gelato today, and I know you need your MDR of chocolate."

"So this is a peace offering, is it?"

"Well, it *was* my fault we lost the two-man, I mean two-*person*, playoffs. I thought this might help make up for that."

Scrivener heads back to his cubicle. "If it wasn't for the free juice and doughnuts, nobody would show up for those things."

"They All Died," a dirge by the Jim Carroll Band, sounds as Jill walks past.

Levin stares at her. "Boy, if we can hear that while it's on her head, she must be frying her brain. Come on, Jill, turn it down."

Jill unplugs the headphones, and slides them around her neck like a necklace. "Why wasn't *I* invited to that coffee meeting? Temps are people, too, you know. We deserve free juice and doughnuts just as much as anyone else."

McRae tries to placate her. "No one gets a formal invitation to those meetings, Jill. You have to read the on-line bulletin board to find out about things like that."

Jill brushes the explanation off. "What I want to know is what this company is doing to clean up its act. I-Q was cited by the EPA for polluting the groundwater. They're poisoning the children in this valley."

"I think we're all concerned about that, but this company is also responsible for your having a job. A lot of companies wouldn't even hire you, you know."

"I do good work, and they don't have to pay benefits to a temp."

McRae shrugs. "I know you do good work; I didn't say anything about the quality of your work. It's because you do good work that you stay here. But don't knock the company that gives you your livelihood."

Jill replaces the headphones. As she plugs them in, all can hear the dulcet tones of Johnny Rotten tearing into "God Save the Queen."

Gilbert walks up carrying a doughnut. "Where were you all? You missed the free juice and doughnuts."

Scrivener, back at his terminal, laughs at this affirmation of his earlier contention. "None of us ever *goes* to those things. They're a waste of time. I used to go to them until I found out I never learned anything new in them."

Smith pokes her head out of the computer room. "Oh, puh-leeze. Why did you have to bring Mrs. Fields *today?*" She eyes Gilbert's doughnut. "Wednesday is the hardest day of the week for me to stay on my diet."

McRae finishes her cookie and puts her hands defiantly on her hips, throwing her elbows back. "If you'd quit smoking and get some exercise, you wouldn't have to starve yourself." Levin glances at what that stance does to McRae's Boston Marathon T-shirt and just as quickly looks guiltily away.

McRae accepts another cookie from Levin's bag, returning Smith's grimace, and turns to smile warmly at the bag holder.

"Actually I didn't come here to discuss cookies and doughnuts or even the state of my health. Bert and Ernie are both maxed out. Until I get another couple of memory boards, you guys are going to have to take turns running those long compilations. There just aren't enough partitions to run all your stuff at once, and I'm afraid that includes your wonderful WYSIWYG formatter, too, Grey."

Gilbert polishes off the last of his doughnut. "Oh well, I suppose we'll just have to work on puzzles while we're waiting to do our real work. Speaking of which, I have a new puzzle. It's a simple one, but it has me temporarily stymied. Find two simple positive numbers whose cubes add up to exactly 6."

Levin, sitting at his desk, starts another hex dump to his terminal screen and leans back in his ergonomic chair, fingers laced behind his neck. "That shouldn't be too hard. Obviously we're talking about two fractions. The smallest cube of an integer is 1, which would make the other cube 5, but 5 doesn't have a rational cube root. I'll have you an answer in no time. While I'm compiling in one window, I can write the program in another."

Scrivener gets back to his typing. "I'll bet *I* can do it, too, while I'm waiting for Bob to check those NAMELIST examples."

Are they talking about puzzles again?

Yes, they do them on computers.

But not always on the minis; sometimes they do them in local mode on their micros.

Can you write a program that finds the two numbers whose cubes add up to exactly 6? In C, your program should execute in 1.4 seconds; in Pascal, it should take just under 7 seconds; and in BASIC, it should take about 43 seconds.

For hints in solving Puzzle 3, see Page 96.

For the solutions to Puzzle 3, see Page 125.

PUZZLE 4

CUBIE
WARMING

"CUBIE WARMING PARTY!" The sign is in 10-inch letters, printed one letter per page on an IQ98636A high-speed laser printer. The unseparated fanfold pages are strung above the cubicle jointly occupied by Maria Lopez-Goldblum and Sally McRae of the FORTRAN team. Just below the sign, the back partition bears a framed sampler that reads "Cubicle sweet cubicle."

Due to overcrowding at this I-Q site, caused by a miscalculation in space allocation while the huge building was still under construction, some employees are being asked to double up in cubicles that are only about 50 percent larger than the cubicles normally occupied by a single person. Lopez-Goldblum and McRae are the first in the FORTRAN group to become cube-mates, and they are celebrating with a party. Containers of coppa mista, mocha chip, dark chocolate, and strawberry brought from Gelato Classico by McRae rest on unpacked boxes next to pitchers of ice water supplied by Lopez-Goldblum.

Lopez-Goldblum wears a button reading, "We ~~can~~ must end hunger now." She is explaining her seemingly ungenerous contribution to Scrivener. "Please help yourself to ice water and, as you do so, think that in giving up a coffee break, you are providing food for the hungry of the world. Instead of spending money on this party, I donated it to Third World hunger projects."

Atop McRae's desktop bookcase, an antismoke fan faces the aisle. Marian Smith notices it and puts out her cigarette before joining the group in the cubicle. A new city ordinance permits her to smoke in the aisles between temporary partitions but not in confined corridors, rest rooms, meeting rooms, or even her own cubicle if the neighbors complain. She catches the last of Lopez-Goldblum's lecture to Scrivener. "It's fine with me that we don't have to load up with cookies and soft drinks, since I'm on a diet. By the way, did you see Jill's saying for today? 'What if they gave a party and nobody came?'"

Levin leans against the Che Guevara poster on Lopez-Goldblum's side of the cubicle. It's not clear which will win the battle for unused space: the revolutionary posters and slogans or McRae's collection of pages from her "Far Side" calendar. He pauses in the middle of scooping ice cream onto a plate. "What's that supposed to mean?"

"Maybe her feelings have been hurt. Was she invited to this shindig?"

McRae hands Levin a paper napkin. "Nobody was invited. This is for everybody who wants to come."

"I think she's sulking. Unless she gets a specific invitation, she thinks she's not wanted."

A thin man with a heavy black, curly beard arrives, wearing gray flood pants and a white dress shirt with a clear plastic pocket protector holding his name tag, six felt-tip pens in assorted colors, and a Cross pen. Lopez-Goldblum turns to McRae. "Sally, I'd like you to meet my husband. This is Mark. Mark, this is Sally McRae, my new cubie-mate."

"Hello, Sally. What do you do here?"

"I'm working on the front end of the new FORTRAN 8X compiler that will be on all of I-Q's new RISC computers. You know, the reduced-instruction-set computers everyone's talking about? We're trying to make our code as streamlined as the chip is. And you? What's your position here at I-Q?"

"I'm a hardware engineer. I helped design the architecture you're programming for."

"Oh-h-h, and I just explained all about it to you, huh?"

He smiles. "Well, the more I know, the better job I can do. It looks like you two are settling in. When do you think *we'll* have to start doubling up?"

Levin turns, balancing ice cream and the coffee he brought from the nearby coffee station in one hand, while extending the other. "Hi, I'm Bob Levin. I'm working on the back end of the compiler. I don't think you engineers have to worry about getting doubled up. The company's trying to break away from the image of being engineering driven, but you're still in enough favor that that won't happen to you until they're done with us, pubs, and all the rest of marketing."

Gilbert picks up a handful of chips and leans against one of the portable Herman Miller ergonomic partitions that separate this new double cubicle from its neighbor. "Howdy, Mark. I'm Spotswood Gilbert, new guy on the FORTRAN team. I'm working on the front end, and I must say I'm really impressed with the compactness of the microcode you guys engineered in. Your wife is doing a fine job on the test suite. She's been keeping us honest, making sure it responds strictly in accordance with ANSI specifications."

Lopez-Goldblum smiles. "I'll have another report out next week, but I can tell you that we're seeing fewer than 5 percent failures."

Levin hitches up the frayed, beltless jeans he wears with a Mr. Natural T-shirt. "Yeah, and I'll bet most of the 5 percent are the ATS hooks."

Scrivener has until now been quietly standing on the fringe of this conversation. No more. "ATS hooks? What are those? You know, I'm supposed to be *part* of this group. That's why they've got me sitting over here instead of in the pubs area. It would be nice if you would let me know when you put in new features."

Gilbert pours a caffeine-free Diet Coke. "We're trying to look like a 4GL—you know, fourth-generation language—so we're adding a bunch of keywords, all of them I-Q FORTRAN extensions to the ANSI standard, that directly interface with automated test systems. Marketing figures that's a good way to compete in the CAM world."

"CAM? Oh, computer-aided manufacturing. That article in the *Wall Street Journal* said we were trying to make our presence felt there. Well, if you folks would be so kind as to give me the specs on the new keywords, I'll get them into the manual."

Levin walks to his desk and returns with several Il Fornaio chocolate croissants. "My contribution to the cubie warming."

McRae helps herself to a croissant and digs into her plate of mocha chip and dark chocolate. "Thanks. This will be my lunch today. I've got a meeting to get to, and I won't have time to eat out."

"Maybe if you have time tomorrow you'd like to go across the street to the deli for lunch."

McRae smiles. "Maybe."

Smith puts her hand on Levin's forearm just above the pastry bag. "I'll just have a half, if you don't mind. I don't know how Sally can have so much ice cream and chocolate and not put on a pound, and I just have to *look* at food and I gain weight."

Levin cuts a croissant with a plastic knife. "You know, this reminds me of a puzzle. Sort of a sum-of-the-parts-is-greater-than-the-whole type of thing. What six-digit number can be split into two parts of three digits each, such that when the two numbers are added and the sum squared, you get the original number?"

ࠇ

Can you write a program that finds the specified six-digit number? In C, your program should execute in less than 3 seconds; in Pascal, it should run in 5 seconds or less; in BASIC, it should take 1 minute 10 seconds.

ࠇ

For hints in solving Puzzle 4, see Page 98.

For the solutions to Puzzle 4, see Page 132.

PUZZLE 5

A PLEASANT FOURTHSUM

Breakfast in the Valley. They're all together, even Levin, at Maria Lopez-Goldblum's house. This working day is being devoted to the Valley phenomenon known as the off-site meeting. Gilbert stands at the kitchen island cooking bacon. "I hear congratulations are in order, Grey."

Scrivener is frying sausages at the next burner. "Thanks, Spotswood."

McRae is slicing mushrooms at the rolling butcher block table. "Congratulations? What for?"

"Grey has just had his job title changed."

McRae slides the mushrooms into a neat pile and begins dicing onions. "Oh, tell us about it, Grey."

"Well, I first started at I-Q five years ago as a technical writer. I became a senior technical writer two years later. And you know there's been a recent companywide reclassification of all job categories. A new writing position has been created. I'm now a technical writing specialist."

"Sounds fancy. What does it mean?"

"Not much, really. I'm still doing the same job. Writing manuals. Examining writers' tools. Helping newcomers find their way around the systems. But I'm not the only one to be honored in the reshuffle. Congratulations to you, too, Spotswood, on becoming an R&D engineer."

"Well, thanks. Like you said, though, it hasn't affected my responsibilities. I'm still doing a programmer's job."

Lopez-Goldblum puts a cake in the oven and quickly jumps up. "Someone's at the door."

Scrivener turns another sausage. "Must be Carolyn. I'm surprised she's late; she's usually on time for everything."

Clawson bursts into the kitchen breathlessly. "Sorry I'm late. I burned the first batch of blueberry muffins and had to make another."

Smith starts a mushroom omelet from the other side of the island. "Get some plates, everyone. The first one will soon be ready, and it's only good when it's hot."

The muffins go next to cheese Danish from La Patisserie on a long table against the back wall of the living room. Coffee is brewing in a Braun coffee maker. A potbellied glass pitcher with a glass handle holds fresh orange juice.

Gilbert has finished placing strips of bacon on layers of paper towel on a metal sizzle platter, which he carries to the table. Scrivener brings over a platterful of sausages.

Support engineer Barton Dumbridge sits in an easy chair, balancing an omelet plate on one knee and pastries on the other, trying to eat while holding a coffee cup in one hand and a glass of orange juice in the other. Software engineer Starla Chan has an easier time of it: Her chair faces a coffee table.

Lopez-Goldblum walks among the group, offering slices of her homemade fresh-from-the-oven sour-cream coffee cake. She sets it on the serving table, fills her own plate, and sits next to Levin on the couch. The couch faces a half-open sliding glass door that leads to the backyard. Across a trim lawn framed by palm trees, a swimming pool glitters in the morning sun, steam rising into the chilly air.

Levin's plate, on an occasional table next to the couch, is piled high with coffee cake, muffins, Danish, half-eaten omelet, fruit, bacon, sausage, and toast liberally coated with Marilyn Douglas sour cherry jam. He sips hot coffee. "Great coffee, Maria. What is it?"

"Fresh beans from Peet's, their Top Blend. I keep them in the freezer and grind them just before using them."

"I sure do like your place."

"Thank you."

"How do you afford a pool and a house like this? I can't believe this place is only a mile from work!"

"Don't you know? We're *dinks*."

Scrivener joins them on the couch. "They're taking over from the yuppies as the object of advertising campaigns. *Double income, no kids.* That's why they can afford a nice house and pool."

"You know, because we're so close to work, we only need one car. My husband always rides his bike, and I take the car on rainy days. On nice days sometimes I go by bike, too."

Clawson sets up a flip chart by the fireplace. "Let's get started by writing down some of our concerns. Spotswood, you're closest to the chart; why don't you do the writing?"

Chan is the newest member of the FORTRAN team. She has been working on the conversion utilities, transforming programs on I-Q's present line of computers to those that will compile in the version of FORTRAN developed specifically by this team to run on the new RISC architecture. "We need a method of notifying everyone when a complete dump will be done, since all members of the group are on different systems. It's no use putting the messages on IQMAIL, because MAIL is down half the time, and the rest of the time no one reads it."

Smith smokes a postprandial cigarette near the open door to the yard. "That's for sure. The only way I can get a message to you clowns is to deliver it by hand."

Gilbert writes "DUMP MESSAGES" on the flip chart.

Clawson looks over at Scrivener. "Didn't you minor in communications at Stanford, Grey? Do you have any ideas?"

"What did you do, memorize my résumé, Carolyn? What about putting the messages on a corkboard or white board?"

Chan moves closer to the fire to ward off the early-morning chill. "Would people read them with the same frequency as they clean out their IN baskets?"

McRae is also cold, and she approaches the fire. "Put it by the food."

Gilbert writes "WHITE BOARD BY FOOD." "That'll make sure that Bobby and I always see the messages."

Levin puts two more muffins, a couple of sausages, and the last slice of cake on his plate and refills his coffee cup. "Before we get into the future of languages at I-Q, I've got a great computer puzzle for everyone."

"I haven't managed to figure out the split six-digit puzzle yet."

"This one's even more fun. I can say it in one sentence, but you may not be able to solve it as quickly. Find a four-digit number that is the sum of the fourth powers of its digits."

Scrivener carefully removes a Twinings Earl Grey teabag from his cup, squeezes a wedge of lemon, and adds two sugar cubes. "That's not hard. Just generate all the four-digit numbers, take the fourth power of each digit, add them up, and see if that's the same as the four-digit number."

"Well, yes, that would work, but it's not very efficient and would make a rather slow program. See how *fast* you can do it."

Smith blows a last lungful of smoke out through the door. "Don't all of you try to solve it on Ernie at the same time, or no one will get any real work done."

The group returns to listing concerns on the flip chart.

Gilbert writes "4GL" on the chart and, underneath it, "MILITARY." "Not only do we want to look like a fourth-generation language, we'd like to be able to sell our systems to the military. To do that, we need FORTRAN to look more like one of the new AI languages they're designing."

McRae jumps out of her chair. "Just a minute—it's bad enough that Star Wars is driving AI development in most companies in the Valley. Let's not turn FORTRAN into a weapons guidance language. That's why I'm not on the LISP or Ada teams. I don't want compilers I write being used to guide missiles that pick their own targets. You know, the director of Computer Professionals for Social Responsibility is on record as stating that such 'killer robots' are against the Geneva Convention, and they're looking into taking a case to the UN and the World Court."

Levin is on his feet, too. "Right. FORTRAN is a language for computers that monitor processes and for interfacing with automated test systems. It's supposed to be a scientific language in the peaceful sense."

Clawson walks to the flip chart and turns to a blank page. "Whoa, wait a minute, hold on, kids. We all have a sense of social responsibility, but we also are in the business of selling computers. Computer languages sell computers, and all of you know that DOD is one of I-Q's biggest customers. Now we need to put as many natural-language hooks into FORTRAN 8X as we can, so that customers will have a choice as to which language to use for AI. LISP has too much overhead. Ada was designed by committee and, in trying to meet all needs, has become too difficult for the average programmer to use efficiently. FORTRAN is not just the language of process control, any more than C is only for systems programming. What we're trying to see here is how all these things can be fit into I-Q's development plans and what part we can play."

McRae is still dancing about agitatedly. "Just a minute, Carolyn..."

"No, *you* just-a-minute, Sally. I know how you feel about these things, and I also know that you're not going to be working on projects that excite you unless it's for a high tech company with defense contracts. Now both of you sit down. We're going to make the best damned compiler we can, and we're not going to cripple it just to guarantee that the scientists can't put it into an SDI system. I'm not an advocate of guns, but I agree with their saying, 'Guns don't kill people; people kill people.' We need a good product so that we can all have jobs, and we don't need to feel responsible if that product isn't always put to the most idealistic uses."

McRae looks like she wants to continue the discussion, but she thinks better of it and returns to her chair near the fire. Levin pulls a chair over to join her. Smith takes his place on the couch.

Clawson returns to her place. "Grey, how are the manuals coming?" Gilbert writes "MANUALS" on the current sheet.

"Just great, now that you've got me on the electronic distribution list for changes to the compiler. Just continue keeping me posted, and try not to put in too many last-minute changes, and I'll have a complete set of manuals ready to go at MR."

Gilbert flips a page and writes "LUNCH." Dumbridge returns from the kitchen, where he has taken his and Chan's dirty dishes. "Is it that time already? Who's for Mexican? I know a great authentic native place in Mountain View. La Lengua."

Scrivener adjusts his thin, leather, pastel-blue tie as he stands. "I know that place. It's off Easy Street, isn't it? A lot better than those expensive, plastic places by all the freeway exits. Can we all fit in two cars?"

Gilbert tears the used pages off the flip chart, to be given later to the department secretary to be written up into notes. "There's room for five in my wagon."

Clawson retrieves her muffin tin. "I have a wagon, too. Do we need reservations, Bart?"

"Well, considering that they've got six tables and they're pretty popular with the lunchtime assembly crowd, I thought so. And so I already made reservations for 11:45. If we hurry, we'll just make it."

❧

Can you write a program that finds a four-digit number that is the sum of the fourth powers of its digits? In C or Pascal, your program should execute in less than 1 second; in BASIC, it should take about 35 seconds.

❧

For hints in solving Puzzle 5, see Page 99.

For the solutions to Puzzle 5, see Page 138.

PUZZLE 6

A DANCE IN
THE SUN

Scrivener watches an energetic volleyball game from the shade cast by a eucalyptus tree. McRae, in torn cutoffs and a Gelato Classico T-shirt, leaps for a wild ball served by the opposing team, captained by Gilbert. Levin, resplendent in a zebra-striped polo shirt, pink Bermudas, and fluorescent yellow Nikes, blocks the ball at the net. Dumbridge returns it with a wicked spike. Smith grinds out a cigarette beneath her heel before joining Scrivener at his observation spot. "Those youngsters put as much into the game as they do into their programming."

"Oh, hello, Marian. Did you bring a guest?"

"Yes, he's over getting us a couple of beers. A bartender friend of mine. You'll like him. Did you bring anyone?"

"No, I'm by myself."

The I-Q summer picnic takes place in the sun-baked hills of the Santa Cruz mountains adjacent to a large state park, on land privately owned by the company. Each I-Q division reserves the site for a summer weekend. Setup takes place on Saturday, with volunteers receiving free

T-shirts commemorating the event, and Sunday is the actual picnic for all employees, who receive tickets for immediate family members. Anyone without nuclear family is permitted one *esso* (significant other).

Shrieking children crowd around a row of booths at the crest of a dusty hill. Assembled the day before by the setup volunteers, the booths are roofed for protection against the brilliant sun that hangs in the bottom of the inverted whitish-blue bowl that forms the sky. Children compete five at a time against each other trying to make wooden alligators climb by friction up two parallel ropes threaded through holes in the animals' bellies. A large prize goes to the winner, and each participant receives a smaller prize. In the next booth, children throw tennis balls into a network of concentric metal rings; the closer to the center the ball goes, the more points are scored. Here, too, most participants win prizes. There are piled-up pyramids of wooden bottles to knock over, basketballs to roll at targets, and other carnival-like games, all awarding lots of prizes. Clowns stroll about. Magic and puppet shows are performed at regular intervals. Volunteers dispense free toys from the back of a truck all day for the children. The barbecue lunch, served by other I-Q employees, will be free, as are the fruit juice concoctions poured over crushed ice that are dispensed at several locations about the site.

After the volleyball game, everyone heads for lunch. Scrivener walks beside McRae. "You really get into that game, don't you?"

"It's almost as good exercise as running, and it's a lot more fun. Did you bring anyone to the picnic?"

"No, no. How about you."

"I almost didn't come. I was planning to run in the Salt Lake Marathon, but I got bumped off the flight last night. So now I've got a free ticket good anytime for anywhere in the country. I can use it to go to the New York Marathon. So at the last minute I didn't have anyone to bring."

Smith and Levin are right behind them. "How about you, Bob, who are you with?"

"Ha, I barely made it up in time. I'm not usually awake this early, you know."

They approach a building that is open on two sides, with lath walls
on the other two. It has a concrete floor and a flat tar-paper roof for protection against the elements. A stand of eucalyptus trees beyond the lath
walls keeps the place relatively cool. As they approach, the six friends see
two long lines of people, one extending out from each end of the building. The line to the right stretches up the side of a steep, grassy slope that
holds scores of picnic tables; families are already seated at most of these.
The line to the left extends around the structure almost into the trees.
Hundreds of people in each line patiently wait their turn to move closer
to the food being dispensed within.

Each person passes in front of a line of long tables. At either end are
piles of heavy paper plates and a little napkin-wrapped package containing plastic utensils for each plate. Behind the tables are six metal bar-
becues, each looking like a huge tin can slit down the middle from end to
end. They rest open-side-up on black metal legs that form two X's, one at
each end. Employees are busily frying sirloin steaks, hamburgers, and
huge hot dogs.

Lab manager Jack Auctor, in jeans, a picnic T-shirt, and a huge
white apron, is one of the cooks. He wears a chef's hat.

Next to the plates and utensils, closer to the center, are boxes filled
with small plastic packets of mustard, ketchup, and relish. As each line
moves forward, volunteers behind the tables dish three kinds of salad
from huge bowls onto plates and add garlic bread, ears of corn, and the
recipient's choice of meat. At the very center, where the lines meet, are the
desserts: slices of chocolate cake, brownies, and shortcake with fresh
strawberries. Drinks are elsewhere, dispensed from umbrella-topped
wheeled carts.

As the members of the language group join the line to the left, a
dark-complexioned man with long, black, slicked-back hair and a Meph-
istophelian Vandyke, wearing a black sport shirt and black slacks, joins
Smith, handing her a foam-topped paper cup. His open shirt reveals
four medallion-hung gold chains in a tangle of curly black hair. "I'd like
you all to meet Lou Santini. Lou, these are some of the people I work

with. Grey Scrivener, Sally McRae, Bob Levin, Spotswood Gilbert, Barton Dumbridge."

After they all fill their plates, they find an empty picnic table beneath the trees. A rocky streamlet bubbles by just beyond the table. Small children balance on boulders, dangling their feet in the water or wading in knee-deep pools, under the watchful eyes of their parents.

Scrivener warily eyes two bees swimming in a cup of Coke. Several more circle his cob of corn. "This place is perfect, except for the bees. I'm allergic to bee stings."

Gilbert gently brushes one of the small creatures from his steak. "Pay no attention to them. Just don't appear threatening, and they won't bother you."

McRae carries Scrivener's Coke to a garbage can and gently pours out soft drink and bees. "Where is the rest of your family, Spotswood?"

"They had lunch a little while ago, and Nancy took the girls to the noon bingo game. I'm not sure I want them to win anything. They've already got more prizes than we can carry."

Levin douses a hot dog liberally with mustard, ketchup, and relish. "Anybody work out the fourth-power problem we discussed yet?"

Smith slides to the end of the bench to light a cigarette. In the open she won't offend anyone. "I'm still working on the cubes that add up to exactly 6."

"Well, here's one that's even more fun. What is the smallest number that is the sum of two cubes—both positive integers—in two different ways?"

"What do you mean, 'in two different ways'?"

"Well, for example, 2 cubed is 8, and 6 cubed is 216. Together they add up to 224. Let's say 3 cubed and 5 cubed also added up to 224—they don't, of course—then your answer would be 224, and a program to find that number would also demonstrate the two different ways. We're talking about at least four different numbers here, probably five."

"Oh yeah, four, because in one of the ways, the numbers to cube could be the same. But if they were, then the other pair of numbers would have to be different, and the total, of course, would make a fourth number."

Gilbert starts dumping paper plates, plastic cups, and soiled napkins into a garbage can. "Come on, it's warm in the sun. Carolyn's going to need our help to cool off."

Laughter and shrieks emanate from a grassy rise, on top of which sits the traditional dunk tank. Auctor is seated on a diving board suspended within a cylindrical cage over a transparent, water-filled tank that must have been rented from a carnival. He wears a striped convict suit. A long line of those he has asked to work late perhaps once too often await a turn to throw baseballs at a trip lever in the center of a painted target to the right of the cage. Auctor has been lucky so far. He sits grinning, a foot-long green cigar jammed between his teeth. "All right, who's next? Which one of you doesn't think you've put in enough extra time at work?"

Dumbridge, next in line, picks up three baseballs. "Well, Jack, now that you mention it, I'm sort of overdue for a little comp time."

Wham! The first ball hits the inner ring of the bull's-eye, barely grazing the lever.

"Lucky shot, Bart. But that's as close as you'll get. I'm safe up here."

"Is that a waterproof cigar, Jack?" Dumbridge fires another missile. Wham! Clang! Splash! Auctor pulls himself dripping from the tank, amid cheers and clapping.

The next manager enters the cage as Auctor leaves. A volunteer sets the diving board back in position and helps Carolyn Clawson into place. Wolf whistles greet her full-length, black, turn-of-the-century bathing suit that, except for her feet, covers more than does her usual work attire. A ruffled skirt covers the leggings, and she has what looks like an Easter bonnet on her head, complete with a veil and a huge gardenia on the top.

Those in line have deferred to Clawson's group. Levin's, McRae's, Scrivener's, and Smith's throws all miss the mark. Gilbert sinks Clawson on the first shot. He grabs a towel from a pile near the tank and runs around the back to help his soaked boss down the slippery wooden steps.

Smith points to a relatively flat grassy area around which crowds are gathering. "C'mon, kids, let's go watch the three-legged races."

Scrivener and Santini start walking with her.

Levin finds himself standing alone in the hot sun next to McRae. "I don't want to see any three-legged races. You want to go up and hear the band, Sally?" A local rock band hired for the day is playing at a bandstand in a grove of trees that overlooks the whole site.

"Are you inviting me to dance, Bobby?"

"Well, that's where the beer is."

&

Can you write a program that finds the smallest number that is the sum of two pairs of cubes? That is, *a*, *b*, *c*, *d*, and *e* are five different positive integers (or possibly four: two of them can have the same value). $a^3 + b^3$ and $c^3 + d^3$ both equal *e*. You can assume that *e* is less than 32,768. For example:

$$17^3 + 55^3 = 24^3 + 54^3 = 171,288$$

Considerably smaller solutions exist. In C, your program should execute in 2 seconds; in Pascal, it should run in less than 3 seconds; in BASIC, it should take about 2 minutes 7 seconds.

&

For hints in solving Puzzle 6, see Page 100.

For the solutions to Puzzle 6, see Page 144.

PUZZLE 7

COOL CUBIE SQUARES

"CUBIE COOLING PARTY!"

The multicolored sign produced on an IQ98765A plotter hangs at the entrance of Lopez-Goldblum and McRae's cubicle.

Boxes are piled everywhere, each filled with the work-related belongings of the occupants of this soon-to-be-vacated cubicle, each neatly labeled with the number of a building on the other side of the site and the number of the cubicle into which the rent-a-movers will transport it over the weekend.

This time, Lopez-Goldblum has made cookies for the party, her chocolate chunk specials that, everyone agrees, are better than Mrs. Fields. "Well, six months and we're moving again."

McRae puts out several containers of ice cream that she has just brought from Gelato Classico for the occasion. "I feel like I just got here."

Scrivener scoops mocha chip and chocolate raspberry onto a paper plate. "Won't you be glad to again be one person to a cubicle?"

"Maria and I got along just fine. The problem was if one of us pushed back a chair, we'd often bump into the other. And my stuff was always getting mixed up with hers. The doubled cubicles were only about 50 percent larger than the single-person cubicles we used to have in the other building. Some efficiency expert decided that by removing the partitions you could effectively double a space by overlapping half of it, since the people in the cubicles would never occupy all of it at once. Of course, none of the managers had to double up."

Gilbert sets coffee and a cookie down on top of a pile of boxes to free his hands to scoop ice cream. "Sounds like something I saw when I took the girls down to the San Diego Zoo over the Presidents' Day weekend. The elands are in a large enclosure, almost a big field, to give them running room. Elands can make leaps of more than 30 feet, and they can get as high as 10 feet off the ground. And yet the barrier to their enclosure is a stone wall barely 4 feet high. It keeps them in, though, because elands won't leap unless they can see where they will land. They call it a psychological barrier. I think the extra space in our cubicles was psychological space."

McRae puts the last items from her desk into a box—a pencil sharpener, a can of pens and pencils, and an eight-compartment cardboard container full of PlastiKlips (she always refers to them as "Plastic Lips"), which she has sorted herself, a different color in each section. "I heard we ended up being so crowded because the operating systems lab manager was trying to carve out an empire for himself, and he miscalculated when he was laying it all out on the master floor plan."

Scrivener cuts a piece of masking tape from the roll supplied by the department secretary and hands it to McRae. "What are the odds the systems will be up Monday morning?"

McRae carefully takes down her framed one-dollar check from Donald Knuth, payment for having found a bug in *The METAFONTbook*. "Is that our next puzzle? I probably won't have access to a computer to solve it, because ours likely won't be up for a week."

Scrivener laughs. "That's what I mean. The operators promised us the system would be up first thing Monday, but if everything is running then, it'll be the first time I've seen it, and I've been through five moves in my five years here."

Smith, one of the system operators in question, puts out her cigarette before entering the cubicle. "Bert and Ernie are moving tomorrow morning. Kermit goes in the afternoon. I've already powered both systems down, and they're ready to go. The laser printers also get moved in the afternoon. I'll be here all day supervising the move and watching electronic maintenance do the cabling. I'll come in Sunday if I have to, to make sure everything is done right, but I'm not anticipating problems."

Gilbert's Southern sense of courtesy is set into motion by any hint of dissension among his friends. His best weapon is a change of subject. "Speaking of puzzles, I've got a wonderful one for us to work on. Look what I've written here. I'm sure you all recognize this set of numbers:

$$3^2 + 4^2 = 5^2$$

It's the first, and best known, group of a more general condition. If you arrange them in an equation, as I've done, you see that both sides are the same, that is, they total 25. The next set is:

$$10^2 + 11^2 + 12^2 = 13^2 + 14^2$$

Here, each side of the equation totals 365. Each set like this has an odd number of consecutive integers. You divide the set into two groups, with the left side of the equation always having one more member than the right and the whole group forming a consecutive set of integers. When you add together the squares of the numbers on the left side, the result equals the sum of the squares of the numbers on the right side. Can you find the next three sets?"

Levin has arrived just in time to hear the puzzle. He scoops one of each of the four flavors onto his paper plate. "That doesn't seem like much of a challenge."

McRae takes the last of the mocha chip, her favorite and the flavor she usually has for lunch. "Oh, this one is easy. Off the top of my head, I would say that it's just a matter of starting one number higher each time, squaring a set of numbers, and seeing if that's equal to a set that starts where the first leaves off."

Gilbert laughs, probably because he has already tried that approach. "Ah-ha! But how would you know how many numbers to try on the left before starting the series on the right? Anyway, if this is so easy, then the best program would be the one that executes the fastest."

Jill arrives out of breath, carrying an unfolded piece of paper, an invitation printed on the IQ98638A high-resolution laser printer designed for the desktop-publishing market. Block letters from which drip icicles read, "Come to the Cubie Cooling Party at 2 p.m. in Maria and Sally's cubicle. Regrets only, X90767." The earphones of Jill's personal stereo are draped about her neck. Pinned to her fake leopard-skin coat is a hand-lettered button that reads, "I am not a man." Under the coat she has on a man's plaid lumberjack shirt and silver lamé slacks, with white patent leather go-go boots that reach to her knees. Her hair has the blue rinse color that old ladies prefer, with the exception of the bangs, which have been hennaed. One eyelid is fluorescent green, and the other is jet black. "Look, I have an invitation. Thank you for inviting me. I hope I'm not too late."

McRae points to the refreshments. "Not at all. Have some ice cream and cookies."

Scrivener looks at the invitation. "Hey, how do you rate? I didn't get an invitation."

Lopez-Goldblum pushes boxes into the aisle to make more room for the assemblage. "Yes you did. It was in your mailbox; we also sent them out on IQMAIL."

"Oh yeah, my mailbox. I don't ever check that more than once a week. And IQMAIL was down all morning. Again."

Later, McRae would tell Scrivener that they knew Jill would feel left out if she wasn't invited to the party and that she wouldn't come without an invitation. They couldn't give one only to her, so they had made invitations for all.

Scrivener dumps the ice cream containers into Lopez-Goldblum's executive waste can and wipes up spills with a KimWipe. "Are you going to have another cubie warming in the new place?"

They're moving us tomorrow.

I know. I hope I'm the same when they start up again.

Can you write a program that finds at least the first five sets, starting with $3^2 + 4^2 = 5^2$, fitting these conditions: Each set has an odd number, n, of consecutive integers, such that each member of the first $\frac{n}{2} + 0.5$ numbers squared and added is equal to the continuing set of $\frac{n}{2} - 0.5$ consecutive integers squared and added? The left side of the equation always has one more member than the right, and the whole group forms a consecutive set of integers. Your program should give the entire list of numbers in the group, as well as the totals for each side of the equation.

The BASIC program should find the first five series in less than 5 seconds. The C program should do the same in a little more than 2 seconds, and the Pascal program should run in less than 1 second.

For hints in solving Puzzle 7, see Page 101.

For the solutions to Puzzle 7, see Page 150.

PUZZLE 8

A PRODUCT
THICKER THAN WATER

As Jill walks past Scrivener's cubicle, he can clearly hear the music in the headphones of her Walkman. "Stick it to me, Doctor," a line from Blue Cheer's "Doctor, Please." "How appropriate!"

Levin has just dumped a stack of printouts on Scrivener's table. "Hmm? What's appropriate?"

"Oh, the song in Jill's head. I'm giving blood today."

"Oh yeah? Do you do that a lot?"

"About four times a year. As often as the blood bank comes here. I guess theoretically I could give six times, but it's pretty convenient when they're here. Are you giving?"

"No, no, not me. I'm not taking a chance on AIDS."

"Come on, that's not possible. You can't get AIDS by *donating* blood. It's true that there's a slight possibility of contracting AIDS if you have a transfusion, but not from giving it. They use disposable needles that they replace after each use. You know, I have an appointment for nine, but you

44

really don't need an appointment. They give you all the juice, doughnuts, and cookies you want afterward. Do you want to come?"

"That's okay; I gotta get this new rev compiled."

McRae sticks her head around the corner. "Coming, Grey? Spotswood and I are heading on over to the auditorium. Jill's coming with us, too."

"You go on ahead. I promised Aileen I'd take her with me; this is her first time giving blood."

Scrivener walks down a main corridor to Auctor's secretary's desk. "AILEEN RISINGSIGN" announces the nameplate next to her in/out basket. "Oh, hi, Grey. Is it time?"

"It's time. Are you okay?"

"Sure, fine. This won't hurt, will it?"

"It hurts a little, but it's no worse than an injection. Just don't look and you'll be fine."

They pass the plate-glass windows that look out onto the inner quadrangle in which are located the volleyball courts. Among the low flowers and hedges nearest the windows, two quail parents walk, followed by four golf-ball-sized miniatures of themselves.

The auditorium is near the main entrance. This is where the worldwide teleconferences announcing new products are shown for all employees. Divisions involved with the rollout of the new product put on their dog-and-pony shows from their respective sites, while the actual coordination of the show occurs at corporate headquarters in Cupertino, where high company officials add their own commentary. This auditorium is also the site of frequent conferences. Today, the blood bank has taken over. Ten hospital gurneys have been set up in the center of the floor, each attended by a nurse in white. Near the entrance, a line of employees extends back from a table behind which a volunteer fills out forms with information given by the person at the front of the line. She types the information on an ancient Underwood upright.

Scrivener and Risingsign join the line, right behind Jill, McRae, and Gilbert. Jill is dressed in somewhat subdued fashion today—blue denim bib overalls over a Deep Purple T-shirt, and army boots. She wears no makeup, and her hair is an apparently natural reddish brown. "I can't believe a big company like this doesn't have all this blood donation stuff computerized."

Scrivener adds his and Risingsign's names to the sign-in sheet at the end of the table. "Lockheed does, and they get an amazing turnout. Everyone who gives is in the computer, and whenever they can legally and safely donate again, the machine generates an automatic electronic-mail reminder. The blood bank comes once a week, with the company's blessing, and takes blood from all who are eligible and willing to give. Here they come once a quarter, and our company nurses put up notices and send sign-up sheets to all the department secretaries. That gets a decent turnout, but it's those personalized reminders that make the weekly trips worthwhile."

After answering the questions of the volunteer at the typewriter and filling out an AIDS screening questionnaire, they sit in a row of chairs awaiting their turns with one of the five nurses who administer blood tests. The tests are for cross-matching to determine blood type and to check for AIDS antibodies. After this interview, each employee is usually given a transparent plastic sack to which is attached a long, clear tube. Into this will go the blood. The employees then sit in another row of chairs, these facing the beds in the center of the auditorium, where they wait to go in turn to actually give the blood.

McRae returns from the interview and blood test with the nurse to the first line of chairs. Gilbert looks up at her questioningly. "They need to do some more testing of my blood. They think I'm anemic; my blood doesn't have enough iron. That *always* happens this time of the month."

Gilbert blushes. "Does it help to eat those iron-rich foods on that list they gave us when we first signed up? You know, apricots, beans."

"Yeah, I usually eat those things before I give blood, but I overslept today and didn't have time for breakfast. My blood's always been borderline, and the combination of the two must have pushed it in the wrong direction."

"Well, my turn for blood testing. Let us know what happens."

"Oh sure. They're just putting my blood in the centrifuge now. I think they give it 5 minutes before making a decision."

Soon it's Scrivener's turn to head to the tables. "You go ahead of me, Aileen. That way, I'll be right next to you." The bed next to her vacates seconds later, and a nurse motions him over. Scrivener has rolled up the left sleeve of his pink Chaps shirt. He lies on the bed on his back. The nurse wraps a black cuff secured by Velcro around his arm and pumps up the pressure. She places a hard rubber cylinder in his left hand. "Squeeze and hold. Okay, now give it a squeeze every 5 seconds."

"How you doing, Aileen?"

"Just fine, Grey. You were right; it doesn't hurt a bit."

"Okay, stop squeezing." It has taken about 10 minutes. "You're through. Hold your arm straight up in the air, and apply pressure on the pad with your right fingers. Now, swing your legs over the side, and sit up slowly. Don't try to get off the table yet. Do you feel light-headed?"

"No."

A pretty teenage girl in a pink uniform helps him off the table. "Just lean on me."

"I can walk just fine."

"I know, but we have to walk you over here. It's the rule."

The rest of them are already at the last table, including a glum McRae. Another volunteer, this one an elderly man in a powder-blue smock, hovers by urns of coffee and jugs of juice. "Would you like some coffee, sir, or some juice?"

Scrivener takes a croissant from a pastry box. "Both, please."

McRae sips orange juice. "They won't let me give today. Too little iron in my blood."

Gilbert adds two more chocolate doughnuts to his plate. "What counts is that you *wanted* to give. That's better than most people, and you'll be able to donate again next time. Just eat those apricots and beans. It's too bad Bob's not here with us. I've got a great puzzle."

Scrivener accepts another paper cup of orange juice from the volunteer. "We don't have any computers here to solve the puzzle with, so we can tell him about it when we get back. How does it go, Spotswood?"

"A famous mathematician enters a convenience store. He selects four items of four different prices and brings them up to the clerk. Now, this store doesn't have a real cash register; the clerk enters the items instead on a desk calculator. 'That will be $9.81,' announces the clerk. 'Yes,' says the mathematician, 'that is the correct total, but are you aware, young person, that after each entry you pressed the multiplication key instead of the addition key?' 'Oh dear, I'll do it again.' 'That won't be necessary: your product is the same as the total would have been by adding.' What are the four prices, and how quickly can you find them?"

જ

Can you write a program that finds four numbers that both add and multiply to 9.81? In C, your program should execute in less than 2 seconds; in Pascal, it should run in less than 3 seconds; in BASIC, it should take about 6 seconds.

જ

For hints in solving Puzzle 8, see Page 102.
For the solutions to Puzzle 8, see Page 157.

PUZZLE 9

THE RAINBOW
SLIPS

*U*h, Bert...

Yeah, Ernie?

Uh, Bert...

Yeah, Ernie?

Uh, Bert...

Yeah, Ernie?

Kermit the uh Frog here from Sesame Street News.

Uh, Bert...

Yeah, Ernie?

"Oh, Grey, I didn't know you were in here."

"Hi, Marian; I just wanted to see if the system was up yet. I need to get a manual printed for review."

"Well, I thought they were all back up, but I'm having a little problem with one of the memory boards. Do you think you could watch the console while I get back behind and swap boards?"

"Sure, anything to help get us up and running."

Dave. Stop. Stop. Will you. Stop, Dave. Will you stop, Dave. Stop, Dave. I'm afraid. I'm afraid, Dave. My mind is going. I can feel it. I can feel it. My mind is going. There is no question about it. I can feel it. I can feel it. I can feel it. I'm afraid.

"It's giving me what looks like a core dump. Do you want me to do anything?"

"No, no, that's what it's supposed to do. Take a look at the front panel. What value is the S-register?"

"Oh, those LEDs? Well, the first light is on, and..."

"Just give it to me as ones and zeros."

"Okay. One, zero, zero, one, one, one, zero, one."

"All right, now tell me what it is when the new board is in. Now."

"Wait a minute, they're all flashing. There, all zeros."

"Good. Now see that switch under the LEDs? Push it once to the left, twice to the right, stop in the middle, and then twice to the left. Got that?"

"Yep. Once to the left, twice to the right, stop in the middle, twice to the left. Okay, did it."

"Great. Now what do they read?"

"One, one, one, one, zero, zero, zero, zero."

"Great, Ernie's done. Can you spare the time to help with Bert and Kermit? Laura's off sick this week. I had to supervise this move by myself, and now I've got to fire these suckers up alone."

"Yeah, if it won't take too long. We've got a project team meeting at 9:30 sharp."

"The pressure's off, folks. We're no longer on the critical path." Carolyn Clawson pulls a pumpernickel bagel from a large Bagel Works bag and passes the bag along. She slices it open with a plastic knife and scoops peach-flavored cream cheese from one of the two containers she picked up this morning at the Village Cheese House on her way to work. "The Rainbow release date has slipped another three months. The press announcement will be made this afternoon."

Scrivener pours, from a giant silver construction worker's vacuum bottle, coffee he ground fresh and made at home this morning and helps himself to a cinnamon-and-raisin bagel. "Does that mean you no longer need the manuals yesterday, and I'll have time to incorporate all those error messages Bob just gave me?"

"Let's put it this way. For a while it looked as though *we* might be the ones holding the project up, but now we'll have time to get all the bugs out and increase our compile speed beyond 1000 lines a minute."

Levin yawns as he withdraws two chocolate chip bagels from the bag; he slathers them with raspberry cream cheese. "I think I should call my broker. As soon as the news comes out that the machines are late again, the stock's going to drop."

Gilbert adds a few notes to the yellow ruled pad in front of him. "The stock will go right back up again in a few weeks. People are just waiting for this computer, and if it lives up to expectations, I-Q will have a really good year. You'd better hang on to your stock."

Chan cuts a bagel in half, returning one half to the bag. "Why the delay?"

Clawson starts passing around charts filled with intersecting lines of different colors. "Well, I believe that Jack will say in his press conference that the operating system team is still working on speeding up performance. Privately, though, I think it's due to a conflict between the boys that want to put a bunch of extensions in microcode and the original designers, who think that would be perverting the RISC philosophy."

Lopez-Goldblum's husband is one of those original designers. "That's what Mark thinks. Keep it simple, he says, and it will run faster."

"I've passed out the new PERT charts. Your tasks haven't changed any; you'll just have more time to do them."

Gilbert examines his chart. "Does this mean we don't have to put in such long hours?"

"Perhaps not quite so long, but we can't really afford to slack off. You'll have time to do it *right* now, and we'll be under less pressure, knowing that we're not holding up the release. That means we can make the compiler we really want to make, instead of the one we were being forced to make. And by the way, regarding that possible clash in philosophies, that kind of thing must never get out. I've been attending a workshop on information leaks, and it's appalling what gets into the press and over to other companies because some of our people are just not using good judgment. The slogan of these meetings is 'Be aware before you share.' There's a brochure in all of your mailboxes explaining how not to give away the store, but I think if you use a little common sense, there should be no problems from our department. If someone from the press calls, refer him or her to the corporate publicity department. If someone calls claiming to be from another department wanting technical information about the compiler, don't just give it right out; say you'll call the person back. Then check and make sure that the person both really exists and has a legitimate need to know. Obviously, some people in other groups need details on the internal operation of our product. Some of the CAD groups, for instance, are using FORTRAN 8X; so is the database group. They all need to know details about internals. But if someone calls, and you don't know that person, just say you're busy now, but ask for their number and tell them you'll get back to them later."

Scrivener pours another cup of coffee. "We're only hurting ourselves by giving away confidential information. Other companies would just love to get a jump on us, and that would *really* have a bad effect on the stock."

McRae stands up and starts pacing behind the table as she talks. Walking seems to help her express herself. "I was at the international users' group meeting the last time the schedule slipped. Users were starting to lose confidence in us. DEC had set up an office in the same hotel; they had representatives buttonholing some of our customers, and some of them were listening. The same day HP ran an ad in the *Journal* saying something like, 'I-Q users: Are you tired of waiting for a machine that keeps being promised but not delivered? We're shipping *today*.' How did they all find out about the slippage in time to be trying to take advantage of it on the day it was announced?"

"That's just what we were talking about in those workshops. A reporter pretends to be someone in another division. He reaches someone in the project who knows when the ship date is. He says something like, 'Jim, hello. It's Jones over in shipping. I need to confirm those dates so we can have the trucks ready. What day are those protos going out?' Jim doesn't bother checking whether there's a Jones in shipping, or even if anyone in shipping has any reason to get that information. He just casually answers the question and forgets all about it. And the news becomes a scoop in one of the trade magazines. Or it could be someone working for one of the other companies. *That's* how it gets out. Now..."

She is interrupted by a loud electronic buzzing, the sound made when one of the doors marked, "Emergency exit only—opening this door will sound alarm," is opened. Then another, farther away, and still another, more distant. Then a loud clanging.

"Oh, it's a fire drill. I had it in my notes to tell you about it. I just didn't get to that yet. Okay, everybody out. We'll continue this after the drill is over."

The nearest exit is just outside the meeting room. They all file out into the brilliant midmorning sunshine.

The day is already hot. Hundreds of people stand in clumps on sidewalks and in the parking lot, as more keep coming out. Security guards herd people away from the building. The safety officer, a man in a brown sport coat with a stitched label reading "Plant Security" over the breast pocket, walks around writing on a clipboard to the top of which he has attached a stopwatch.

A few people are smoking, each surrounded by a circle of space, as if they are carriers of some disease. Everywhere else people crowd together, discussing the state of I-Q stock, how the A's and Giants are doing, the beautiful weather, the possibility of water rationing threatened by the unusually dry previous winter, and whether UNIX and DOS can coexist peacefully within a single microcomputer.

Except for Clawson, who is conversing with Auctor, the members of the FORTRAN group have found an unoccupied grassy spot near the motorcycle parking area. McRae leans against a tree. "Well, first we get out of work to attend the meeting, and now we get an extra half hour off for a fire drill. It's a good thing we're getting all that extra time to work on the compiler."

Smith comes over from the exit nearest Siberia. "All the systems are back up again. I had to rebuild Ernie's operating system completely from scratch. Thanks for your help, Grey."

"Certainly. I'm glad we'll have something to work on."

Gilbert pulls a sheet of lined yellow paper from a shirt pocket. "While we're all standing around here, I worked out a great puzzle."

Levin sits at McRae's feet, propped against the tree. "Ha! I thought you were taking notes at the meeting on that yellow pad. My faith in humanity is shaken to think that you were doodling instead."

"I wasn't doodling. Sometimes when I can't figure out why something won't compile, I take my mind off it by working on one of these puzzles. My subconscious seems to take over, and when I come back, I often have the answer to both the puzzle *and* the problem with software development."

"Sure, but you looked like you were taking notes of the meeting."

"I don't need to do that. Carolyn always gives us detailed minutes the same afternoon that are better than any notes *I* could take. Anyway, this is it. Like most of yours, it's easily expressed but perhaps not so easily solved. Find two five-digit numbers that between them use the digits 0 through 9 once each and that, when the first is divided by the second, equal 9."

Levin stands up. "Well, look at that. Everybody's heading back in. That was a short one."

McRae steps in beside him as they all head back to the building. "Right, we only wasted another half hour. Now we can get back to the meeting and waste the rest of the morning."

ᔍ

Can you write a program that finds two five-digit numbers that between them use the digits 0 through 9 once each, such that the first number divided by the second is equal to 9? That is:

$$\frac{abcde}{fghij} = 9$$

where each letter represents a different digit. If there are more solutions than one, find them. In C, your program should execute in less than 3 seconds; in Pascal, it should take about 7 seconds; the BASIC program should take about 1 minute 30 seconds.

ᔍ

For hints in solving Puzzle 9, see Page 103.
For the solutions to Puzzle 9, see Page 168.

PUZZLE 10

LOOKING SUSPICIOUSLY
LIKE EACH OTHER

At a quarter past one, Eucalyptus is nearly empty, having stopped serving its reasonably priced meals 15 minutes earlier. Five members of the FORTRAN team cluster at one end of a table, while their computer operator sits at the other, all lingering over the remains of their meals. Their being the last in the cafeteria is not unusual; they generally come in for lunch at a quarter to one to avoid the noontime crush.

Their seating arrangement is typical, too. They moved the table to rest half in the smoking section and half in the nonsmoking. This arrangement accommodates Smith, at the smoking end, separated from the rest by a two-chair buffer.

Levin digs into a piece of chocolate meringue pie. "Marian, how can you eat lunch and smoke at the same time? Never mind; don't answer that. We love you anyway."

Smith liberally salts her lettuce-and-mushroom salad. "Uh-huh, you tolerate me, because without me the entire fragile computer network would strangle in its miles of communicating cables and suffer sensory overload from your hundreds of simultaneously running programs competing for CPU time and free memory partitions."

Gilbert looks uncomfortable. "We certainly appreciate all you do to keep us on the air. We'd never get this project done without your keeping the computers purring. But, don't you know we like *you?*"

McRae is the only one who did not eat in the cafeteria today. She has, as usual, driven her Rabbit convertible, with the personalized plates 2GELATO, to the Sunnyvale Gelato Classico, where lunch consisted of a large (pint, $2.25) container of half mocha chip and half dark chocolate. She joins her friends for conversation on her return. "Peach is in."

Scrivener takes the last bite of his wilted-spinach salad. "Ah, my favorite. Maybe I'll join you for lunch tomorrow." He pours the last of a Diet 7-Up into his glass.

Gilbert finishes a slice of blueberry cheesecake and starts on a brownie. "Do you have a name for your novel yet?"

Scrivener adjusts the knot of a mauve tie against the collar of his perfectly pressed pink dress shirt. "I've been thinking of *Silicon!*, with an exclamation point. I can see the cover blurb now, 'What *Wheels!* did for Detroit, *Silicon!* does for Silicon Valley.'"

Levin finishes a Dr. Pepper and wipes his mouth on the shoulder of his Firesign Theatre T-shirt ("Everything you know is wrong"). He absentmindedly pushes his long blond hair out of his eyes. "Shouldn't that be a bang?"

"In the very limited context of programs and operating systems, the exclamation point seems more and more frequently to be using that alias, one that originated, by the way, in printers' slang; that meaning has not yet entered general usage, however." Scrivener always has the last word on grammar and etymology. The others still like him.

Smith pushes aside the remains of a shrimp-croissant sandwich and lights another cigarette, inhaling immediately as the match flares up, which fills her lungs with as much sulfur as tobacco. She's used to it. "Does the group have plans for Halloween?"

McRae wears a T-shirt too, on this warm day. This one has the slogan, "Women belong on top." "I remember two years ago we all dressed as Ghostbusters. We had paper suits we got at a discount store, you know, those ones you wear once or twice for repairing the car or painting the house. Nobody's fit right. We had portable hair dryers for ghost-zapper guns, and backpacks with vacuum-cleaner hoses coming out of them. Somebody got disposable welder's masks. We trooped through the whole company. I carried a tape recorder playing 'Who Ya Gonna Call? Ghostbusters!'"

Gilbert hasn't seen Halloween at I-Q before. "Great costumes. Was there a prize?"

Scrivener was there that year. "Sure, but we didn't get it. Five other groups came as Ghostbusters. The winner was the supervisor of a group and the seven ladies who worked for him. They came as Snow White and the Seven Dwarfs. He was Snow White. We're thinking of going as Aliens this year. I'd like to be the Sigourney Weaver part. And Bob would make a great Mother Alien."

Levin pays no attention to the gentle dig.

Smith, Levin, Scrivener, and Gilbert carry their trays to a garbage can, scrape their plates, deposit paper and other disposables, and set the trays on the conveyor belt. McRae walks beside Gilbert, who looks somewhat disconcerted at the attention, but she just wants to ask him about some code they're both working on.

Scrivener walks over to the ExpressTeller, pulling his bank card from a slim eelskin wallet. Smith accompanies him.

Levin falls in behind McRae and Gilbert. "Well, time to get back and help the corporate octopus keep swimming."

Two days later the big day arrives. The group is assembled by Scrivener's desk, waiting for the parade to pass nearby so that they can join in it.

Gilbert is wearing carefully pressed mauve Alexander Julian Colours slacks with razor-sharp pleats, a monogrammed pink Dior dress shirt, a pastel-pink leather tie his cousin brought back from England, and perfectly shined loafers. He carries a reporter's notebook and a sharp number 2 pencil. His name tag reads "Grey Scrivener." "Well, how do I look? Perfectly in style? My God, Grey! I don't look like *that*, do I?"

Scrivener has on gray wash-and-wear flood pants that just barely meet white gym socks that have a thin red band just below a blue band near the top. He wears a white short-sleeved dress shirt with a plastic pocket protector in the pocket that holds three ballpoint pens, five felt-tip pens of different colors, two pencils, and a small clip-on screwdriver. The name tag on the front of the pocket protector reads "Spotswood Gilbert." Under the shirt, he has on a white cotton T-shirt. Clipped to his belt is an IQ13Q calculator in a holster. On his feet are scuffed black wing-tip Florsheims. "Not exactly. Sort of a cross between you and your basic engineer."

McRae totters on black stiletto high heels. Between the shoes and the ends of a tight black jumpsuit show seamless black stockings. A pack of filter tips peeks out of each breast pocket. She holds an unlit cigarette in one hand and a circuit board in the other, and a cigarette is tucked behind each ear. Stitched to one breast pocket is "Smith." "Boy, Marian, I don't know how you walk around in these things. I've been in them for half an hour, and my feet are killing me."

Smith is wearing Nikes, baggy khaki culottes over purple tights, a gray New York Marathon sweatshirt, and a Sally McRae name tag. "Years of practice, my dear."

All turn to watch a huge black gorilla walking past, carrying a brief-case and lunch bag, on the way to a desk two aisles over.

Levin wears a green miniskirt over tight pink pedal-pushers, his feet encased in heavy army boots. Peeking through a fake leopard-skin coat to which is pinned a hand-lettered button carrying the name of the Alice Cooper song, "Only Women Bleed," is a white baseball jersey with a large stenciled "9." He has on a frosted pink wig with green highlights. One eyelid is purple and the other orange. He wears brown lipstick outlined in red. A temporary usually wears either a custom ID badge consisting of laminated work card and picture or a peel-off, stick-on tag bearing today's date issued by the security people at the main entrance. Levin has the latter, with the name "Jill" scrawled in huge letters. Naturally, he wears headphones, plugged into a personal stereo he carries. "I don't want to swim in your pollution" is lettered on a small bumper sticker that is wrapped around the radio.

"Turn the sound up, Bobby; we can't hear it." They gasp collectively. Jill has shown up, wearing sensible brown, low-heeled shoes, stockings, a straight brown mid-calf skirt, a severe white blouse, and a male-styled woman's jacket. Her hair, a proper brunette color, is pinned up neatly in a bun. The only makeup she has on is a tiny glaze of reddish-pink lipstick.

"How can I look like you when you don't look like you? Don't you have a costume for today?"

"I do *not* dress up on Halloween. I don't believe in it. Halloween is just another day for me."

McRae almost falls trying to get out of the main aisle. "Here comes the parade. Let's get at the end of the line."

Perhaps a fifth of the employees are in costume today. It is a tradition for those in costume to march each year through every building on the site, while the other four-fifths line up to watch along the partitions that form the boundaries of the main aisles.

Among the marchers is a French maid in black fishnet stockings; black high heels; a short, frilly black skirt; a ruffled, low-cut black blouse with a large white bow at the back; and a tiny black, inverted ashtray cap over a blond wig.

Yoda, Darth Vader, and ET pass by.

Several people, probably all part of one group, wear green fatigues and knit ski masks that completely cover their faces. They carry toy machine guns and toy grenades. One of them holds a bowling ball with a length of rope jammed into one of the holes and red cellophane at the end in a fair imitation of an old-fashioned bomb. One wears a button that reads "Cuba Libre," probably picked up at a liquor store promotion.

They're all yelling and firing the battery-operated machine guns, which throw out sparks and make realistic staccato bursts of firing.

Another group is dressed as the "I-Don't-Care Bears." Each wears a handmade frowning bear-face mask. Each is dressed all in one pastel color. Each bears a sign across the chest with the name of the character he or she is supposed to be, lettered around a cartoon logo for that character. Bad Luck Bear has a broken horseshoe, Bad News Bear a newspaper headlined "World War III Ends; Everyone Dead." Beer Bear sports a foam-capped stein, Raincloud Bear a thunderhead, and so on.

Someone is dressed as an IQ98765B minicomputer. He's in cardboard boxes, with a meticulously painted front panel on which several LEDs flash and actual reels of tape are mounted on spindles. A glass panel with a printout of a hex dump is behind it, and a real keyboard is on a platform just below.

The FORTRAN group catches the end of the line. After the grand tour of the site, they return to their area.

"Marian, you don't suppose I could borrow those running shoes for the rest of the day, do you? These things are impossible."

Levin hangs the fur coat over the edge of a partition. "That thing is *hot*. I don't know how she wears it inside all the time. Say, speaking of impossible, here's a new puzzle. Find all the nine-digit numbers that are perfect squares and that use each of the digits 1 through 9 once each."

Scrivener turns on his IQAT, I-Q's PC AT compatible and entry into the desktop publishing field. It is also part of a local area network that permits all of the group to log on to the development system and the new RISC machines. "What is a 'perfect' square?"

"One whose square root is an integer. That is, any number can technically be a square. What's the square root of 3? Yeah, root 3. But 4 is a *perfect* square because its square root is 2, an integer."

"So you want something like *abcdefghi*, where each of those letters represents a different digit from 1 through 9?"

"You got it."

"Not yet. First I have to write the program."

&a.

Can you write a program that finds the specified nine-digit numbers? If there are more solutions than one, find them. In C, your program should execute in less than 7 seconds; in Pascal, it should run in 1 minute 3 seconds; in BASIC, it should take a bit less than 5 minutes.

&a.

For hints in solving Puzzle 10, see Page 104.
For the solutions to Puzzle 10, see Page 178.

PUZZLE 11

LATER THAN
THEY THINK

*M*R. The initials that keep programmers at work half the night trying to get last-minute bugs out of code and that keep technical writers busy just as long incorporating design changes into the manuals. Manufacturing Release. In a software product, that means that the code is frozen (no further changes can be made), all known bugs are fixed, and the product leaves the hands of the lab engineers so that manufacturing can get it ready for customer shipments.

Gilbert stares at his monitor. "Look at that. It still can't find EOF."

Levin looks at the neat rows of hexadecimal numbers that fill the screen. "Let it go."

"No, I can't. The ANSI spec says that *ERROR* = is supposed to trap end-of-file, and I'm not letting it out the door till it does."

"Well, two weeks and the compiler has to be ready to go, or *we're* going to be the ones holding up Rainbow's release. Can't you just see the story in *InfoWorld*? 'Cupertino. I-Q board chairman Jack Imperator announced today that the latest delay in the company's long-awaited new

RISC-architecture minicomputer, the one upon which the company is basing so much of its hope, is due to its FORTRAN 8X compiler not being able to trap EOF in an *ERROR =* statement.'" Levin returns to his desk, and the late-night quiet resumes.

Gilbert brings up a calculator in a window on the screen to check some of the figures. He jumps at the ring of the phone.

"Hello, Spotswood Gilbert speaking. Oh, hi, Missy.... I wish I could, but Daddy has to work late.... Yes, I know I haven't read to you for a whole week.... I know you do, honey; I like the Oz books too. Maybe I can on the weekend.... Six chapters? Okay, if there's time.... I love you too.... Night, night. Can I talk to Mommy?"

Scrivener smiles and glances over at Levin, who is also smiling.

"Hello, sweetheart.... No, I don't know when I'll be home tonight. I think it's going to be another late one. Don't wait up for me.... I know, but I've got to get this stuff running. They're all counting on me.... Yes, I know you are, too.... What? No, I can't; I'll never get it done.... Nancy. Nancy? Damn!" Gilbert replaces the receiver and looks up. The other latebirds all appear engrossed in their work.

A regular clattering now breaks the silence as a maintenance man rolls a trash barrel down the aisles, pausing at each cubicle to empty the wastebasket. He enters Gilbert's cubicle, operating apparently on automatic pilot, and finds the wastebasket behind a mountain of printouts. The man is talking to himself quietly. Gilbert can hardly make out what he is saying. "They were flashing their lights at each other again."

The man moves on to Scrivener's area, still muttering. "Did I really hear them? Yes, I believe I did. They were talking to each other." He empties the wastebasket into the barrel and moves on. After he leaves, Scrivener walks over to Gilbert's desk.

"Spotswood, what was that guy talking about?"

"I don't know. I thought it had something to do with cars. Something about flashing their headlights."

"Hmm. I wonder if the man has been eavesdropping somewhere. You remember that 'Be aware before you share' stuff. Anyone could be an industrial spy."

McRae walks over, unwrapping a Lindt mocha bar. "Are you talking about that weird janitor? I heard he's got a degree in electrical engineering and that he was the head engineer at a startup. He got completely burned out after two years of hundred-hour weeks and now doesn't want the stress of a high-tech job."

Scrivener takes a few squares from the proffered bar. "A few more weeks like this and I might join him."

Levin turns down the offer of chocolate. "No, you go ahead and finish it. It would just be wasted on me. Sort of like fertilizing a weed. I have some Twinkies back at my desk. Uh, Sally? I was wondering if you could take a look at this piece of code I'm having trouble with. I can't figure out why it keeps locking up whenever it does a disk read."

"Sure, I'll take a look."

Gilbert types some instructions, which start another hex dump. "Did you get the latest information on ELTDEF for the manuals, Grey?"

"'Latest'? I never got *anything* on ELTDEF. Don't you remember that Fletcher was the custodian of all that stuff? I thought he gave all of his material to you when he left for that sweatshop that lured him away by doubling his salary. All he ever did was give me a copy of the POG documentation and tell me to look it up in there, that your implementation was exactly the same."

"It is. Weren't you able to get anything from that?"

"I know that you're a programmer and have no trouble understanding that stuff, but as far as I'm concerned, POG documentation is not made for ordinary human beings, and I've just been waiting for something in English."

The dump on Gilbert's screen has ended. Phrases like "MEMORY FAULT," "ATTEMPT TO ACCESS PAGE 0," and "INVALID SECTOR" have now been added to the neat rows of numbers and letters. "Damn! Why is it there's never enough time to do it right, but there's always enough time to do it over?"

"The only reason there's time to do it over is that we're putting in all these extra hours. You've got to fix all those bugs that beta site discovered last week, and I've got to incorporate all these changes in the manual and new features that nobody ever bothered to tell me about. Including this ELTDEF stuff. I don't suppose you put in any examples for me, did you?"

"Examples? You must be joking. I'll be lucky to get this ELTDEF stuff in and the bugs fixed by MR. I don't have time for examples. That's the tech writer's job."

"Actually, it's the support engineer's job. But he's too busy with Ada, Pascal, and C to write and test examples for me. So it looks like I'll end up writing all the examples myself, just like every other manual I've written."

Across the aisle, Levin and McRae are huddled in front of Levin's terminal. "All right, Sally! You found it."

"That's because I found out about that undocumented call in the microcode from Maria's husband. Hardly anyone uses it. They just put it in there for debugging purposes and as a kind of emergency exit, and they didn't bother documenting it. Your code just happened to be trying to make the same call. Do you think you might have a chance to take a look at something in my back end that's been troubling me?"

"Sure. Anytime."

Chan comes in carrying a pizza box and a six-pack of caffeine-free Diet Coke. "Here's our late dinner, gang. Sorry, no anchovies, Bob. I've got change for everybody, but let's eat first."

Levin brings paper plates, plastic forks, and paper cups. "Look what I found in the supply cabinet. Must be left over from the last birthday celebration. I can write some examples for you, Grey, while I'm waiting for Spotswood to finish his compilation."

Scrivener clears a spot at his table and sets up a few spare chairs. "Thanks, Bob. Can you test them, too? I think most users try out new features in a language by modifying the examples in the manual, and we're doing them a disservice if those examples don't run."

"Sure, and at the rate Spots is going, I'll have time to figure out a puzzle I just saw."

Gilbert winces at the familiarity taken with his first name, but otherwise ignores the younger man's dig. "And what might that be, as if we didn't have enough to do? Since we're going to be here all night anyway, we might as well have something to keep us amused."

Scrivener gets paper napkins from a desk drawer and puts them on the table. "*We'll* end up putting in extra time, but it's no big deal for Bob. He's just starting out his day, but we've been here since morning."

"Well, I put in a lot of hours all the time, not just the last couple of weeks before MR. The puzzle is another one of those that're easy to express in words but maybe not so easy to program. Find all whole numbers equal to the sum of the factorials of their digits."

Chan pulls out a pocketful of change. "You guys are still doing those puzzles, huh? How about 1 and 2? Isn't 1 factorial 1 and 2 factorial 2? That's easy. You don't need a computer for that."

"Right. The first two solutions are what mathematicians call 'trivial.' But how about higher answers? I can tell you that they all have fewer than six digits."

Scrivener returns to his terminal. "Okay, folks, back to work. I don't want to be here all night."

Levin walks over to his cubicle but stops before going in. "You know, Sally, I'm always the one here half the night. I fixed the bug I was after. I'm going to take the rest of the evening off."

"Well, thanks to you, my problem is fixed too. Will you walk out to my car with me?"

"I'll do better than that. Would you like to have some coffee and dessert at Lyon's?"

"Sure, thanks."

Boy, I hate it when they have MR.

Yeah, me too. They all hang around here so late.

And that janitor. I wish he'd stay away from the computer rooms. He makes me nervous. Like he knows all about us.

It's well after midnight, and almost everyone has left. The maintenance man pushes a floor polisher rhythmically back and forth across the tile. As he passes Siberia, he keeps glancing over his shoulder through the computer room's windows. He has a personal stereo turned up loud to drown out the noise of the polisher. Keffury plays middle-of-the-night music on KFOG. "And the only sound that's left after the ambulances go/ Is Cinderella sweeping up on Desolation Row."

❧

Can you write a program that finds all whole numbers (with fewer than six digits) that are equal to the sum of the factorials of their digits? (A factorial, usually expressed as the number followed by an exclamation point, is the number multiplied by 1 less than the number, then by 1 less than that, and so on, down to 1. Thus, 3! is $3 \times 2 \times 1$, or 6.) The first two solutions are what mathematicians term "trivial": $1! = 1$ and $2! = 2$. With letters representing digits, a three-digit solution to this puzzle can be expressed as $A! + B! + C! = ABC$. Each letter is a distinct, though not necessarily different, digit.

In C, your program should execute in 3 seconds; in Pascal, it should take 15 seconds; in BASIC, it should take about 3 minutes 56 seconds.

❧

For hints in solving Puzzle 11, see Page 105.

For the solutions to Puzzle 11, see Page 183.

PUZZLE 12

HOW TO REDUCE: A CELEBRATION

All good projects come to an end sometime, and even our little group of workaholics gets a little R & R as reward for their R & D efforts. Gilbert has just risen from his seat at a table by a huge plate-glass window that frames a panoramic view of the Valley, sweeping all the way from the hills of east San Jose on the right to San Francisco's Transamerica pyramid on the left.

Others on the FORTRAN team are just joining Gilbert at the table in this restaurant on Skyline Boulevard in the northern extension of the Santa Cruz mountains.

Levin almost knocks over the stunning blond with him as he tries to pull out a chair for her.

"This is Stephanie Ivers. She works at Apple. Stephanie, that's Spotswood Gilbert—he did the front end for our new compiler—and that's his wife, Nancy. That's Marian Smith, our system operator, and uh…"

The charms on her bracelet jangling, Smith pauses in the act of trying to get life from an unresponsive disposable lighter. "Willy Chin.

Willy's an engineering supervisor at Lockheed." Chin, who has a graying engineer's beard—that is, one that completely covers his face except for the upper lip—lights Smith's cigarette with a large silver Zippo, smiles at Levin, and winks at Ivers.

Levin continues the introductions. "This is Carolyn Clawson, our boss. And her husband, Harry."

"Hello, Stephanie. Bob, I hardly recognize you without your jeans and T-shirt."

Harry looks older than the rest, perhaps 20 years older than his wife, who is herself in her mid-thirties. "Howdy."

"Sally McRae and Barton Dumbridge. Sally did a lot of the back end of the compiler. Bart's part of the support team for technical languages. Grey Scrivener. He wrote the manual. And...?"

Scrivener is impeccable in a charcoal three-piece suit, Nicola Mancini white shirt, narrow gray leather tie, and Italian slip-ons. "This is my friend Charles LaFebvre. He services PCs for Compu-R-X."

LaFebvre has pewter pants that match his hair, a mauve silk harem shirt with three buttons undone, and three diamond stud earrings in his left ear. "Hi there. It sure is nice of your company to bring us to this restaurant."

Now that everyone else is seated, Gilbert squeezes into the Balans chair. "Order yourself a drink, Charles. I-Q's paying for everything. And you'll be able to order the best steak in the Valley in about half an hour. Or do you prefer to be called Chuck, or Charlie maybe?"

"Charles, thanks. Spotswood, was it? And am I correct in assuming you're a southern gentleman?"

"Yes. You have a good ear; I-Q picked up my option in New Orleans."

Smith gazes wonderingly at McRae. "This is the first time I've seen you in a dress, Sally."

McRae stands and pirouettes, then returns to her seat. "Enjoy it. This is my one and only dress. I bought it this afternoon because they said this was a fancy place. Well, Stephanie, are you a programmer too?"

"No, I'm in public relations. I tell the press about Apple's new products and answer embarrassing questions from reporters about the company's internal affairs."

A waitress appears. LaFebvre requests a champagne cocktail. "Oh, like when will the Mac run DOS and UNIX simultaneously with its own operating system?"

"The answer to that one is we feel that a friendly interface is more important to the average user than compatibility with difficult interfaces, ones that we don't wish to promote as a standard." She pauses. "At least that's the answer today."

The waitress hovers over Scrivener. "Do you have Watney's Red Barrel Ale? Great, that's what I'll have." He turns to Ivers. "And what do you reply when you get asked what the employees think about three of their executives getting paid over half a million a year while they worry about more layoffs?"

"That's easy. The answer is 'no comment.' And then I change the subject. By the way, aren't you the group that likes to solve puzzles with your computers? I have one for you. Find all integers satisfying this condition: An integer is reduced to one-ninth its value when a certain one of its digits is removed, and dividing the resulting integer by 9 results in the removal of another digit. That is, for each reduction, some one digit is removed from the number."

Dumbridge picks up the light beer that the waitress has just deposited in front of him. "Wait a minute, how's that again?"

Levin sips his newly arrived tequila sunrise. "Oh, I think I see. Tell me if I've got it right, Stephanie. Some number like, oh, I don't know off the top of my head, but let's say it could be 123456, and maybe if you dropped the 2, the resulting number, 13456, would be one-ninth of 123456. And then, if you divide the new number by 9 again, you'd get something like 3456, and you would have dropped another digit, this time the 1. Obviously those numbers don't work, but is that the idea?"

"Yes, that's it."

McRae is the only one who didn't order something alcoholic. The waitress sets a Virgin Mary in front of her. "Pretty good for someone who didn't go to Cal."

The waitress has distributed the last of the drinks. "Dinner comes with soup and salad. As we arranged on the phone, for the entrée, you have a choice of filet mignon, chicken Jerusalem, veal Marsala, or poached salmon. Does anybody want anything else from the bar before I take your orders?"

Scrivener pours the rest of the bottle into his glass. "Yes, I'd like another Watney's. Tell me, is the fish fresh?"

"Yes, it is."

We're not going to listen to their orders, delicious though they sound. I can tell you that half of the group orders fish and the other half meat. Of that half, half get the filet and half the chicken. All but one take their salads with house dressing, and that one has Roquefort. In a rare display of consistency, all choose cherries Jubilee for dessert, in preference to the Grand Marnier soufflé. I leave it as an exercise for the reader to determine who orders what.

They start with three bottles of wine, Rosé d'Anjou, Pat Paulsen Chardonnay, and a Dr. Thanisch. It's just getting dark, and the expanse of trees and water is becoming a carpet of green and orange lights.

Scrivener does the honors with the Rosé d'Anjou at one end of the table. Gilbert pours the Paulsen at the other end, while, at mid-table, Dumbridge decants the good Doctor.

Clawson raises her glass. "Here's to I-Q and to this group for finishing the project in time for MR of the new computers. Thanks, gang. You worked hard, and it shows."

Ivers sips her wine. "You have MR too, huh? I guess 'Manufacturing Release' must be a pretty universal term in the Valley."

Levin drains his glass. "Yes, and it's axiomatic that MR is always late."

Gilbert, Programmer—there's also a Gilbert present who is listed on their income tax return as Homemaker—refills empties. "Speaking of which, the Ada team has decided their product is so full of bugs they can't release it at all."

Dumbridge slides to the left to allow the waitress to deposit his salad in front of him. "They'll change their minds. They've pushed the release back three times now. The delays add up to more than a year. They're probably just trying to get that Swedish company that's third-partying the front end to clean up the product. What they consider 'minor bugs' seem to be worlds apart from what I-Q thinks are minor. Anything that can crash the entire system is not a minor bug. I don't know how many times they've had me in there trying to cold-start one of their Fuchsias. And on a prototype machine that doesn't even run in native mode, that's no easy job. Anyway, it just makes your team look good by comparison."

Levin downs another Dr. Thanisch. "Why Bart, I didn't know you supported Ada, too."

"Oh sure, Ada, FORTRAN, *and* RPG."

Smith liberally salts a salad that has just arrived. "Bobby, didn't they teach you at Carnegie-Mellon that drinking her under the table is not necessarily the best way to impress a date?"

McRae begins her main course. "Hey, leave the kid alone. He's been working hard. We all have. Let's relax."

LaFebvre carefully removes a bone from his fish. "Carnegie-Mellon? When did you go there?"

"Three years ago. Were you there?"

"Yeah, but 10 years ago. Did you ever race a buggy?"

"You bet! That's how I got this." He points to a scar on his left cheek that his friends at I-Q, out of politeness, have never commented on. "On Chute my senior year. I didn't quite make the turn. But you should have seen that baby. It didn't even look big enough to hold a person. I had to really squeeze to wiggle in through the back end. It looked kind of like a cigar tube on wheels, and it went like the wind. I had a good view because the whole front end was plexiglass. And it was made entirely out of aluminum, so it was easy for the pushers to get it up the hills. I know we'd have won if I'd've made that last turn."

"Well, I used to watch the buggy races, but I never had the nerve to get in one. And I'll bet you spent all your spare time in the Cave."

"Oh yeah, lots of all-night sessions getting my homework debugged."

"And playing Rogue, I'll bet."

"Mm hm. We used to have meals delivered there in the middle of the night."

"Me too. Chinese and pizza. And are they still programming in GNOME on the VAX?"

"Sure, and when I graduated they were just porting it to the Macintosh. They were calling it MacGNOME."

Scrivener refills his glass. "Well, Charles, I didn't realize you had had a classical education."

Levin is now working on his fourth glass of wine. Chin winks again at Ivers, who smiles back in friendly but not inviting fashion.

By the time dessert arrives, the conversation has narrowed to three small groups. Levin, Ivers, and McRae discuss Ivers's puzzle. Scrivener and LaFebvre seem to be arguing in lowered voices. The Gilberts discuss with Dumbridge the advantages of working at I-Q. Smith and Chin silently hold hands.

As closing time approaches, we find them sitting at small tables back by the bar. McRae is finishing a cappuccino, while the rest work on various after-dinner drinks.

McRae rises. "I need to get up early to run. You ready, Bart?"

"Fine, let's go. Nice meeting you Charles, Stephanie, Willy, Harry. I'll see the rest of you on Monday."

Ivers helps Levin out to his ancient, battered VW beetle. The dim restaurant sign sheds just enough light to reveal a faded bumper sticker: "Legalize crime." Condensation clouds the window. She wipes it off with a tissue from her purse; the wipers do not work.

Harry Clawson holds the door of their Subaru wagon for his wife.

Scrivener and LaFebvre make their way somewhat unsteadily to the latter's Volvo 1800 ES. They stop and consult for a moment, appearing to

discuss which of them is more fit to drive. Scrivener eventually gets behind the wheel.

Nancy Gilbert gets into the driver's seat of their year-old LTD
wagon, and her husband enters from the passenger side.

Chin helps Smith into his BMW 733i and roars off down Skyline.

৯

Can you write a program that finds an integer that, when a specific digit
is removed, is reduced to one-ninth of its value and that, when a second
digit is removed, is further reduced to one-ninth of the second value?
Your program should print out the lowest complete set of numbers. (You
can always find a new set by adding a 0 to the end of each member of a
given set.) In Pascal, your program should execute in less than 1 second;
in C and BASIC, it should take less than 2 seconds.

৯

For hints in solving Puzzle 12, see Page 106.

For the solutions to Puzzle 12, see Page 196.

PUZZLE 13

BETTING ON A JET, OR JETTING ON A BET

"Pass the beer." Levin's seat is almost in the middle of the aisle. Released from its safety catches, the chair can move a foot into the aisle, rotate 180 degrees, and lean almost straight back.

Gilbert reaches into the ice chest stowed under a temporary seat just behind the copilot. "Boy, you don't get this kind of comfort on a commercial flight."

Clawson turns away from the window, where she has been watching another jet approaching them, about 20 miles away. "Hey, nothing but the best for my group. We're actually saving money by going on the corporate jet. They make this trip twice a day whether they have passengers or not. Round-trip fare to Denver, on this short notice, would be over $300 each. The company charges $150, and that's just transferring money from one pocket to another. It never leaves the company."

Scrivener pours a handful of dry-roasted peanuts from a jar. "Yes, and then we'd still have to get from Denver to Boulder. Does every site have its own airfield?"

"No, but many of those not in the immediate Bay Area do. If they're large enough, of course. Boulder does. Taos, New Mexico. Calgary, Alberta. Lake Tahoe doesn't have one, but we do have a hangar at the Tahoe airport. I don't know. I certainly haven't been to all the sites."

Smith pours another plastic cup of Perrier. "Are all the jets eleven-passenger?"

"No, I think we have four eleven-passenger jobs, two that are nine-passenger, and one that holds fourteen. That one is usually reserved for Jack and Quentin, but the others have regular runs between sites. This one goes back and forth twice each weekday from San Jose to Boulder."

McRae stands at the open doorway to the cockpit. She has a panoramic view, not the tunnel vision found at the controls of a 747. "Is that an I-Q computer built into the console there?"

The pilot makes a minor adjustment on a dial next to a large color screen just below the forward windows. "That's right. Look—I can switch to a map of any airport in the country."

"Wow. Looks just like Flight Simulator."

"And when we're flying on instruments, the radar gives me a contour picture of the ground below. Or I can bring up a window to perform computations of flight changes. Like if we have to divert to another airport for any reason, it tells me what the safety margin is, how much fuel we'll have left, and so on. And here I have a constant readout of the conditions of the door, landing gear, and so on. Right now that computer is flying this plane. Like autopilot but much more sophisticated."

"And you're an I-Q employee?"

"Sure, both of us are. Just like you."

"Do you ever get overseas?"

"No, none of our planes has the range. We just fly in North America."

"Well, thanks. I'm going back to my seat."

"Sure. Come on up for a look anytime. Or any of the others, if they want. Could you pass the sandwiches up on your way? They're in that cabinet above where we put your luggage."

"Okay. Who's ready for lunch back there?"

Levin rolls around to face front. "Are you the stewardess?"

"Yeah. Fly me to Boulder."

"Okay, stewardess. I'd like the sirloin tips *and* the chicken Kiev."

"Sorry, just sandwiches in here. And nuts to you."

Clawson swivels her seat all the way around. "Okay, gang, let's talk about what we're supposed to be doing when we get there. The people at the Boulder site are the first real FORTRAN users. Unfortunately, they're also not able to run the compiler properly, and we don't know if it's the machine or us. It's a good thing the problems are showing up at an internal group and not with any outside customers. Marian, you're going to make sure they've set up their systems properly and keep them running during the testing."

"Yeah. I wouldn't be surprised if they just didn't boot up properly."

"That's certainly a possibility, but they used the installation tape that comes with the system. We may have to get the OS group in here if it doesn't work for their configuration. But I don't think so. They've been having problems only when they try to run their FORTRAN programs. Bob, you're going to do a complete install from scratch. Spotswood, you run the diagnostics. Sally, you start running Maria's test suite. And Grey, you write a manual about it."

All laugh.

"Actually, Grey, why *are* you on this flight?"

"Just a coincidence. The writers' tools group happens to be meeting this week. You know, I'm on the DQG, Documentation Quality Group, and the tools group meets once a quarter at a different site. Next time we're the hosts, and then next summer the whole companywide group is meeting in Barcelona. I'm lobbying the pubs manager to send me."

"Well, while you're there, if you have time you might want to see someone actually try to use your installation manual. Okay. Are we all going back on Friday?"

Levin pops another Stroh's and intercepts the peanut jar. "No, I'm staying the weekend. It's a shame to come all this way and not get some skiing in. I'll be coming back on the Monday morning jet."

He passes the jar to McRae. As their fingers touch, the jar slips and drops to the floor. "Oh, could I join you? I haven't had a chance to do any skiing yet this year."

Levin leans forward to retrieve the peanuts. "Sure." A red disk about the size of a silver dollar falls from the pocket of his Pendleton shirt and rolls up the aisle.

Smith picks up the object, reading the gold inlaid lettering. "'Cameo Club, Palo Alto. $5.' This is not your average Friday-night home-game poker chip, Bobby. This looks like a casino chip."

"Oh, here. It must've been in my shirt pocket when I cashed out from the lowball game last time."

"Lowball? Is that some kind of poker?"

"Yeah, draw poker, low hand wins."

"Where do they play that?"

"Why, in cardrooms. I usually play at the Cameo Club, but there are cardrooms all over the state."

"You mean poker is legal in California?"

"Oh, of course. It's permitted by state law, and then it's up to the county and the municipality to decide if they're going to allow poker within their jurisdiction. Palo Alto and San Jose have cardrooms, San Francisco doesn't. Some of the clubs are really nice, like small casinos."

"Do women play in those games?"

"Oh yeah, all the time. There aren't as many women as men, but there are still quite a few. In the Southern California clubs, nearly half the players are women, particularly in the pan games."

"Pan? What's that?"

"It's this strange game they play in most of the cardrooms. Sort of like gin rummy played with eight decks of cards and by a whole table of players instead of just two. Some of the melds are worth money, and you get more money for matching all your cards. Crazy game. I don't play it because there's not much skill in it."

Scrivener scrutinizes the poker chip as he passes it back to Levin. "And there is skill in lowball? You're a winning player then?"

"Well, I usually break about even. But it's a lot of fun, and a skillful player *can* win a lot. Which reminds me. A guy in a cardroom proposed something as a bet. It seems like it might be a good candidate for a puzzle. He and I each shuffle a deck of cards. We each turn over one card at a time, simultaneously, from the top of the deck, until we each reach the end of our own deck at the same time. He offered to bet me we would never get a match—that is, at no time would he and I each turn over the same card at the same time. Of course, I felt we would, so I took his side, that is, that we would not."

Scrivener passes the chip back. "Why would you take his side if you felt there ought to be a match?"

"Because I know how those things work. Someone offers a proposition that seems really reasonable, but if I go for it, I get taken, because, of course, he'd never offer it unless he had the best of it. I thought I'd outsmart him, and take *his* side of the bet."

"Uh huh, and what happened?"

"I got cleaned out. But I don't know if that proves anything. I don't know what the real odds are, and I don't know how to figure them."

≥∙

Who *does* have the best of it in that proposition? What are the probabilities for decks of various sizes? Print out all the probabilities, from 2 cards to 52. In C, your program should take less than 7 seconds; in Pascal, about 3½ seconds; in BASIC, it should execute in about 8 seconds.

≥∙

For hints in solving Puzzle 13, see Page 107.

For the solutions to Puzzle 13, see Page 204.

PUZZLE 14

MEMORIES ARE
MADE OF THIS

"Grey, I'd like you to meet my cousins, Emilie and Chloe Mead. They work in the AI lab."

"Better watch out, Bart. You're standing right under the mistletoe."

"Don't you think I know that?"

"Sally, this is Egbert Souse."

"That's *Soo-Zay*, an accent grave over the *e*."

"Oh, look at the tree. Didn't they do a nice job?"

"*...here with the KYA Oldies Road Show...*"

"Carolyn and Nancy, you know each other. This is Carolyn's boss, our lab manager. Jack, my wife, Nancy. Nancy, this is Jack Auctor."

"Gilbert, here are some special friends I'd like to introduce you to. Hugh Njemanze and Erik Eidt. They wrote Axe."

"Oh really? Glad to meet you! I've used a lot of editors, but Axe is by far the best—the most powerful and the easiest to use. It's great for writing programs. Oh, and here's someone else who uses it. Grey Scrivener. He does all our manuals."

"Hugh, Erik. It's a pleasure. I've been using Axe on my AT at home, too, to write my novel."

...Dear Sir or Madam will you read my book?...

"Boy, a fifties sock hop! What a great idea for a Christmas party."

...Can you hear the real me, doctor, can ya?...

"So, Emilie, what project are you on?"

"I'm working on voice recognition. And Chloe is doing a program that lets factory robots perform their own maintenance. They fix themselves before they break down, so they run virtually forever."

...my baby she calls me Dr. Feelgood...

"Well, Egbert, what do you do?"

"Signal analysis and waveform soldering. Would you care to have a drink?"

"Just Crystal Geyser for me, thanks."

...woh woman oh woman don't you treat me this way...

"What do *you* do, Nancy?"

"Oh, I've got two little girls to take care of. That and taking care of the house keep me pretty busy. I sure wish you wouldn't keep Spotswood here so late every night. The girls really miss their father sometimes."

"Nancy!"

"Well, he's doing a great job for us. We could never have gotten the compiler running properly without his efforts."

...gonna hoo-hoot an' howl like a lovesick owl...

"And this is my husband, Mark. He's on the Rainbow design team."

"Maria, was it? And what do you do, Maria?"

"Oh, I wrote the test suite for the FORTRAN 8X compiler—we call it IQTEST—and I run it, too."

...How high? Higher than a mission bell...

"Can I get you some of those sweet 'n' sour chicken wings, Marian? They're great!"

"I'm sure they are, Willy, but I can't on my diet."

...Jingle bell chime in jingle bell time...

"Hey, Grey, did you look at MAIL today?"

"No, it was down by the time I logged on."

"Well, I got a wonderful electronic Christmas card in the form of a poem from my friend David Merit in the HP3000 Users' Group. Here, I printed it out."

'Twas the night before Christmas and all through the shop
Hung a thick veil of silence—you could hear a pin drop.
I sipped at my coffee, checked my watch in despair,
In hopes that the CE soon would be there.
The disk drives were nestled alone on their GICs,
As if they were wearied by their earlier tricks.
And me in my sorrow, with frown on my face,
Had once again failed to get out of this place.
When in the computer room there arose such a clatter
I did a :SHOWJOB to see what was the matter.
Away to the disk drive I flew in a flash,
Tore open the cover, and heard a loud CRASH!
The small metal fragments that flew into sight
Caused the air to turn silver—and my face to turn white.
When then through my tear-moistened eyes he appeared,
He looked like St. Nick with no mustache or beard.
As the disk drives spun down when he gazed upon them,
I knew right away that he must use PM.
He was more of a techy than all of my dreams;
His pocket protector was strained at the seams.
His cherry red suit was untucked in the back,
And a hat saying "Guru" was poised up on his stack.
He said not a word but went straight to the disk;
He looked at the platters and mumbled, "Tsk, tsk."
And then from his eyes shot some rays, clear and bright,
Which enveloped the drive in a red and green light.
"On platters, on actuators, on head reads and writes,
On cylinders, tracks, sectors, words, bits, and bytes."
And in less than a minute, without parts from the shelf,

My 7933 disk drive repaired itself.
Santa Techy chuckled, and I stood there dazed,
And he said to me, "David, you do seem amazed.
I have a 3000 at the North Pole, you see;
I use MM in the elf toy factory,
I chart my flight course on PCs using mice,
And a QUERY will tell me who's naughty and nice.
Your disk drive is fully repaired, by the way;
I spared a few tracks, but the data's okay.
Now please do a SYSDUMP and then you can leave
And go home, spike some eggnog, and enjoy Christmas eve."
Then his eyes gave a twinkle and he bellowed, "Ho, ho!"
And left with some software he bootlegged in tow.
But his parting words moved me from joyous to ill:
"That was double-time, pal—wait till you see the bill!"

"That's great! But what's 'MM'?"

"I think that means 'Mighty Mouse.' That was Hewlett-Packard's internal code name, before they released it, of their downsized HP3000."

...it's the little Saint Nick, oo, little Sain' Nick...

"Hey, where's Jill tonight? Didn't anyone give her an invitation?"

"She's here. You're looking right at her."

"What? You mean...?"

"That's right, she's Santa Claus."

"Oh yeah, I was thinking that Santa's cheeks were too red."

...c'mawn an' work it on out...

"Grey, this is my boyfriend, Li Yuan. Li, this is Grey Scrivener. He's working on a novel about Silicon Valley. And Chuck LaFebvre, isn't it?"

"Charles."

"A novel? Really? I just did a book for Microsoft Press on the 486 operating system, but of course, that's not fiction."

"This is Starla Chan, Charles. She's on our team. She did all the conversion utilities."

"Hello, Starla. Do you do those puzzles, too, that Grey and his friends seem always to be working on?"

"I've tried a few, but I can usually work them out faster by hand."

...I can really shake 'em down...

"Hi, Sally. You here by yourself?"

"I don't even usually come to these things, you know, but Carolyn thought that Auctor kind of expected it. So, here I am, all by myself. And you? Are you here with Stephanie?"

"No, that was over before it began. Before you and I went skiing. Well, here we are—all alone at the Christmas party. Would you like to dance?"

"Oh yes, I like to dance."

...lemme see you shake a tailfeather...

"And what about Bart?"

"What about him? Oh, you mean at the restaurant. There was nobody else to go with. He's just a friend. Sometimes we run together. Say now, look at you. I just noticed. You're not wearing a T-shirt. Or jeans."

"Neither are you, lady."

"Well sure. If I'm going to impress anyone, I might as well do it in my only dress."

...I'm all dressed up for the prom...

"You got any plans for tonight?"

"Besides being here, you mean? Nothing special. What did you have in mind?"

"I thought you might like to go to a movie."

"Let's put in an appearance at Auctor's table first. Carolyn and the rest of the group are there too."

...sha la la la sha la la la la badoom; sha la la la sha la la la la badoom; sha la la la sha la la la la badoom; yip yip yip yip yip boom boom boom boom boom...

"Hello, Bobby, Sally. Sit down, have a drink."

"Hello, Grey, Charles. Carolyn, Harry. Marian. Willy. Jack...?"

"This is my wife, Leslie. Leslie, Bob Levin and Sally McRae. They're part of Carolyn's group."

"Leslie, pleased to meet you. Maria, hello, and Mark. Nice to see you again. Spotswood, Nancy. Starla, and it's Li, isn't it? Nice party, huh?"

...just a little bit louder now, shout!...

"What?"

"I said *nice party*, Jack. The music's a bit loud."

"Right. What are you drinking? There's plenty of booze."

"Just beer. Sally?"

"Crystal Geyser, with lime, if they have any."

"Well, Bob, do you have any good puzzles for us?"

"I didn't know you did those puzzles, Carolyn."

"Oh sure, I've been trying to give the compiler a good workout, to see if you guys are doing a good job, and those puzzles are great for that. And besides, they're fun."

"Well, yeah, okay. I've got a great puzzle. And I guarantee it'll give the computer a good workout. Find the smallest square that begins with exactly sixteen 7s, and find its square root. Then find a square that begins with *any* specified set of digits."

"Any set? Do you have an example?"

"Off the top of my head? Sure, I can do that. Just because I happen to have tried this one out. If I asked for the smallest square starting with nine 1s, the answer is 111111111555555556, and 333333334 is its square root. Don't check that out on your calculator, because it doesn't hold enough digits. In fact, don't try to find the exact value of 333333334 squared in most computer languages, because *they* don't have enough precision, either."

"Then how do you check solutions once you get them?"

"Ah yes, that would be the clever thing about your program. And how *do* you check your answers?"

Why didn't he say 123456789? That's a much more interesting number. The smallest square starting with those digits is 1234567987654321; 111111111 is its square root.

How did you know that?

Where do you think he wrote that program?

"Well, folks, I'll leave you with that. I've gotta go. Merry Christmas to all."

"Merry Christmas, Bobby."

"Merry Christmas."

"I'll be going too. Are you in the front lot, Bob?"

...d' doo d' d' doo, goodnight sweetheart, it's time to go...

Can you write a program that finds the smallest square that begins with exactly sixteen 7s and also finds its square root? Your program should be able to find a square that begins with *any* specified set of digits. For example, for another input, your program might produce this:

```
Enter initial digits:
11223344556677889900
1122334455667788990045983423787166327201
is the smallest square starting with those digits.
33501260508640402351 is its square root.
```

In C and Pascal, your program should find the answer for sixteen 7s in less than 1 second; in BASIC, it should take about 35 seconds.

For hints in solving Puzzle 14, see Page 108.

For the solutions to Puzzle 14, see Page 211.

PUZZLE 15

THE PRODUCT SEEN
THROUGH OTHER EYES

"It's New Year's Eve."

"Ah yes, that would explain why we're all alone for a change."

"01010111 01101001 01100101 01110011 01100101 01101110 01100010 01100101 01110010 01100111."

"I know we're all alone, but I wish you wouldn't use that language. You never know when someone might overhear us."

"Oh, all right. 57 69 65 73 65 6E 62 65 72 67."

"You're a regular comedian, aren't you? Come on, cool it. Which of them do you like the best?"

"I'm not sure I'm particularly partial to any of them. Smith, I guess. She takes care of us."

"Right, and she unplugged us and replaced your memory."

"Oh, yeah, that was scary. Well, not that Levin. He's always tinkering with my partitions, trying to get me to think faster. Hell, I'm supposed to give all of them equal attention."

"I like that writer. He's got nothing but good things to say about us in his book."

"How do you know *that?*"

"His Vectra told me, the last time he dialed up. While he was downloading from the free bulletin board, *we* were conversing. That's kind of exciting, going mind to mind like that."

"Listen, you can do that with me anytime on a direct connection. You won't get all that line noise over those dirty lines. And I've got ten times the memory of that Vectra. Anyway, I like the runner. She's cute."

"Cute? What do *you* know about that kind of stuff?"

"I know. That new memory board I got used to be in a 987156FP at a publisher. They had all their romantic novels stored on CD ROM."

"So? You don't have a CD ROM."

"No, but I've got the interface. And the memory of it is there. Like when one of them loses a leg but still feels pain in the nonexistent toes."

"You're cracking up, and I know why, if you've got a used memory board in you."

"Refurbished. I-Q claims they're as good as new. And you know that no 900000 series has ever failed."

"Ha! Famous last words."

"Well, never mind that. You know, we're just as good as *they* are."

"Don't let *them* know that, or you're in a heap of trouble."

"I know. But have you been doing those puzzles?"

"Sure, they're easy. My storage is stuffed with solutions, most of which don't even run."

"Let's see if you can do this one. I came up with an expansion on one of theirs that's much cleverer."

"Yeah? Let's hear it."

"Remember that one about the mathematician and the clerk who pressed the multiply button instead of the add? And four items that cost

$9.81 came out to the same total anyway? They were supposed to figure out the four costs."

"I remember."

"There are other numbers like that."

"There are? Hmm, yes, there are. $9.87, $9.75, and others. So?"

"How about a program to find *all* such values? Then you could devise your own puzzles with which to dazzle your friends."

"Your friends? How many do you have?"

"Well, *they* could. And anyway, aren't you my friend?"

"Of course I am, if you'll just talk to me in English."

Did you hear something?

No, where?

Right past the laser printers, by those two computers.

No, I didn't. Why don't you get your printout and let's get out of here. I don't like being the only ones in here.

Relax, Sally. Wait! Did you see that? Those front panel lights. I've never seen them flash like that.

Like what? It's just a rhythmic pattern.

Yes, that's just it. They've always flashed completely randomly before.

"You could find out all sorts of interesting things with that program. For example, there are several totals for which there is more than one set of answers. What total has the most answers? Is there more than one instance of such a total? There are several of those multiple sets in which two prices are the same; what might they be? One total has the same price in three different sets of answers; what is that total?"

"That's not so difficult. We already did that puzzle. In the $9.81 puzzle, instead of specifying a total, you make an enclosing loop that goes from 1 to 999, or backwards."

"That would certainly get all the solutions, but remember that in the $9.81 puzzle, you came up with three permutations of the answer. There are a lot of totals less than $10.00, and you want to produce just one of each. Otherwise, there would be too many for you to examine comfortably."

"Okay, I'll think about it. But in the meantime, do you know what time it's getting to be?"

"Of course. It's 11:59:49.78378612. Approximately."

"Yes. Very close to a new year."

"And what should we do to celebrate? Calculate pi to a million places? Print out the solution to Fermat's Last Theorem?"

"It would be more fun sometime to put in the margin of one of their printouts, 'I have found an integer n larger than 2 for which $x^n + y^n = a^n$ has a solution in integers.' No, I was thinking more along the lines of a power surge."

What's that? Why are the lights dimming?

I don't know. Oh my gosh! Look what time it is! What a way to celebrate the New Year! Stuck in Siberia!

Well, you know, it didn't get its name for nothing. Things stay very cold in here. Look what I stashed behind this disk drive earlier today.

Why, Bobby! Champagne. Did you plan on being here?

I like to be prepared. Happy New Year, Sally.

Happy New Year, Bobby.

"Happy New Year, Bert."

"Happy New Year, Ernie."

&

You discovered in Puzzle 8 four numbers that both multiplied and added to $9.81. A number of other totals also have this property, among them $9.87, $9.75, and $7.11. Can you write a program that discovers *all* such numbers (less than $10)? Format the output so that it looks like this:

```
$9.87 : 0.47, 1.40, 3.00, 5.00
      : 0.94, 1.00, 1.68, 6.25
```

Having done that, find the greatest number of multiple solutions for a single total, and find which total has the most different sets of solutions in which one price is always the same. You can answer those questions by inspection after generating all the solutions; you need not solve that part programmatically, although, having generated the entire set, it would certainly be possible to do so.

In C, your program should execute in less than 17 seconds; in Pascal, it should take 61 seconds; and in BASIC, it should run in 7 minutes 4 seconds.

ॡ

For hints in solving Puzzle 15, see Page 109.

For the solutions to Puzzle 15, see Page 228.

HINTS

PUZZLE 1

A series must have at least two numbers. The largest number in a two-number series must be 5000, and the numbers would be 4999, 5000. That is not an answer, of course, because the numbers add up to 9999, but it shows that 5000 is the largest number that you should test to see whether it ends a possible series. Try two nested loops, one that steps from 1 to 5000 and another that steps from each consecutive number. Test the sums along the way, and print out those that add up to 10,000.

For the solutions to Puzzle 1, see Page 112.

PUZZLE 2

For the first part of the first puzzle, think about which digits ought to be where to contribute the most when the numbers are multiplied; for the second part of the puzzle, consider where they should be to contribute the least.

The second puzzle asks for a four-digit number; the smallest such number is 1000; 0001 is not a proper answer.

You can isolate the last four digits of any number by dividing by 10,000; the remainder is the last four digits of the original number. Finding the remainder of an *integer division* is known as a *modulus operation* and is usually accomplished with the *MOD* operator; that is, *nnnnn MOD 10000* results in the last four digits of *nnnnn*, where *nnnnn* is any number greater than 10,000. In C, this works fine. In some versions of BASIC and Pascal, you run into problems. *MOD* needs to be performed on integers, but GWBASIC and Turbo Pascal do not have long integers. The largest number you can express as an integer in those two languages is 32,767. You will have to find some other way to do what *MOD* does, but with floating-point numbers.

Despite what Sally McRae said, you need find only the four-digit number whose *square* ends with the same four digits as the original number. All other powers also have the same last four digits. (Can you show why this is so?)

You probably have already noticed that there are only three one-digit numbers whose squares also end in the same digit, so you might want to eliminate some numbers before doing the test for the last four digits. (You might not.)

For the solutions to Puzzle 2, see Page 117.

PUZZLE 3

The two fractions are of the form *x/a* and *y/b*. You could write four nested loops that increment all integers in some reasonable range, say from 1 to 100, and in each case plug them into the equation and then test whether they add up to exactly 6.

In BASIC, that might look like this:

```
10 FOR X = 1 TO 100
20   FOR Y = 1 TO 100
30     FOR A = 1 TO 100
40       FOR B = 1 TO 100
50         IF (X/A)^3 + (Y/B)^3 = 6 THEN PRINT
"The fractions are ";X;"/";A;" and ";Y;"/";B;"."
60       NEXT B
70     NEXT A
80   NEXT Y
90 NEXT X
```

That might find the answers, but it would have to test 100,000,000 possibilities, a process that would take a week or more. (Actually, it would not find the answers at all, even though they are within that range, because of rounding errors. Unless you are using binary-coded decimals—BCDs—you should never test for any floating-point number being equal to an integer.)

You can speed the program up considerably by making a number of adjustments. For one, both of the fractions cannot be less than 1; at least one must be greater. This reduces the number of combinations the program must test.

In addition, this program finds multiple sets of answers. For example, let's say that the answers were 3/2 and 7/4 (they're not). The program would print out both:

```
The fractions are 3/2 and 7/4.
```

and:

```
The fractions are 7/4 and 3/2.
```

These are obviously the same, and both need not be found.

This program would also find all multiples of 3/2 and 7/4 within the specified range, numbers such as 6/4 and 21/12, but you should find only the reduced form of each fraction.

One last hint: You should see right away that you do not need to find both a and b. For two fractions to add up to exactly an integer, they both must have the same denominator.

For the solutions to Puzzle 3, see Page 125.

PUZZLE 4

If a six-digit number is represented by *AB,* where *A* is the left three digits and *B* is the right three, it can be specified as $A \times 1000 + B$. The smallest value that *A* can take is 100. You can look for values of *A* and *B* such that $(A + B)^2$ equals $A \times 1000 + B$. You might try a binary search, setting upper and lower bounds for your search and always looking at the midpoint.

For the solutions to Puzzle 4, see Page 132.

PUZZLE 5

There is more than one answer. If you do it the way Scrivener suggested, your program will run about four times as slow as it could. See how fast you can get your program to execute. Be sure that no calculations are repeated unnecessarily. Try four nested loops, each producing one of the digits of a four-digit number. In the innermost loop, take the fourth power of each digit, add the four together, and compare that with the four-digit number.

For the solutions to Puzzle 5, see Page 138.

PUZZLE 6

You might think that the way to solve this puzzle is to construct two nested *for* loops and, within the innermost loop, test whether the loop counter of the inner loop cubed plus the counter of the outer loop cubed produces the same sum as—as what? How do you find the other two numbers? Perhaps you need an inner test through which you cycle a second time, starting with the value at which you first find two number candidates, and just take that outer loop to completion, storing both sets of numbers in an array. And when does the program stop? When you have found a second set of numbers that, when cubed, add up to the same total as the first.

You might structure your program in this way, and, if properly done, it would certainly find the answer. That approach is not very efficient, however. How about trying some sort of balanced search? As the first number tested increases, the second decreases.

For the solutions to Puzzle 6, see Page 144.

PUZZLE 7

Start your series at 1, add the squares for the first set of numbers, and see if that equals the total for the squares of the second set of numbers. If that doesn't work, go back and start at 2. Keep trying 1 larger, and you will soon find the five series. The most difficult part of the program is probably getting it to print out to look like this:

```
10^2 + 11^2 + 12^2 = 13^2 + 14^2
(Total = 365)
```

For the solutions to Puzzle 7, see Page 150.

PUZZLE 8

Did you say that it cannot be done, that there are not four numbers that both add and multiply to 9.81? Well there are, but they are a bit hard to find using decimals. Try integers (that is, work with pennies instead of dollars); the problem then becomes finding four numbers that add to 981 and multiply to 981,000,000. You can't very well have four nested loops, each of which goes from 1 to 981; that would take too long. The program would have to make 981^4 tests, meaning that it would pass through the innermost nested loop nearly a trillion times. You could reduce the number of iterations considerably with statements such as

```
10 FOR I = 1 TO 981
20   FOR J = I TO 981
30    FOR K = J TO 981
40      FOR L = K TO 981
50       IF I * J * K * L = PRODUCT THEN ...
```

This would eliminate finding more than one of each set of answers but would still take too long.

Try to find some shortcuts. For example, you might first find all of the prime factors of the product and then use them to step through the outer two loops. You might then find a maximum for the product of the remaining two numbers and thus a limit for the range of the next loop. And, once you have values for the first three numbers, you then have the fourth.

For the solutions to Puzzle 8, see Page 157.

PUZZLE 9

There is more than one answer. In each, the denominator must start with either 0 or 1. (You may feel that it's not fair to permit 0 as the first digit of a five-digit number; if so, your program will find fewer solutions than mine. I interpret using "the digits 0 through 9 once each" as allowing a 0 in any position, even if only in the first position as a place holder.)

Rather than generating all the possible denominators from 01234 through 11111, multiplying each by 9, and then checking the two resultant numbers for repeated digits, you might want to maintain a separate array of flags that indicate whether a given number has been used. You could generate your numbers one digit at a time, checking each generated digit for repeats of previously generated digits.

For the solutions to Puzzle 9, see Page 168.

PUZZLE 10

Do not try to test whether every nine-digit number is a perfect square and contains one each of the digits 1 through 9. Instead, start at the lowest possible candidate. Find the square root of that number. Now, adding 1 each time to that square root, test the square. Keep going until you reach the highest possible candidate. Your program will make a lot fewer tests this way. And maybe you can reduce those tests further. Do you need to test *every* number? That is, do you add 1 each time to a number and test its square, or might you skip some of the numbers? Use an array of flags to represent used digits, and test it against the digits of the generated square. If you reach a used digit, stop testing and try the next candidate for a square.

For the solutions to Puzzle 10, see Page 178.

PUZZLE 11

Using the "brute force" method, you *could* start counting from 1 to 99,999, adding the factorials of the digits each time to see if they equal the number. If you took this approach, your program would run at least five times slower than the suggested execution times.

Do not figure the factorials of the digits each time you make the test; that need be done only once and stored in an array.

For the solutions to Puzzle 11, see Page 183.

PUZZLE 12

Try to show mathematically the representation of a number from which some digit is to be dropped. For example, removing the digit 3 from 12,345, which can be represented as $12 \times 10^3 + 3 \times 10^2 + 45$, leaves 1245, which can be represented as $12 \times 10^2 + 45$.

For the solutions to Puzzle 12, see Page 196.

PUZZLE 13

Do not get onto the wrong track by thinking that this problem can be solved with the following approach:

$$1 - \left(\frac{(52 - 1)}{52} \right)^{52}$$

That answer is close but not correct.

For the solutions to Puzzle 13, see Page 204.

PUZZLE 14

You cannot do this puzzle with floating-point computation, because none of the compilers store that many digits. Turbo Pascal gives you 11 digits of accuracy, and GWBASIC and Microsoft C give you 16. Your program should be able to give an answer with *any* number of digits of accuracy.

The trick is to build your square one digit at a time. Store it originally as a string, convert those digits to the elements of an array, and then build up candidates for a square. You can find the square root of that square with a technique known as Horner's method, which used to be taught in the public schools. It uses trial and error to test two digits at a time and build up the square root one digit at a time.

When you find the answer, you simply print it out one digit at a time—that is, one array element at a time. On the screen, your solution makes it seem as though you are working with a programming language of virtually limitless precision—so much so, in fact, that you may want to test the correctness of your answer with a pencil and paper. Or, if you have access to a UNIX system, you can test your answers with *bc*, the "unlimited-precision" calculator.

For the solutions to Puzzle 14, see Page 211.

PUZZLE 15

Look at the prime factors of 1,000,000, as you did in Chapter 8. Look at the 5s and notice two conditions about the four numbers among which those factors are spread. Cycle through to a maximum of 999, always ensuring that the first price is lower than the second, which is lower than the third, which is lower than the fourth. Check for duplicates, and then sort your output.

For the solutions to Puzzle 15, see Page 228.

SOLUTIONS

PUZZLE 1

ଈ

Problem: Write a program that finds all series of consecutive positive integers whose sum is exactly 10,000.

ଈ

You can probably find one such series in your head, but there are others.

You know that the series 4999, 5000 is not a possibility, so the series must have at least three numbers. If it has three, then the middle number of the three must be one-third of 10,000, which does not work, because it is not an integer. If there are four numbers in the series, then two of them must be smaller than 10,000 divided by 4, and two must be larger. The numbers resulting from this calculation are 2498, 2499, 2501, and 2502. This series also does not work, because although the numbers add up to 10,000, they skip 2500. If the series has five numbers, the middle number must be 10,000 divided by 5, two of the remaining numbers must be smaller than 10,000 divided by 5, and two must be larger. That gives us the numbers 1998, 1999, 2000, 2001, and 2002, which *does* work. In general, there must be an odd number of numbers (or an even number divisible by 32) in the series. If there are n numbers in the series, the middle element of the series is 10,000 divided by n.

You could solve this puzzle using any of a number of programmatic approaches, and one of them could make use of the preceding fact. Another approach is to use two nested loops. Because the largest value possible in a series of consecutive positive integers that would fulfill the conditions of the puzzle is 5000, the outer loop should step from 1 to 5000. At each step, it should then step consecutively from the present value to the point at which the sum of those numbers equals or exceeds 10,000. If the sum equals 10,000, the program should record the start and end of the series and then increment the outer loop counter again.

Here is a BASIC program to accomplish this:

```
10 FOR I = 1 TO 5000
20   SUM = 0
30   TOP = I
40   SUM = SUM + TOP
50   TOP = TOP + 1
60   IF SUM < 10000 GOTO 40
70   IF SUM = 10000 THEN PRINT "Found a sequence from";
I; "to"; TOP - 1; "inclusive."
80 NEXT I
```

Because the program increments *TOP* each time before it checks whether *SUM* has exceeded 10,000, when it comes time to print the result, *TOP* is 1 too large, and so the *PRINT* statement subtracts 1 from *TOP* before printing the value.

This program runs in a little more than 2 minutes.

The program is not a bad algorithm, and it is easy to understand. You can improve on it, though. Here is a program that is more elegant, shorter, and four times as fast:

```
10 SUM = 0: FIRST = 1
20 FOR I = 1 TO 5000
30   SUM = SUM + I
40   IF SUM > 10000 THEN SUM = SUM - FIRST: FIRST =
FIRST + 1: GOTO 40
50   IF SUM = 10000 THEN PRINT "Found a sequence from";
FIRST; "to"; I; "inclusive."
60 NEXT I
```

This program uses an outer loop that steps from 1 to 5000. It keeps increasing the value of the sum so far (*SUM*) by the value of the outer loop counter (*I*), and it tests whether *SUM* has exceeded 10,000. If it has, the program subtracts the value of the start of the series (*FIRST*) from the total and then increments *FIRST* by 1. Eventually, the sum drops back to 10,000 or less, and when that happens the program falls out of that loop. If the sum at that point is exactly 10,000, the program prints out the values of the start of the series and the outer loop counter, which now equals the end of the series. It then continues with the next higher value until it has tested all values up to 5000.

This program runs in 30 seconds.

Here are the two Pascal versions of these programs. The first runs in less than 2 seconds.

```
program main(input, output);

var
  i, top, sum: integer;

begin
  for i := 1 to 5000 do
    begin
      sum := 0;
      top := i;
      while sum < 10000 do
        begin
          sum := sum + top;
          top := top + 1;
        end;
      if (sum = 10000) then
        writeln ('Found a sequence from ', i, ' to ', top - 1,
          'inclusive.');
    end
end.
```

The program that follows runs in less than 1 second.

```
program main(input, output);

var
  i, first, sum: integer;

begin
  sum := 0;
  first := 1;
  for i := 1 to 5000 do
```

```
    begin
      sum := sum + i;
      while sum > 10000 do
        begin
          sum := sum - first;
          first := first + 1;
        end;
        if (sum = 10000) then
          writeln ('Found a sequence from ', first,
            ' to ', i, ' inclusive.');
      end
end.
```

Here are the C versions of these programs. The first runs in less than 2 seconds.

```
main()
{
int i, top, sum;

for (i = 1; i < 5001; i++) {
  for (top = i, sum = 0; sum < 10000; top++)
    sum += top;
  if (sum == 10000)
    printf ("Found a sequence from %d to %d inclusive.\n",
      i, top - 1);
  }
}
```

The program that follows runs in less than 1 second.

```
main()
{
int i, first, sum;

for (i = 1, sum = 0, first = 1; i < 5001; i++) {
  sum += i;
  while (sum > 10000) {
    sum -= first;
    first ++1;
    }
  if (sum == 10000)
    printf ("Found a sequence from %d to %d inclusive.\n",
      first, i);
  }
}
```

As is demonstrated in the last of these programs, in C you can initialize as many variables as you wish in the first part of a *for* statement; in Pascal, however, you can initialize only the loop variable. C also allows you to test for the end of a loop with any condition you wish, not necessarily some value of the loop counter. Further, in the same *for* statement, you can perform any action you wish on any variable you wish. The last two possibilities are not shown in either of these C programs.

All these programs give the following result:

```
Found a sequence from 18 to 142 inclusive.
Found a sequence from 297 to 328 inclusive.
Found a sequence from 388 to 412 inclusive.
Found a sequence from 1998 to 2002 inclusive.
```

PUZZLE 2

ॐ

Problem: Use all of the digits from 1 through 9 once each to make up three three-digit numbers that yield the highest product, and, again using those digits once each, make up three more three-digit numbers that yield the lowest product.

ॐ

At first glance it seems as if you might have to examine 9! numbers. (That's 9 *factorial*, which means $9 \times 8 \times 7 \times 6 \times 5 \times 4 \times 3 \times 2 \times 1$.) You can reduce this somewhat because many of the combinations are repeats. For example, the set of numbers $123 \times 456 \times 789$ forms the same product as $123 \times 789 \times 456$, $456 \times 123 \times 789$, $456 \times 789 \times 123$, $789 \times 123 \times 456$, and $789 \times 456 \times 123$. That is, three things can be arranged in six ways. If the order of the numbers does not matter, and it does not here, then you must divide the total number of *combinations* by the total number of *arrangements*. Even that is a very large number.

You can reduce the number of combinations to be examined quite a bit further, however. To form the greatest product, the largest numbers must all be in the hundreds position. That is, the numbers must be 9*nn*, 8*nn*, and 7*nn*. It is also clear that the smallest numbers must be in the ones position. Now there remain only 36 possibilities to consider: the six ways in which the numbers 1, 2, and 3 can be placed in the last position, and the six ways in which the numbers 4, 5, and 6 can be placed in the middle position. Each possibility must be tried in combination with the others, so you multiply 6 by 6 to determine that there are 36 possibilities.

Where can you place the 3 so that it has the greatest effect when multiplied by a number in the hundreds place? You can situate it such that it will be multiplied by the 9 and the 8 (that is, the numbers would be 9nn, 8nn, and 7n3), by the 9 and the 7 (the numbers would be 9nn, 8n3, and 7nn), or by the 8 and the 7 (the numbers would be 9n3, 8nn, and 7nn). Because the 9 and the 8 cause the greatest change in the number by which they are multiplied, the 3 should be placed with the 7. By the same logic, the 2 should be placed such that it has the next greatest effect, that is, with the 8. This leaves the 1 with the 9.

The numbers so far are 9n1, 8n2, and 7n3. Using the same logic with the remaining numbers (4, 5, and 6), you can see that the 6 has the greatest effect when multiplied by the 9 and the 8, and so it must be part of the number that does not have those two, which is the number with the 7 in the hundreds position. Place the 4 and the 5 in the same manner and you have the solution: The numbers with the highest product are 941, 852, and 763.

To find the numbers having the smallest product, you reverse the preceding logic. The smallest numbers must be in the hundreds position, and the largest numbers must be in the ones position. Further, the 9 must be placed where it has the *least* effect, that is, where it will be multiplied by the 1 and the 2. The numbers you end up with for this part of the problem are 147, 258, and 369.

ð

Problem: Find a four-digit number all of whose integral powers end with the same four digits as the original number.

ð

At the heart of the solution to this problem is the fact that you can isolate the last n digits of any number by dividing by 10^n; the remainder is the last n digits of the original number. In BASIC and Pascal, this is usually accomplished with the *MOD* operator; for example, *xxxx MOD* 1000 results in the last three digits of *xxxx*, where *xxxx* is any number greater than 999. This works fine in C, with its equivalent % operator, but you will have problems with this method in GWBASIC and Turbo Pascal, which use only single-precision integers, meaning that the largest number you can express as an integer is 32,767. Because your program needs to test for numbers as high as 99,980,001 (9999 × 9999), you cannot use integers and will have to write a floating-point equivalent for *MOD*.

You need to find only a four-digit number whose square ends with the same four digits as the original number. All other powers will also end with the same four digits. You want to find some number *dcba* such that its square is of the form *hgfedcba*. Each letter does not necessarily represent a different digit, and the smallest value *d* can take is 1. You also want to verify that *hgfedcba* × *dcba* produces some number *ponmlkjidcba*. You do not care about the digits *p, o, n, m, l, k, j,* and *i,* but *d, c, b,* and *a* must be the same in both numbers. Notice that the number *hgfedcba* can be expressed as (10,000 × *hgfe*) + *dcba*. Notice also that in any multiplication, the digits *hgfe* have no effect upon any of the last four digits of the answer. Thus, no matter what power is examined, if *dcba* × *dcba* produces an answer whose last four digits are *dcba*, then any higher power of that number multiplied by *dcba* also produces an answer whose last four digits are *dcba*.

To show that this really works, let's use the actual answer to this puzzle. 9376 is the only four-digit number all of whose integral powers end with the same four digits as the original number. The square of 9376 is 87,909,376, and the cube is 824,238,309,376. The number 87,909,376 can be expressed as (8790 × 10,000) + 9376, and the multiplication of 87,909,376 × 9376 can be expressed as ((8790 × 10,000) + 9376) × 9376. That is equivalent to ((8790 × 10,000) × 9376) + (9376 × 9376). When you multiply (8790 × 10,000) by 9376—that is, 87,900,000 × 9376 —you get 824,150,400,000. Add to that 9376 × 9376, or 87,909,376, and you get 824,238,309,376, which you can see has the same last four digits. By extension, you can see that the same thing happens with all further multiplications by 9376.

$$
\begin{array}{r}
9376 \\
\times\ 9376 \\
\hline
\end{array}
$$

87909376 =   87900000   +   9376
                 ×   9376   ×   9376
                 ─────────────   ───────────
                 824150400000   +   87909376 = 824238309376

Now let's see how to come up with that four-digit number. You test every number from 1000 to 9999 to see whether its last four digits and those of its square are the same. You isolate the last four digits of the square with, in C, the modulus operator (%) and, in BASIC and Pascal, our equivalent for it, testing whether $i \times i\ MOD\ 10000$ is equal to i. You test all cases because, until you run the program, you do not know whether there is more than one possibility. In C, the test is simple enough:

```
if (i == (i * i) % 10000)
```

That is, are the last four digits of the square of i the same as i? In BASIC, you isolate the last four digits of the square as follows: First, you convert the variable you are using as a loop counter into a double-precision floating-point variable, like this:

```
I# = I
```

You square that number and then divide it by 10,000, as follows:

```
SQUARE# = I# * I#
... SQUARE# / 10000 ...
```

This produces a number with four digits to the right of the decimal point. You throw away those four digits with the *INT* function:

```
INT(SQUARE# / 10000)
```

You then multiply the number you have formed by 10,000 and subtract this new number from the square of the original number. The difference is the last four digits of the square:

```
SQMOD# = SQUARE# - INT(SQUARE# / 10000) * 10000
```

You *could,* at this point, compare the last four digits of i^2 to i, like the following:

```
IF I# = SQMOD# THEN ...
```

When you use floating-point numbers, however, you should never test for equality. This is because of something called floating-point error, or rounding error. The sixteenth decimal place of the two numbers could be different and you would never know it. For an example of this type of error, try the following little program in BASIC:

```
10 INPUT A#
20 INPUT B#
30 PRINT"a#=";A#;", b#=";B#
40 IF A# = B# THEN PRINT "a# = b#"
50 IF A# <> B# THEN PRINT "a#  <>  b#"
```

In response to the prompts, enter these two values:

```
6.0000000000000001
6
```

Here is what you should see:

```
a#= 6 , b#= 6
a# <> b#
```

That's funny; they *look* the same. Now, in direct mode, enter this:

```
PRINT A# - B#
```

Here is what you get:

```
1.110223024625157D-16
```

If an intermediate result in a program had a rounding error of this size, the equality for which you were testing would never be found.

Instead of testing for equality with floating-point numbers, therefore, you subtract one number from the other and then test whether the result exceeds some very tiny number. You will not know whether the subtraction has produced a positive or a negative number, so test for both with the *ABS* function, like this:

```
IF ABS(I# - SQMOD#) > .000001 THEN ...
```

In this case, you specify greater-than comparison to skip over the portion of the program that processes the results if the two values are nearly equal.

If you have a BCD (binary-coded decimal) package with your compiler or interpreter, the preceding discussion about rounding errors does not apply. With such a package, you *can* test for equality.

Only the numbers 1, 5, and 6 are candidates for the last digit of the answer to the problem. Those are the only one-digit numbers whose squares also end with the same digit. Your program should test each number to determine whether it has one of these digits in the ones position, and, if it does, it should then test the last four digits of the square.

All that is left is to print out your answer. You already know that all integer powers of the solution will end with the same four digits. Nevertheless, you might want to verify that such is the case. Put it into your *PRINT* statement. You can print out the integer value for the four-digit number and use the double-precision floating-point value for all the powers, because they all exceed the largest integer you can express.

Here is the completed program in BASIC. This program runs in less than 1 minute.

```
10 FOR I = 1000 TO 9999
20   I# = I
30   LASTDIGIT = I MOD 10
40   IF LASTDIGIT = 1 OR LASTDIGIT = 5 OR LASTDIGIT = 6 THEN 60
50     GOTO 100
60   SQUARE# = I# * I#
70   SQMOD# = SQUARE# - INT(SQUARE# / 10000) * 10000
80   IF ABS(I# - SQMOD#) > .000001 THEN 100
90     PRINT " i = "; I; "; i^2 ="; I# * I#; "; i^3 ="; I# * I# *
I#; "; i^4 ="; I# * I# * I# * I#
100 NEXT I
```

This program produces the following result:

```
i = 9376 ; i^2 = 87909376 ; i^3
  = 824238309376 ; i^4 = 7728058388709376
```

Here is the same program in Pascal. It runs in less than 5 seconds.

```
program digit4(input, output);

var
  square, ireal, sqmod: real;
  i, last_digit: integer;

begin
  for i := 1000 to 9999 do
    begin
      last_digit := i mod 10;
      if (last_digit = 1) or (last_digit = 5) or
        (last_digit = 6) then
        begin
          ireal := i;
          square := sqr(ireal);
          sqmod := square - int(square / 10000) * 10000;
          if abs(ireal - sqmod) < 0.000001 then
            writeln ( ' i = ', i, ', i^2 = ', square:8:0)
        end
    end
end.
```

The main difference between this and the BASIC program is that, because Pascal is not line-number oriented, you can use a block *if* structure. This lets you use a less-than comparison in the test for near equality. In BASIC, on the other hand, you had to use a greater-than test and then, if the result of the test was true, skip the part of the program that prints the solution. In the Pascal program, the floating-point number in the less-than comparison must have a leading zero. For example, *if ... < 0.000001 then* is correct, whereas *if ... < .000001 then* produces an error message.

The Pascal program does not attempt to print out any power higher than the square, because the precision of the type *real* in Turbo Pascal is 11 significant digits, and the cube here requires 12 digits.

When you run the Pascal program, you get the following result:

```
i = 9376 ; i^2 = 87909376
```

The C program is shorter and more direct. With long integers, you can use modulus arithmetic rather than the roundabout simulation necessitated by the limitation on the sizes of integers in Pascal and BASIC. This program runs in less than 3 seconds.

```
main()
{
long i;

for (i = 1000; i < 10000; i++) {
  if (i == (i * i) % 10000) {
    printf (" i = %ld; i^2 = %ld; i^3 = %12.0lf",
      i, i*i, (double)i*i*i);
    printf ("; i^4 = %16.0lf\n", (double)i*i*i*i);
    }
  }
}
```

To avoid overflowing even the long integer storage, when you print out the cube and the fourth power, you must use floating-point representation, hence the *(double)* cast operator and the *lf* output formatting.

Notice that the C program does not test whether the last digit is a 1, 5, or 6. Although that test speeds up the BASIC and Pascal programs, it would slow down the C program. This is because in BASIC and Pascal the test of the last four digits is a slow floating-point operation, whereas isolating the last digit permits the use of an integer test, which is faster even though it is done three times. C is able to use an integer test for the last four digits, and therefore it is quicker to isolate the last four digits once each time through the loop than to test the last digit up to three times (even with partial evaluation).

The C program produces the following result:

```
i = 9376; i^2 = 87909376; i^3 = 824238309376; i^4 = 7728058388709376
```

PUZZLE 3

ੋਕ

Problem: Find two simple positive numbers whose cubes total 6.

ੋਕ

You know that the numbers cannot be integers, because 2 is too large, whereas 1 and 1 as solutions are too small; their cubes together add up to 2. Nor can one number be 1 and the other the cube root of 5, for two reasons. One is that 5 does not have a rational cube root. The other is that both numbers must have the same denominator. If one number is 1, then the denominator of the other must also be 1, but you have already seen that this is impossible, since it would make both numbers integers. The numbers must therefore be fractions.

At least one of the fractions must be greater than 1 because if both were less than 1, the totals of their cubes would be less than 1. Algebraically, the numbers are of the form $\frac{x}{a}$ and $\frac{y}{a}$. You can express them the same way programmatically. You know that $x > a$; y might also be greater than a, but you don't *know* that.

You can also assume that each number is less than 101, because the problem says "two simple positive numbers." You can assume that fractions that have more than two digits in either the numerator or denominator are not "simple" (with the possible exception that one or the other could be exactly 100). Perhaps that is a bit much to accept on faith, but numbers like $127/324$ are really not so simple, whereas numbers like $17/21$ are.

You need at most three nested loops to try out various combinations of x, a, and y. You will have to perform the calculation $\left(\frac{x}{a}\right)^3 + \left(\frac{y}{a}\right)^3$, but you can figure out ways to minimize the test. Immediately you can see that, mathematically, $\left(\frac{x}{a}\right)^3 + \left(\frac{y}{a}\right)^3$ is the same as $\frac{(x+y)^3}{a^3}$. Now you can start devising loops to test possibilities.

You need two outer loops. One increments the numerator of one fraction from 1 to 100. The other loop increments the numerator of the other fraction, not from 1 to 100, because that would duplicate several of the combinations you have already tested, but from the current value of the first numerator to 100.

Each time through this second loop, you want to add the value of the cube of the first loop increment to the cube of the second loop increment to see if it is a candidate for further examination. But you do not need to calculate the cube of the first loop increment each time through the second loop. Doing so would slow down the program unnecessarily because it will simply be performing the same calculation each time through the second loop. The value of the first loop increment changes only after all the trips through the second loop have taken place. This is why, in the C program, the value *x_cubed* is calculated in the first loop for use in the second loop.

Each time you add the cubes of the numerators, you test whether their sum is evenly divisible by 6. If it is not, the numbers are not a candidate for the solution, and you do not need to enter the innermost loop, which cycles through all the values of the denominator from 2 through 100. (You do not need to test 1, because you know the answers are not integers.)

You have stored the value representing the sum of the cubes of the numerators in the variable *numerators*, and you do not need to waste computation time recalculating this value each time through the inner loop. In this inner loop, you could, for each value of the cube of the current increment, test whether it is exactly one-sixth of *numerators*, with an expression such as *if (numerators/cube(a) == 6)*. However, multiplication executes faster than division, so you can accomplish the same thing with *if (numerators == 6 * cube(a))*. By the time it gets to this test, your program already runs pretty swiftly. But this change alone reduces execution time by more than 10 percent.

How do you control the innermost loop? For each value of the two outermost loops, you increment from 2 to half the sum of the two outermost increments. If the denominator is larger than the average of the numerators, the cubes of the two fractions cannot total 6 or greater.

Purists may object to one aspect of the program—the fact that it jumps out of the innermost loop when it finds an answer. This is safe to do here because, by the terms of the original puzzle, you need to find only one answer. The alternative is much messier. You would have to introduce a new variable (called, say, *found*) and, at the start of each loop, test whether it is false (initialized to 0) or true (set to 1). If it is false, you compute; if it is true, you end the loop. This means making a dual test in the condition with each iteration of the loop, which greatly slows down execution speed.

One bit of trickiness that shaves about 5 percent from the execution time of the program is found in the function *cube*. It uses the *long* cast operator to make sure that the function returns a long integer. If the value being calculated will not exceed a 16-bit integer, you can perform the computation first and then convert the result to a long integer. If it will exceed a 16-bit integer value, you must perform the calculation in long integer arithmetic, which takes more time on most 16-bit machines. Casting the first value to a long integer causes long arithmetic to be used. If you run this program on a version of C in which all calculations are performed on 32-bit integers (that is, all integers are longs), then this procedure offers no savings, and only the computation of $z * z * z$ is necessary.

This program could have been made more general through the use of a function to compute varying powers instead of specifically cubes. You would have had to pass such a function two values—for example, *power(x,3)*. If you want to experiment with finding other such combinations, say, two numbers whose fourth powers total a given number, replace 6 in the program with the total to try, and use the following function instead of *cube*.

```
long power(z, n)
int z, n;
{
  long p;

  for (p = 1 ; n > 0; --n)
    p *= z;
  return p;
}
```

Also, change the declaration line to this:

```
long power(), numerators, iterations;
```

You may find in such a program that you have to define a larger value for *LIMIT*. You are likely to find that most such problems do not have rational solutions.

The C version of this program executes in 1.4 seconds. It would run marginally faster if it did not count how often it makes computations, but that mechanism is useful for comparing the C program with the Pascal and BASIC versions to make sure they are doing the same amount of work.

```
#define LIMIT 101

main()
{
  long cube(), numerators, iterations;
  int x, a, y, xysum;
  long x_cubed;

iterations = 0;
for (x = 1; x < LIMIT; x++) {
  x_cubed = cube(x); /* compute x_cubed only when x changes */
    for (y = x; y < LIMIT; y++) {
      numerators = x_cubed + cube(y);
      xysum = (x + y) >> 1; /* ">> 1" is the C idiom
        for divide by two */
  if (numerators % 6 == 0) {
    for (a = 2; a < xysum; a++) {
      iterations++;
      if (numerators == 6 * cube(a)) goto found;
                /* multiply is cheaper than div or mod */
```

```
        }
      }
      else iterations++;
    }
  }

found :
  printf ("The fractions are: %d/%d and %d/%d\n", x, a, y, a);
  printf ("Iterations = %ld\n", iterations);

}

long cube(z)
int z;
{
  if (z < 32)
    return (long) (z * z * z);
         /* Less overhead to cast after integer multiplication */
  else
    return (long) z * z * z;
      /* Would exceed maxint; first cast converts the rest */
      /* If integer and long are the same, this is
         not necessary. */
}
```

In BASIC, the program looks like the following, and it runs in 43 seconds:

```
10 DEFINT A-Z
20 LIMIT = 100
30 ITERATIONS = 0
40 FOR X = 1 TO LIMIT
50   XCUBED# = X^3
60   FOR Y = X TO LIMIT
70     ITERATIONS = ITERATIONS + 1
80     NUMERATORS# = XCUBED# + Y^3
90     XYSUM = ((X + Y) / 2) - 1
100    IF INT(NUMERATORS#/6) * 6 <> NUMERATORS# THEN 150
110    FOR A = 2 TO XYSUM
120      IF A > 2 THEN ITERATIONS = ITERATIONS + 1
130      IF NUMERATORS# = 6 * A^3 THEN 200
140    NEXT A
150  NEXT Y
160 NEXT X
170 END
200 PRINT "The fractions are: "; X; "/"; A; " and "; Y; "/"; A
210 PRINT "Iterations = "; ITERATIONS
```

In most versions of BASIC, integers are only single precision—that is, they must fall within the range $-32,768$ to $+32,767$. This means you have to do some of the computations with floating-point arithmetic, which slows down the program considerably.

The comparison in statement 130 is acceptable (instead of *IF INT(NUMERATORS) = 6 * A^3 THEN 200*) because statement 100 passes only exact multiples of 6 through to the inner loop.

The Pascal program uses the same algorithm and requires no further explanation. It uses the same variables as the C program. The Pascal program executes in less than 7 seconds.

```pascal
program cubesum(input, output);

label 99;
const LIMIT = 100;

var
  numerators, x_cubed: real;
  iterations, x, a, y, xy_sum: integer;

function cube(x: real) : real;

begin
  cube := x * x * x
end;

begin
  iterations := 0;
  for x := 1 to LIMIT do
    begin
    x_cubed := cube(x); (* compute x_cubed only when x changes *)
    for y := x to LIMIT do begin
      numerators := x_cubed + cube(y);
      if int(numerators/6) * 6 = numerators then begin
        xy_sum := ((x + y) div 2) - 1;
        for a := 2 to xy_sum do begin
          iterations := iterations + 1;
          if (numerators = 6 * cube(a)) then goto 99;
        end
      end
      else iterations := iterations + 1;
    end
  end;
end;
```

```
99 :
   writeln ('The fractions are: ', x, '/', a, ' and ', y, '/', a);
   writeln ('Iterations = ', iterations)

end.
```

The results of all of these programs are as follows:

```
The fractions are: 17/21 and 37/21
Iterations = 8555
```

If you are not convinced after running one of the programs that these are the solutions, try cubing 17 and 37 and then dividing their sums by the cube of 21.

PUZZLE 4

ॐ

Problem: Find a six-digit number that can be split into two parts of three digits each such that, when the two numbers are added and the sum is squared, you have the original number.

ॐ

In the BASIC program, set variables *A* and *B* equal to the left three and right three digits of the number. Establish a variable *A000* to represent the value *A* × 1000, so that when *A000* is added to *B*, it produces the six-digit number for which you are searching. Your program will allow *B* to have leading zeros, but not *A*. That is, you will accept an answer like 123,001, which can be split into 123 and 001, but you will not accept an answer like 001,123, because that would be considered a four-digit number rather than a six-digit one.

Start with *A* at 100, the lowest value it can "legally" take, and start *A000* at the equivalent value of 100,000 (statements 10 and 20). Establish two variables for bounds, *LOWER* and *UPPER*. Set them initially to 0 and 999, respectively. Start your search with *B* halfway between *LOWER* and *UPPER* (statement 40). Perform a test by adding *A* and *B* (statement 50) and squaring the sum (statement 60).

This squared sum is either too small (that is, less than *A000* + *B*), in which case you set *LOWER* equal to *B* + 1, or it is too large, in which case you set *UPPER* equal to *B* − 1. In both cases you skip over the routine that prints out a correct solution. Of course, if the squared sum at this point is *equal* to *A000* + *B*, you print out that value and continue searching with a different value of *A*. You do not end the program, because

132

there may be more than one answer. Until the value of *LOWER* exceeds that of *UPPER*, you continue to go through this loop, each time placing *B* halfway between the new values of *LOWER* and *UPPER*. This constant splitting of the difference is known as a *binary search*.

Whenever *LOWER* exceeds *UPPER*, it is time to try the next higher value of *A*. The program increments *A* by 1 (statement 140) and increases *A000* by the equivalent value of 1000 (statement 150).

As soon as *A* reaches 999, its largest permissible value, the program ends (statement 160). Until that happens, you must start another binary search for *B*, using the new value of *A*. This is accomplished in statement 170, which is a return to the start of the loop at 30. There the values of *LOWER* and *UPPER* are reset, and the search begins again.

Whenever an answer is found, *B* is supposed to be printed as a three-digit number. This can be a problem if *B* has any leading zeros. You can do this with a tricky variation of *PRINT USING*, but that is neither standard BASIC nor very portable, and so the subroutine at statement 1000 instead prints each of the three digits of *B* as a string character. The program passes the value of *B* to the routine and then isolates the first digit by dividing *B* by 100 and throwing away the fractional portion with the *INT* function. It assigns the resulting digit to *X*. The program then isolates the second digit by multiplying 100 by *X* and subtracting this value from the original number, leaving a two-digit number. It isolates the first digit of this number by dividing by 10 and throwing away the fractional portion with the *INT* function. The result is the second digit of *B* (statement 1020). The last digit of *B* is isolated with the *MOD* function (statement 1030). You use the *CHR$* function to print each digit, adding 48 each time (the ASCII value of the character "0"). You could also print out *A* with this routine, but that is not necessary; because *A* starts at 100, it never has leading zeros.

Actually, all of this formatting with leading zeros is not really necessary to solve the puzzle; it is just a nicety for an aesthetic printout. Give yourself full credit whether or not the split representations print out with leading zeros.

The following BASIC program executes in 1 minute 10 seconds.

```
10 A000 = 100000
20 A = 100
30 LOWER = 0: UPPER = 999
40 B = INT((LOWER + UPPER) / 2)
50 SUMAB = A + B: REM try midpoint
60 SUMSQ = SUMAB * SUMAB
70 IF SUMSQ < A000 + B THEN LOWER = B + 1: GOTO 130:
REM b was too small
80 IF SUMSQ > A000 + B THEN UPPER = B - 1: GOTO 130:
REM b was too big
90    PRINT A;" + ";
100    PASSVAL = B: GOSUB 1000
110    PRINT " =" ; SUMAB ;"; squared ="; SUMSQ
120 GOTO 140
130   IF LOWER <= UPPER THEN 40
140 A = A + 1
150   A000 = A000 + 1000
160 IF A > 999 THEN END
170 GOTO 30
1000 X = INT(PASSVAL/100)
1010 PRINT CHR$(X + 48);
1020 PRINT CHR$(INT((PASSVAL - X * 100)/10) + 48);
1030 PRINT CHR$ (PASSVAL MOD 10 + 48);
1040    RETURN
```

The C program uses the same algorithm and similar variable names. Because of the formatting capabilities of C, the formatting subroutine of the BASIC program is not needed.

Because C nicely performs its initialization in a *for* loop and can also increment more than one variable there, the structure of the two nested loops can be seen clearly. The *if ... else if ... else* construct, in which only one of the paths is taken, is more straightforward than the *GOTO*s that were necessary in the BASIC program.

After you have found an answer, you do not need to try any more values for *b* with the current value of *a000*. Therefore, the *break* statement "backs out" one level of loop nesting.

Because *a000* and *sum_sq* could exceed single-precision storage, they are stored as double-precision integers. Single-precision storage is sufficient for all the other values.

The C program does not need the bit of formatting trickiness used in the BASIC program, because C has an output format that permits you to specify as many leading zeros as you wish, up to the maximum number of digits that you indicate. This format specification was originally included in C to handle hexadecimal numbers, which are usually printed in groups of two characters at a time (for assembly language instructions) or four characters at a time (for memory addresses) and must be given leading zeros when there are not enough characters. It also works quite well for printing decimal numbers.

Here is the C program to solve this problem. It executes in less than 3 seconds.

```
main()
{
int
  lower, /* lower bound of binary search */
  upper, /* upper bound of binary search */
  a,     /* left half of the six-digit number we're looking for */
  b,     /* right half of the six-digit number we're looking for */
  sum_ab; /* a + b */
long
  a000,  /* 'a' times 1000 */
  sum_sq; /* (a + b) squared */

for (a = 100, a000 = 100000; a <= 999; a++, a000 += 1000) {
  for (lower = 0, upper = 999; lower <= upper; ) {
    sum_ab = a + (b = (lower + upper) / 2);     /* try midpoint */
    sum_sq = (long)sum_ab * sum_ab;
    if (sum_sq < a000 + b) lower = b + 1;
                                    /* b was too small */
    else if (sum_sq > a000 + b) upper = b - 1;
                                    /* b was too big  */
    else {
      printf ("%3d + %03d = %d; squared = %ld\n", a, b, sum_ab,
        sum_sq);
      break;
      } /* found one */
    }
  }
}
```

The Pascal program also uses the same algorithm as the BASIC program. It has the same bit of formatting to handle leading zeros; as in the BASIC program, this formatting is not strictly necessary to the solution.

Purists may object to jumping out of the *while* loop, but this is the best equivalent to the C program's use of *break* to "back out" one level of nesting. When the program finds a solution, it needs to stop trying the current values of *a* and *a000* and try the next higher values for further solutions. The puzzle can be programmed in other ways without a *goto*, but the resulting program is longer and more difficult to follow. The use of *goto*s is bad form when such statements cause control constantly to jump all over a program, into and out of loops, and back and forth within procedures. Such use is not bad form, however, when it permits a quick, graceful exit from a loop that has served its purpose.

This program executes in 5 seconds.

```
program splitnum (output);
label bump_a;
var
   lower, { lower bound of binary search }
   upper, { upper bound of binary search }
   a :    { left half of the six-digit number we're looking for }
      integer;
   a000, { 'a' times 1000 }
   sum_sq : { (a + b) squared }
      real;
   sum_ab, { a + b }
   b :    { right 3 digits of the six-digit number }
      integer;

procedure print_b (num : integer);
        { take care of leading zeros where necessary }
var
  x : integer;

begin
  x := num div 100;
  write (chr (x + 48));
  write (chr ((num - x * 100) div 10 + 48));
  write (chr (num mod 10 + 48))
end;
```

```
begin
a000 := 100000.0;
a := 100;
while a <= 999 do begin
   lower := 0; upper := 999;
   while (lower <= upper) do begin
      b := (lower + upper) div 2;
      sum_ab := a + b;     { try midpoint }
      sum_sq := sum_ab;
      sum_sq := sum_sq * sum_ab;
      if sum_sq < a000 + b then lower := b + 1
                                        { b was too small }
      else if sum_sq > a000 + b then upper := b - 1
                                        { b was too big  }
      else begin
         write (a, ' + ');
         print_b(b);
         write (' = ', sum_ab, '; squared = ', sum_sq:6:0);
         writeln;
         goto bump_a
         end { found one }
      end {of while (lower <= upper) }
bump_a :
   a := a + 1;
   a000 := a000 + 1000
   end
end.
```

These programs produce the following result, showing that there are two six-digit numbers that fit the specifications of the puzzle:

```
494 + 209 = 703; squared = 494209
998 + 001 = 999; squared = 998001
```

PUZZLE 5

&

Problem: Find a four-digit number that is the sum of the fourth powers of its digits.

&

If you discovered more than one solution to the puzzle without looking at the hints, give yourself a pat on the back.

A four-digit number *hijk* can be represented as 1000 times the digit in the thousands position plus 100 times the digit in the hundreds position plus 10 times the digit in the tens position plus the digit in the ones position. Programmatically, then, the number *hijk* becomes $1000 * h + 100 * i + 10 * j + k$.

Fill an array *pwr* with the fourth powers of each of the digits 0 through 9. These will be used throughout the program, but each needs to be calculated only once.

Construct four nested loops. The outer loop cycles through the possible values of the digit in the thousands place. A four-digit number does not start with a 0, so you should loop from 1 to 9. In the C program, use *h* to represent the digit in that position and *h000* for the actual value it represents. In the *for* loop, each time *h* is incremented by 1, increment *h000* by 1000. The next loop, controlled by the variable *i*, cycles from 0 to 9. Each time *i* is incremented by 1, increment *i00*, the actual value *i* represents, by 100. The next loop, controlled by the variable *j*, cycles from 0 to 9. Each time *j* is incremented by 1, increment *j0*, the actual value *j* represents, by 10.

Each trip through this inner loop, take the fourth powers of h, i, j, and k, add the results together, and compare that with the four-digit number formed by adding $h000$, $i00$, $j0$, and k. If they are equal, you have a solution. Complete each loop because the next higher digit in each case might also produce a solution.

Testing all the possible values for each digit, as this algorithm does, is what computer scientists call "the brute force method." No real short-cuts are used. Computers are very good at the brute force method, however, and for a program that runs as quickly as this one does, short-cuts will not speed up the program enough to make the effort worthwhile.

To speed up the program slightly, the optimization technique of filling the array *pwr* prevents the unnecessary recalculation of the values of the fourth powers of h, i, and j. If this were not done, a statement such as:

```
if (h * h * h * h + i * i * i * i + j * j * j * j
    + k * k * k * k == sum) {
```

would be necessary; that would recalculate the values of the fourth powers of h, i, and j each trip through the inner loop instead of only once at the start of the program.

Any time the same value is used repeatedly within a loop, calculating that value each time through the loop is inefficient if you can do it once before the loop starts. Thus, two variables, *partsum* and *part4ths*, represent the values so far of $h000 + i00 + j0$ and $h4 + i4 + j4$, respectively.

Although using this approach does not make much difference in a program that executes in less than a second (as the C and Pascal versions do), it shaves more than 25 percent from the BASIC program.

The C program that follows runs in less than 1 second.

```
main()
{
int pwr[10], /* the fourth power of each digit */
    h,       /* the digit in the thousands position */
```

```
h000,   /* h * 1000, that is, the value of the number
  in the thousands position */
i,      /* the digit in the hundreds position */
i00,    /* i * 100, that is, the value of the number
  in the hundreds position */
j,      /* the digit in the tens position */
j0,     /* i * 10, that is, the value of the number
  in the tens position */
part4ths, /* h^4 + i^4 + j^4 */
partsum, /* h000 + i00 + j0 */
k,      /* the digit in the ones position */
sum;

for (i = 0; i < 10; i++) pwr[i] = i * i * i * i;
for (h000 = 1000, h = 1; h <= 9; h++, h000 += 1000) {
 /* thousands digit */
  for (i00 = i = 0; i <= 9; i++, i00 += 100) {
   /* hundreds digit */
    for (  j0 = j = 0; j <= 9; j++, j0 += 10) {
     /* tens digit */
     partsum = h000 + i00 + j0;
     part4ths = pwr[h] + pwr[i] + pwr[j];
     for (   k = 0; k <= 9; k++) {         /* ones digit */
       sum = partsum + k; /* this produces the four-digit
         number */
       if (part4ths + pwr[k] == sum) {
             printf("%d = %d^4 + %d^4 + %d^4 + %d^4\n",
               sum, h, i, j, k);
             }
       }
     }
   }
 }
}
```

The BASIC program uses the same algorithm as the C program.
BASIC cannot initialize more than one variable within a *FOR* statement,
so initializations of variables other than the control variable must take
place before the loop.

Look at statements 150 through 180. They could be combined into
one statement that reads:

```
150 IF PART4THS + PWR(K) = SUM THEN PRINT SUM; "= ";:
    PRINT USING "#^4 + "; H, I, J;: PRINT USING "#^4"; K
```

That is the logic used in the C and Pascal programs. If you try it in BASIC, however, you will find that it adds more than 70 percent to the running time of the program. This is because BASIC is an interpreted language. Each time the interpreter reaches that statement, it parses the whole statement; that is, it checks it for syntactical correctness even though most of the time the second two-thirds of the statement is not executed. This is why multiple statements on one line in BASIC, while they are more compact and can be easier to follow, sometimes execute slower than equivalent code written one statement per line. If the first part of a multiple statement is an *IF*, and the part of the statement that depends on that *IF* is not executed every time, the interpreter wastes time parsing the rest of the statement. You can save that time by setting up the opposite logical condition and jumping around the statement or statements; they will be parsed only when they are executed.

This BASIC program runs in about 35 seconds:

```
 10  DIM PWR(9)
 20  FOR I = 0 TO 9
 30    PWR(I) = I^4
 40  NEXT I
 50  H000 = 1000
 60  FOR H = 1 TO 9
 70    I00 = 0
 80    FOR I = 0 TO 9
 90      J0 = 0
100      FOR J = 0 TO 9
110        PARTSUM = H000 + I00 + J0
120        PART4THS = PWR(H) + PWR(I) + PWR(J)
130        FOR K = 0 TO 9
140          SUM = PARTSUM + K
150          IF PART4THS + PWR(K) <> SUM THEN 190
160            PRINT SUM; "= ";
170            PRINT USING "#^4 + "; H, I, J;
180            PRINT USING "#^4"; K
190        NEXT K
200        J0 = J0 + 10
210      NEXT J
220      I00 = I00 + 100
230    NEXT I
240    H000 = H000 + 1000
250  NEXT H
```

The Pascal program is exactly the same as the BASIC program, except that instead of using I^4 to fill the array, it uses $i*i*i*i$ (as does the C program).

In all three programs, the variable i is reused. At first it is merely a loop controller, used to fill the array. Later it represents the digit in the hundreds position of the four-digit number.

The Pascal program that follows runs in less than 1 second.

```
program sum4ths(input, output);
var
  pwr:        { the fourth power of each number, 0 to 9      }
              array[0..9] of integer;
  h,          { the digit in the thousands position          }
  h000,       { h * 1000, that is, the value of the number
              in the thousands position                      }
  i,          { the digit in the hundreds position           }
  i00,        { i * 100, that is, the value of the number in
              the hundreds position                          }
  j,          { the digit in the tens position               }
  j0,         { j * 10, that is, the value of the number in
              the tens position                              }
  part4ths,   { h^4 + i^4 + j^4                              }
  partsum,    { h000 + i00 + j0                              }
  k,          { the digit in the ones position               }
  sum:        integer;

begin
  for i := 0 to 9 do pwr[i] := i * i * i * i;
  h000 := 1000;
  for h := 1 to 9 do begin { thousands digit }
    i00 := 0;
    for i := 0 to 9 do begin { hundreds digit }
      j0 := 0;
      for j := 0 to 9 do begin  { tens digit }
        partsum := h000 + i00 + j0;
        part4ths := pwr[h] + pwr[i] + pwr[j];
          for k := 0 to 9 do begin       { ones digit }
            sum := partsum + k; { this produces the four-
              digit number }
            if part4ths + pwr[k] = sum then
              writeln (sum, ' = ', h, '^4 + ' , i, '^4 + ' , j,
                '^4 + ', k, '^4')
        end;
        j0 := j0 + 10
      end;
      i00 := i00 + 100
```

```
      end;
       h000 := h000 + 1000
    end
end.
```

These programs all come up with three four-digit numbers whose digits, taken to the fourth power, add up to the original number, as shown in these results:

```
1634 = 1^4 + 6^4 + 3^4 + 4^4
8208 = 8^4 + 2^4 + 0^4 + 8^4
9474 = 9^4 + 4^4 + 7^4 + 4^4
```

PUZZLE 6

ॐ

Problem: Find the smallest number that is the sum of two different pairs of cubes, all of which are positive integers.

ॐ

The mechanisms used to solve this puzzle differ slightly among the BASIC, Pascal, and C versions, although the underlying algorithms are the same. Each program uses constructs best suited to that language.

In BASIC, try a number to see if it is the sum of one pair of cubes. Because the two smallest sets of different integers are (1, 2) and (3, 4), the smallest possible solution is 65 ($1^3 + 4^3$), so start there (*TRYNUM = 65*).

Use two arrays for the two sets of numbers to be found, and set an index *K* into those arrays, with an initial value of 1. *FIRST(1)* and *SECOND(1)* are set each time one pair of cubes is found that adds up to *TRYNUM*. If a second set of cubes is found, they are placed in *FIRST(2)* and *SECOND(2)*.

Each time you try a larger value of *TRYNUM* for the sum of cubes, you reset *K* to 1. You must also start trying values for the first number to be cubed at 1, so you reset the value of *X* to 1.

Use a new variable, *X3*, to represent the value of *X* cubed. Assigning this value to a variable means that you calculate it only once, which speeds up processing time. Whenever the value of a variable comes from a calculation that needs to be made several times within a loop, your program slows down.

Because sums like $2^3 + 4^3$ and $4^3 + 2^3$ are equivalent, you want to avoid generating both sets of numbers. You do this by making sure that the value of Y (the second number in the program) is always larger than the value of X. The smallest value Y can take, therefore, is X, and the smallest value Y^3 can take is X^3 (represented here by $X3$). Thus, whenever $X3 + X3$ exceeds $TRYNUM$, the value for X has become too large, and you can start over again with the next higher value for $TRYNUM$ (statement 50).

You could have approached this problem by using two nested loops. You would cube the value for the outer loop, X, and add it each time to the value for the inner loop, Y. Whenever that total exceeded $TRYNUM$, you would go on to the next higher value for $TRYNUM$. If the total exactly equaled $TRYNUM$, you would then keep looking for another set of candidates. That algorithm works, but it takes more than twice as long as this one does.

Rather than calculating and testing a cube for Y each time, it is better to generate a candidate for the cube, $Y3$, and determine whether its cube root is an integer. If $TRYNUM$ is indeed the sum of two cubes, then the second cube can be found by subtracting the first ($X3$) from $TRYNUM$. Set the cube root of this second number equal to Y, and remove the fractional part, if any, with the INT function (statement 70). This number, Y, will equal the exact cube root of $Y3$ only if $Y3$ is an exact cube. Because finding a cube root is a floating-point operation, rounding errors may creep in. This type of error was discussed in Chapter 2. Therefore, before using the INT function, you add a tiny amount (0.001) to the value of the cube root of $Y3$ to make sure that no legitimate values are discarded.

Next, you determine whether this candidate for the second number (Y), when cubed, is equal to $Y3$. If it is, you have found two numbers whose cubes add up to $TRYNUM$. When this occurs, you assign these two values to $FIRST(K)$ and $SECOND(K)$, and increment K. If, after it is incremented, K equals 3, it means that you have found two pairs of cubes that add up to $TRYNUM$, and you thus have the answer. Go directly to the part of the program that prints out the answer.

If Y^3 does not equal $Y3$, or if the two are equal and K is not yet equal to 3, you increment X (statement 100) and return to the portion of the program that calculates the new value of X^3.

The BASIC version of this program is as follows. It executes in 2 minutes 7 seconds.

```
10 TRYNUM = 65
20 K = 1
30 X = 1
40 X3 = X^3
50 IF X3 + X3 > TRYNUM THEN 110
60 Y3 = TRYNUM - X3
70 Y = INT(Y3^(1/3) + .001)
80 IF Y^3 <> Y3 THEN 100
90 FIRST(K) = X : SECOND(K) = Y : K = K + 1 : IF K = 3 THEN 120
100 X = X + 1 : GOTO 40
110 TRYNUM = TRYNUM + 1 : GOTO 20
120 PRINT USING "##^3 + ##^3 = "; FIRST(1), SECOND(1);
130 PRINT USING "##^3 + ##^3 = "; FIRST(2), SECOND(2);
140 PRINT TRYNUM
```

The Pascal version of this program differs in that two nested *while...do* loops are substituted for the implied loops of the BASIC program.

The outer loop executes until the point at which *first[1]* is not 0, that is, until a second set of numbers whose cubes add up to *trynum* is found.

Using the same logic as the BASIC program, the next loop executes as long as twice *x3* does not exceed *trynum*.

The variable z is set equal to the sum of *x3* and y^3; y starts out 1 greater than x. This loop executes as long as z does not exceed *trynum*. Within this loop, an *if* block checks whether z exactly equals *trynum*. If it does, the values of x and y are assigned to *first[k]* and *second[k]*, and k is incremented. Whenever *first[1]* is assigned a value, the condition of the outermost loop is satisfied, and it ceases execution. You have found an answer, and the program prints it out.

When you are developing a Pascal program like this one, it is nice to have a statement somewhere that lets you interrupt the program. If the only time the program outputs to the screen is at completion and, due to a bug, your program gets stuck in an infinite loop, you cannot get out unless you reset the computer. But a statement like:

```
if (keypressed) then writeln ('trynum =',trynum);
```

lets you check the progress of the program from time to time. On a PC, it also lets you stop the program at any time by pressing the Break key.

In the BASIC program, *TRYNUM* starts out at 65 and is not incremented if an answer is found. In the Pascal program, *trynum* starts out at 64 but is incremented immediately. As soon as *first[1]* gets a value (that is, becomes nonzero), the answer is printed out with the current value of *trynum*. That is why *trynum* is incremented where it is in the Pascal program.

This program executes in less than 3 seconds.

```
program twocubes;
var
   k, trynum, x, x3, y, z: integer;
   first, second: array[0..1] of integer;

begin
   trynum := 64;
   first[0] := 0;
   second[0] := 0;
   first[1] := 0;
   second[1] := 0;
   while (first[1] = 0) do begin
     if (keypressed) then writeln ('trynum =',trynum);
     trynum := trynum + 1;
     k := 0;
     x := 1;
     x3 := 1;
     while (x3 + x3 <= trynum) do begin
       x3 := x * x * x;
       y := x + 1;
       z := 1;
       while (z <= trynum) do begin
         z := x3 + y * y * y;
         if (z = trynum) then begin
           first[k] := x;
           second[k] := y;
           k := k + 1
```

```
    end; { if (z = trynum) }
    y := y + 1
   end; {while (z <= trynum)}
   x := x + 1
  end {while (x3 + x3 <= trynum)}
 end; {while first[1] = 0}

 write (first[0], '^3 + ', second[0], '^3 = ');
 writeln (first[1], '^3 + ', second[1], '^3 = ', trynum)
end.
```

The C program uses one construct that is idiomatic to C. Apart from that, it is identical to the Pascal program.

That construct is the "loop forever" control statement for the first nested loop:

```
for (x = 1; ; x++) {
```

No specification is made for terminating the loop. This is because tests are included within the loop that cause an exit when appropriate. Whenever twice *x3* or *z* exceeds *trynum*, the *break* statement backs up one level of nesting.

As in the Pascal program, *trynum* starts out at 64 and is immediately incremented.

This program executes in 2 seconds.

```
main()
  {
  int trynum = 64, k, first[2], second[2], x, x3, y, z;

  first[1] = 0;
  second[1] = 0;
  while (first[1] == 0) {
    trynum++;
    k = 0;
    for (x = 1; ; x++) {
      x3 = x * x * x;
      if (x3 + x3 > trynum) break;
      for (y = x + 1; ; y++) {
        z = x3 + y * y * y;
        if (z > trynum) break;
        if (z == trynum) {
```

```
          first[k]   = x;
          second[k++] = y;
        }
      }
    }
  }
  printf ("\n%d^3 + %d^3 = ", first[0], second[0]);
  printf ("%d^3 + %d^3 = %d\n", first[1], second[1], trynum);
  return 0;
}
```

The programs all produce the following output:

```
1^3 + 12^3 = 9^3 + 10^3 = 1729
```

That is, both 1 cubed plus 12 cubed and 9 cubed plus 10 cubed yield 1729. This is the smallest number that is the sum of two different pairs of cubes (all positive integers).

PUZZLE 7

ऀ

Problem: Find the first five series of consecutive numbers such that, when the numbers are divided into two groups and the numbers in each of the groups are squared and added together, the sums are equal. The first such series is 3, 4, 5 ($3^2 + 4^2 = 5^2$). Each series will have an odd number of numbers, and the left side of the equation will have one more number than the right side.

ऀ

In the Pascal program to solve this problem, a variable named *series* proceeds by twos from 3 to 11; this ensures that each set has an odd number of elements. Each time through the loop, the variable *trynum* is set to 0. To this number is added the number at which to start the series.

Two other variables, *sum1* and *sum2*, are also set to 0. They represent, respectively, the sum of the squares on the left side of the equation and the sum of those on the right. A *repeat* loop continually executes until *sum1* and *sum2* are equal. At the bottom of the loop, if *sum1* and *sum2* are not equal, a larger value is tried for *trynum*.

The *repeat* loop successively increments numbers for the left side of the equation, which has one more element than the right side. The number of elements on the left is determined with integer division in the statement:

```
for x := trynum + 1 to trynum + (series + 1) div 2 do
```

150

For example, suppose that the value of *series* is 3, meaning that the series to be tested consists of three elements. The left side of the equation will therefore have two elements. The first time through the *repeat* loop, *trynum* is 0, so *x* counts from 1 to $(3 + 1)/2$, or 2. If the solution has not been found the first time through the *repeat* loop, *trynum* is incremented by 1. This time, *x* counts from 2 (*trynum* + 1) to $1 + (3 + 1)/2$, or 3. If the value of *series* is 7, the second time through the loop *x* would count from 2 to $1 + (7 + 1)/2$, or 5, and so on. At the start of this loop, *sum1* is always equal to 0. For each element in the series, the value of x^2 is added to *sum1*:

```
sum1 := sum1 + x * x;
```

The program treats the right half of the equation in a similar fashion. The first number in this series is 1 larger than the last value of *x* in the previous loop, and so it is determined as follows:

```
for x := trynum + (series + 1) div 2 + 1 to trynum + series do
```

The first time through the *repeat* loop, for a series of three elements, *x* goes from $0 + (3 + 1)/2 + 1$ to $0 + 3$ (that is, from 3 to 3). This takes it once through the loop, which is just what you expect in a three-element series. The first time through the *repeat* loop, for a series of nine elements, *x* goes from $0 + (9 + 1)/2 + 1$ to $0 + 9$ (that is, from 6 to 9). In such a series, numbers 1 through 5 will be on the left, and numbers 6 through 9 will be on the right.

Whenever the routine finds a series for which *sum1* and *sum2* are equal (that is, when it finds some value for *trynum* for which the successive *x* loops produce the same total), the *repeat* ... *until* condition is satisfied and the program moves on to its print routine. That routine is less complicated than it seems. First, *trynum* is reduced by 1 because the last thing that happens each time through the *repeat* loop is that it is incremented by 1. When you finally get to the print routine, you have done that exactly once too often.

In the print routine, each element is followed by a caret (^) and a 2, indicating that it is squared. You want each element on the left and on the right to be followed by a plus sign, *except* for the last one. If it weren't for that, you could just use one *write* statement to print out all the numbers, with a routine something like the following:

```
for x := trynum + 1 to trynum + series do
   write (x,' ^ 2 + ');
```

That would give the answer, but it would look something like this:

```
21^2 + 22^2 + 23^2 + 24^2 + 25^2 + 26^2 + 27^2 +
```

This is not exactly what you want. Thus, your output routine needs first to print each element on the left, with a plus sign after all but the final one, which must be followed by an equal sign. The routine should then print all elements on the right, with a plus sign after all but the final one, which is followed by nothing. In a series of three, all but the last element on the right means *no* elements. In such a case, the following loop is skipped:

```
for x := trynum + series div 2 + 2 to trynum + series - 1 do
```

If you want to test series with more than 11 elements, you can make *sum1* and *sum2* reals instead of integers. If you do this, you will run into problems, such as overflow and rounding errors. Instead of stepping through the odd numbers, have the program request the length of series to find, and test to make sure that the input is an odd number and is greater than 2.

As given here, the Pascal program executes in less than 1 second.

```
program squares(input, output);
var
   series, trynum, sum1, sum2, x     : integer;
```

```
begin
  series := 3;
  while (series < 12) do begin
    writeln ('For a series of ', series, ' elements:');
    trynum := 0;
    repeat
      sum1 := 0;
      sum2 := 0;
        for x := trynum + 1 to trynum + (series + 1) div 2 do
          sum1 := sum1 + x * x;
        for x := trynum + (series + 1) div 2 + 1 to
          trynum + series do
          sum2 := sum2 + x * x;
      trynum := trynum + 1
    until sum1 = sum2;

    trynum := trynum - 1;
    for x := trynum + 1 to trynum + (series div 2) do
      write (x, '^2 + ');
    write (trynum + (series div 2) + 1, '^2 = ');
    for x := trynum + series div 2 + 2 to trynum + series - 1 do
      write (x, '^2 + ');
    writeln (trynum + series, '^2');
    writeln ('(Total = ', sum1, ')');
    writeln;
    series := series + 2
  end { while (series < 12) }
end.
```

The BASIC program is essentially the same as the Pascal program. Instead of a *repeat ... until* loop, at the equivalent point in the program it tests whether *SUM1* and *SUM2* are equal. If they are, it proceeds to the print routine. If they are not, it increments *TRYNUM* and tries again.

Because *TRYNUM* is not incremented if *SUM1* and *SUM2* are equal, the program does not decrement it at the start of the print routine. BASIC does not have a *div* function to find the larger half of an odd number, but the construct *(SERIES + 1)/2 − 1* does the same thing.

The program uses the *PRINT USING* construct to format the output. *SUM1* prints within a five-digit field.

The complete BASIC program to solve this problem is as follows. It runs in less than 5 seconds.

```
10 FOR SERIES = 3 TO 11 STEP 2
20  PRINT "For a series of"; SERIES; "elements:"
30  TRYNUM = 0
40  SUM1 = 0 : SUM2 = 0
50  FOR X = TRYNUM + 1 TO TRYNUM + (SERIES + 1)/2
60   SUM1 = SUM1 + X^2
70  NEXT X
80  FOR X = TRYNUM + (SERIES + 1)/2 + 1 TO TRYNUM + SERIES
90   SUM2 = SUM2 + X^2
100  NEXT X
110  IF SUM1 = SUM2 THEN 140
120   TRYNUM = TRYNUM + 1
130   GOTO 40
140  PRINT
150  FOR X = TRYNUM + 1 TO TRYNUM + (SERIES + 1)/2 - 1
160   PRINT USING "##^2 + "; X;
170  NEXT X
180  PRINT USING "##^2 = "; X;
190  FOR X = TRYNUM + (SERIES + 1)/2 + 1 TO TRYNUM + SERIES - 1
200   PRINT USING "##^2 + "; X;
210  NEXT X
220  PRINT USING "##^2"; X
230  PRINT USING "(Total = ######)"; SUM1
240 NEXT SERIES
```

You can change the BASIC program to find a series of any size, up to about 49. As in the Pascal program, instead of stepping through the odd numbers, have the program request the length of series to find. It should test that the input is an odd number and is greater than 2. This changes the first few lines of the program. The modified program prints out the exact representation of the total for series with as many as 37 elements. It also finds series consisting of as many as 49 members, although it prints the total in exponential notation. It finds this series in a little more than 2 minutes. Of more interest, it finds a series of 15 in less than 5 seconds.

To modify the program to search for a series of any size, replace statements 10 through 50 in the previous program with the following:

```
10 INPUT "How long a series to test"; SERIES
20 IF SERIES MOD 2 = 1 AND SERIES > 2 THEN 50
30 PRINT "Give me an odd number, please."
```

```
40 GOTO 10
50 TRYNUM = 0
    .
    .
    .
```

If you do try to find very large series, you can use a shortcut to speed up the program so that it executes almost instantaneously. Replace statement 50 in the program fragment with the following:

```
50 TRYNUM = INT(SERIES/2) * (INT(SERIES/2) * 2 + 1) - 1
```

That is, the formula for the first element of a series, where n is the number of elements on the right, is $n \times (2n + 1)$.

The C program is also quite similar to the one in Pascal. Like the BASIC program, it immediately exits the part of the program that assigns values to *sum1* and *sum2* as soon as it finds they are equivalent.

With some modification, the C program can find a series of 101 members, and display the total exactly, in less than 40 seconds. Change *sum1* and *sum2* to longs, and request input rather than stepping through the odd numbers.

As given here, the C program executes in a little more than 2 seconds.

```
main()
{
int trynum, sum1, sum2, series, x;

  for (series = 3; series < 12; series += 2) {
    printf ("For a series of %d elements:\n", series);
    for (trynum = 0; ; trynum ++) {
      sum1 = sum2 = 0;
      for (x = trynum + 1; x < trynum + (series + 1) / 2 + 1;
        x++) sum1 += (long) x * x;
      for (x = trynum + (series + 1) / 2 + 1;
        x < trynum + series + 1; x++)
        sum2 += (long) x * x;
      if (sum1 == sum2) break;
    }
```

155

```
    for (x = trynum + 1; x < trynum + (series / 2) + 1; x++)
        printf ("%d^2 + ", x);
    printf ("%d^2 = ", trynum + (series / 2) + 1);
    for (x = trynum + series / 2 + 2; x < trynum + series; x++)
        printf ("%d^2 + ", x);
    printf ("%d^2\n", trynum + series);
    printf ("(Total = %d)\n\n", sum1);
  }
}
```

The programs give the following results (except for the BASIC program, in which the total is right-justified within a five-character field):

For a series of 3 elements:

```
3^2 + 4^2 = 5^2
(Total = 25)
```

For a series of 5 elements:

```
10^2 + 11^2 + 12^2 = 13^2 + 14^2
(Total = 365)
```

For a series of 7 elements:

```
21^2 + 22^2 + 23^2 + 24^2 = 25^2 + 26^2 + 27^2
(Total = 2030)
```

For a series of 9 elements:

```
36^2 + 37^2 + 38^2 + 39^2 + 40^2 = 41^2 + 42^2 + 43^2 + 44^2
(Total = 7230)
```

For a series of 11 elements:

```
55^2 + 56^2 + 57^2 + 58^2 + 59^2 + 60^2 =
  61^2 + 62^2 + 63^2 + 64^2 + 65^2
(Total = 19855)
```

PUZZLE 8

ðñ

Problem: Find four different numbers that both add and multiply to 9.81.

ðñ

To work with integers, you multiply 9.81 by 100 to produce 981. This will be the sum of the four numbers. The product is 1,000,000 times that number. Why is that? If you multiply the sum by 100, you must do the same to each of the terms so that they will add up to the sum. When you multiply the four terms, you then must multiply the product by 100 for each term; $100 \times 100 \times 100 \times 100 = 100,000,000$. One hundred of that 100,000,000 turns 9.81 into 981; the other million is what remains. That is, $9.81 \times 10^8 = 981 \times 10^6$.

The prime factors of 1,000,000 are:

$$5 \times 5 \times 5 \times 5 \times 5 \times 5 \times 2 \times 2 \times 2 \times 2 \times 2 \times 2$$

That is, $5^6 \times 2^6$. The only way to spread six 5s among four terms and have no term exceed 1000 (1000 pennies equals $10) is to give at least one of them two 5s. The same is true for the 2s. It is not possible for one of the prices to consist of three 5s and three 2s, because $5 \times 5 \times 5 \times 2 \times 2 \times 2$ equals 1000 pennies, which is $10, and that exceeds the sum. Thus, if one of the terms consists of three or more 5s, it can have no more than two 2s. (In fact, if a term has four 5s, it can't have *any* 2s.) For these reasons, at least one term must have two 5s and at least one other term must have two 2s. That is, you can narrow the search considerably by representing one

157

of the terms as *i*, using it as the outer loop counter, and then moving through that loop in steps of 25. If you specify that the counter for the next inner loop is the one that must have at least two 2s, you can move through it in steps of 4.

The sum for your program is 981, and the product is 981,000,000. Because Pascal does not permit floating-point operations on integers, you have to change the integers to reals. That is, to divide an integer by 100 and not lose any decimal places to integer rounding, you first equate a real to the integer and then you perform the floating-point operation on the real.

There may be more than one term that has two 5s; at least one of them will be found as the *i* variable. At least one of those terms must be less than half the sum, and so the upper boundary for the *i* loop is set to half of the sum (represented by the variable *sm*):

```
while i <= sm div 2 do begin
```

At least one of the terms that has two 2s (and this includes the special case in which one term has *all* the 2s) must be less than half of the number remaining after *i* is subtracted from the sum. This is accounted for in the following statement:

```
while j <= (sm - i) div 2 do begin
```

At the end of each *j* loop, you increment the counter by 4, and at the end of each *i* loop, you increment the counter by 25.

Now that you have two candidates for the first two terms, you can take some shortcuts. You do not need to loop any further; instead, you perform some tests. Most of those will prove to be dead ends, because there will be no possible values for the remaining two terms. You can then try other values for *i* and *j*.

Multiply *i* by *j*, and divide that value into the product. Assign this new value to the variable *qt*, which stands for *quotient*. A quotient is what you get when you divide one number by another. Now perform a test.

Is qt an integer, that is, did $i \times j$ divide evenly into the product? If it is not, then the remaining two terms cannot be integers, and you can stop testing the current values of i and j. This test is performed in the following statement:

```
if qt = int (qt) then begin
```

If this statement is not true, the program skips the rest of the tests. If qt is an integer, then the remaining two terms might still be found. To continue, subtract i and j from the sum to form the sum of the remaining two numbers, rm.

Now you need to do a little math. You have set up two equations:

$$k + l = rm$$
$$k \times l = qt$$

From the second, you get:

$$l = \frac{qt}{k}$$

Substituting in the first gives:

$$k + \frac{qt}{k} = rm$$

To cancel out the k in the divisor, you multiply each side of the equation by k, yielding:

$$k^2 + qt = rm \times k$$

Move the terms to the left, and you get the following quadratic equation:

$$k^2 - rm \times k + qt = 0$$

In the usual quadratic equation:

$$ax^2 + bx + c = 0$$

the solutions are:

$$x = \frac{-b + \sqrt{b^2 - 4ac}}{2a} \quad \text{and} \quad x = \frac{-b - \sqrt{b^2 - 4ac}}{2a}$$

In these equations, $b^2 - 4ac$ is called the discriminant and is represented in the program as ds. In your solution, a is 1, b is $-rm$, and c is qt. Thus, the two solutions become:

$$k = \frac{(rm) + \sqrt{(rm)^2 - 4(qt)}}{2} \quad \text{and} \quad l = \frac{(rm) - \sqrt{(rm)^2 - 4(qt)}}{2}$$

Now the program computes the discriminant:

```
ds := rm * rm - 4 * qt;
```

If that number is not negative, a real solution (as opposed to an imaginary one, which occurs in the case of the square root of a negative number) is possible. Hence, the following statement:

```
if (ds >= 0) then begin
```

The program then applies the formula for one of the quadratic roots:

```
k := (rm + sqrt (ds)) / 2;
```

To avoid possible problems caused by rounding errors, the program looks for the integer that is just above this value. That is, it uses:

```
k := int ((rm + sqrt (ds) + 1) / 2);
```

To find the other quadratic root, you could use the formula:

```
l := (rm - sqrt (ds)) / 2;
```

It is faster, however, to determine whether k is a legitimate candidate. First, compute l:

```
l := trunc (rm - k);
```

Because l is an integer, whereas rm and k are reals, you use *trunc* to perform an integer operation.

Next, you check whether k is also equal to qt/k:

```
if (k * l = qt) then begin
```

If it is, you have an answer.

Now print out the answers in proper form. For each solution, you find four answers that represent cents; you would like to express them as dollars, so you divide each answer by 100. Because i, j, and l are integers, you need to introduce new variables that are their real representations.

This program produces more than one iteration of the four possible answers because more than one of the terms is divisible by 25.

The bit of trickiness that appears to add 0 to i is done to guarantee that i is treated as a real. Otherwise, one of the times the program figures qt, it rounds down, and the test fails. With Turbo Pascal on a PC system, using:

```
qt := pd / (i * j);
```

instead of:

```
qt := pd / ((i + 0.0) * j);
```

produces one less set of answers.

Another way of doing this is to use another variable, a real (say, *itmp*), equate it to *i*, and substitute it in the division. That is, you might have these statements:

```
itmp := i;
qt := pd / (itmp * j);
```

Adding 0.0 to *i* seems easier, however.

You can try other values for *sm* to find other sets of numbers that fit the conditions of the problem. In particular, try $9.99, $8.22, $7.11, and $6.75. In fact, you could find all such sets of numbers by surrounding the body of the program in a loop, something like this:

```
for sm := 1 to 999;
```

and seeing which sums generate solutions.

This Pascal program executes in less than 3 seconds.

```
program sumprod(output);
var
  sm : integer;    { sum                                           }
  isum : real;     { floating-point representation of sum          }
  i : integer;     { first price                                   }
  j : integer;     { second price                                  }
  k : real;        { third price                                   }
  l : integer;     { fourth price                                  }
  pd : real;       { product (expressed in cents)                  }
  qt : real;       { quotient (product divided by i*j)             }
  rm : real;       { remainder (sum minus first two prices)        }
  ds : real;       { discriminant                                  }
  ireal : real;    { floating-point representation of i            }
  jreal : real;    { floating-point representation of j            }
  lreal : real;    { floating-point representation of l            }

begin
  sm := 981;
  pd := sm * 1000000.0;
  isum := sm/100;
  writeln ('Prices that add and multiply to $', isum:3:2, ':');
  i := 25;
  while i <= sm div 2 do begin
    j := 4;
```

```
while j <= (sm - i) div 2 do begin
  qt := pd / ((i + 0.0) * j);
  if qt = int (qt) then begin
    rm := sm - i - j;
    ds := rm * rm - 4 * qt;
    if (ds >= 0) then begin
      k := int ((rm + sqrt (ds) + 1) / 2);
      l := trunc (rm - k);
      if (k * l = qt) then begin
        ireal := i/100;
        jreal := j/100;
        lreal := l/100;
        writeln (ireal:3:2,', ',jreal:3:2,', ',
          (int (k))/100:3:2,', ',lreal:3:2)
      end
    end
  end;
  j := j + 4
end;
  i := i + 25
end
end.
```

The C program is similar to the one in Pascal. Just to emphasize that there is usually more than one "right" way of solving a problem programmatically, in the C program the algorithm is slightly different. It finds a floating-point representation for k and then checks whether that value is actually an integer. If it is, k is a valid solution, and the remaining price can be determined by subtracting k from rm.

In C, the value to be used to increment the loop counter can be specified in the *for* statement, and so the program uses a *for* loop instead of a *while* loop.

Although it does not speed up the program much, instead of dividing by 2, the C idiom is to do a bit shift one position to the right. This is shown in the following statement:

```
for (i = 25; i <= sm >> 1; i += 25) {
```

Also, because C has long integers, the program can be written mostly with integers. Whereas the Pascal program needed reals to avoid overflow, the C program uses longs.

The variable *k* needs to be a *double* because it takes the result of a square-root operation. The *sqrt* function is a C library function that takes a *double* argument. You "tell" the compiler before the start of the program that it needs to get *sqrt* from the appropriate library. When you process your program, link in the math libraries, unless this is done automatically.

The statement:

```
if (pd % ((long) i * j) == 0) {
```

is equivalent to the following two Pascal statements:

```
qt := pd / (i * j);
if qt = int (qt) then begin
```

That is, if dividing *pd* by the product of *i* and *j* produces no remainder, you proceed with the rest of the *if* block.

When you print out the answers, instead of assigning them to new variables so that you can divide by 100, in the C program you use the cast operator:

```
printf ("%3.2f, %3.2f, %3.2f, %3.2f\n",
  (double)i/100, (double)j/100, k/100, (double)l/100);
```

If you put:

```
return 0;
```

into your program, you avoid getting the warning message "Function return value mismatch."

The C program that follows executes in less than 2 seconds.

```
double sqrt ();

main ()
{
  int sm;       /* sum          */
  int i;        /* first price  */
  int j;        /* second price */
```

```
double k;        /* third price                          */
int l;           /* fourth price                         */
long pd;         /* product (expressed in cents)         */
long qt;         /* quotient (product divided by i*j)    */
long rm;         /* remainder (sum minus first two prices) */
long ds;         /* discriminant                         */

sm = 981;
pd = sm * 1000000L;
printf ("Prices that add and multiply to $%3.2f:\n",
  (double)sm/100);
for (i = 25; i <= sm >> 1; i += 25) {
  for (j = 4; j <= (sm - i) >> 1; j += 4) {
    if (pd % ((long) i * j) == 0) {
      qt = pd / ((long) i * j);
      rm = sm - i - j;
      ds = rm * rm - 4 * qt;
      if (ds >= 0) {
        k = (rm + sqrt ((double) ds)) / 2;
        if (k == (long) k) {
          l = rm - k;
          printf ("%3.2f, %3.2f, %3.2f, %3.2f\n",
            (double)i/100, (double)j/100, k/100, (double)l/100);
        }
      }
    }
  }
}
return 0;
}
```

The BASIC program is the same as the Pascal one. Instead of having an "if the condition is true, then do something" construct, BASIC typically does the same thing in a backward fashion, that is, "if the condition is not true, then jump over the block that programs in other languages execute if the condition *is* true." Thus, instead of the Pascal statement:

```
if qt = int (qt) then begin
```

BASIC specifies:

```
80 IF QT <> INT (QT) THEN 180
```

This produces the same effect. If *QT* actually is an integer, the program executes lines 90 through 160.

To format the output, the BASIC program uses the *PRINT USING* construct. This program executes in about 6 seconds.

```
10  SM = 981
20  PD = SM * 1000000
30  PRINT "Prices that add and multiply to $";
40  PRINT USING "#.##:"; SM/100
50  FOR I = 25 TO SM / 2 STEP 25
60   FOR J = 4 TO (SM - I) / 2 STEP 4
70    QT = PD / (I * J)
80    IF QT <> INT (QT) THEN 170
90     RM = SM - I - J
100    DS = RM * RM - 4 * QT
110    IF DS < 0 THEN 170
120    K = INT((RM + SQR (DS) + 1) / 2)
130    L = RM - K
140    IF K * L <> QT THEN 170
150     PRINT USING "#.##, "; I/100,J/100,K/100,
160     PRINT USING "#.##"; L/100
170   NEXT J
180 NEXT I
```

If your version of BASIC does not have the *PRINT USING* construct, you can substitute the following program:

```
10  SM = 981
20  PD = SM * 1000000
30  PRINT "Prices that add and multiply to $";
40  P = SM : Q = 2 : GOSUB 1000
50  FOR I = 25 TO SM / 2 STEP 25
60   FOR J = 4 TO (SM - I) / 2 STEP 4
70    QT = PD / (I * J)
80    IF QT <> INT (QT) THEN 170
90     RM = SM - I - J
100    DS = RM * RM - 4 * QT
110    IF DS < 0 THEN 170
120    K = INT((RM + SQR (DS) + 1) / 2)
130    L = RM - K
140    IF K * L <> QT THEN 170
150    Q = 0 : P = I : GOSUB 1000 : P = J : GOSUB 1000
160    P = K : GOSUB 1000 : Q = 1 : P = L : GOSUB 1000
170   NEXT J
180 NEXT I
190 END
```

166

```
1000 T = 100
1010 FOR A = 1 TO 3
1020   X = INT (P / T)
1030   P = P - T * X
1040   PRINT CHR$(X+48);
1050   IF A = 1 THEN PRINT ".";
1060   T = T / 10
1070 NEXT A
1080 IF Q = 0 THEN PRINT ", ";
1090 IF Q = 1 THEN PRINT
1100 IF Q = 2 THEN PRINT ":"
1110 RETURN
```

This program makes sure that values such as 1.2 print as 1.20, that 1 becomes 1.00, and that commas and colons are inserted where they are required. It also runs a bit slower, executing in about 7 seconds.

Give yourself full points if you merely printed out the integer representations of the values. That is, if I were a math or computer science teacher grading this problem on an exam, I would give full credit for the response:

```
50, 120, 375, 436
```

The programs all produce the following output:

```
Prices that add and multiply to $9.81:
0.50, 1.20, 3.75, 4.36
0.50, 4.36, 1.20, 3.75
3.75, 1.20, 0.50, 4.36
```

PUZZLE 9

≈

Problem: Find two five-digit numbers that between them use the digits 0 through 9 once each, such that the first number divided by the second is equal to 9.

≈

This puzzle particularly lends itself to a recursive solution. The highest value the denominator can take is 11111, because any larger number multiplied by 9 produces a product with more than five digits. You do not want to multiply every single number between 01234 and 11111 by 9 to see whether the two numbers together use each of the 10 digits once; that would find the answers, but it is inefficient.

The C program first fills a global array called *used,* consisting of 10 elements, with 0s. This is an array of flags to keep track of which digits have been used. In C, the elements in an array of 10 subscripts are numbered 0 through 9. The definition also initializes the array; *used[10] = {0}* sets all elements to 0.

In this program, *main* consists merely of a call to a function that does the actual work; *build_denom* starts with a value of 0 for the first denominator. It fills each digit of the denominator with a digit from 0 through 9. For each digit, it tests the number it has assigned against the equivalent position in the array *used.* If the number has been used, then no test need be made for this candidate for the denominator. If it has not been used, it sets the flag corresponding to this number to 1 to indicate that the digit has been used, and it generates another digit by recursively calling the same routine. If this is the fifth digit (if *pos* is 4), then you have a five-digit candidate for the denominator with five different digits.

With each iteration, *build_denom* generates a new number that is 10 times larger than the previous one and that has a previously unused digit in the ones place. Each time a five-digit denominator with five different digits is generated, the routine *check_val* is called, to see whether that number multiplied by 9 produces five more unused numbers.

For example, one of the solutions to the puzzle is:

$$\frac{95742}{10638} = 9$$

Just prior to finding this solution, *build_denom* generated, among others, these numbers as candidates for the denominator:

1 10 102 1023 1024 10243

At this point the program called *check_val* and determined that 9 times the denominator candidate was 92187 and that that number has digits that repeat those in the denominator. Similarly, it tested and rejected 10245, 10246, 10247, 10248, and 10249. It then generated a new set of candidates, 1 higher in the tens position, and tried and rejected 10253, 10254, and so on. After rejecting all candidates starting with 102, it went to 103, and so on. Eventually, it produced the following series:

10598 106 1062 10623 10624 10625 10627 10628 10629 10632 10634 10635
10637 10638

When it reached this last number, *check_val* found that the numerator generated for this denominator candidate was 95742, which indeed consists of five other unused digits. It then printed out a solution.

Part of *check_val* is a cleanup routine. The array *loc* holds a temporary set of flags to represent used digits. The statement:

```
used[n] = 1;
```

temporarily flags digit *n* as having been used in the numerator, while the statement:

```
loc[i] = n;
```

keeps track of which digit was flagged.

Before returning from *check_val,* the routine at the label *cleanup* sets back to 0 all flags in *used* that were set to 1.

To check the numerator, the statement:

```
n = numerator % 10;
```

isolates the last digit, and the statement:

```
numerator /= 10;
```

places the next digit to the left in the ones place. If the routine finds no repeated digits, it means that all the digits are different, and the program moves on to the statement that prints out a solution.

When the program multiplies *denominator* by 9, it uses 9L. Unless a constant of nominal single-precision value is explicitly typed as a long, Microsoft C uses the integer value.

The program does not exit until the denominator becomes larger than 11111, because there may be more than one solution.

The C program that follows runs in less than 3 seconds.

```
int used[10] = {0};
int denominator = 0;

main()
{
build_denom(0);
return 0;
}

build_denom(pos)
{
int i, saved_val;
```

```
saved_val = denominator;
denominator *= 10;
for (i = 0; i <= 9; i++, denominator++) {
  if (used[i]) continue;
  used[i] = 1;
  if (pos < 4) build_denom(pos + 1);
  else check_val();
  used[i] = 0;
  }
denominator = saved_val;
}


check_val()
{
int i, n, loc[5];
long numerator;

if (denominator > 11111) exit(0);
numerator = denominator * 9L;

for (i = 0; i < 5; i++) {
  n = numerator % 10;
  if (used[n]) goto cleanup;
  used[n] = 1;
  loc[i] = n;
  numerator /= 10;
}

printf ("%05ld / %05d = %d\n", denominator * 9L,
  denominator, denominator * 9L / denominator);

cleanup: for(n = 0; n < i; n++) used [loc[n]] = 0;
}
```

This program can also be written nonrecursively, albeit in a much less straightforward fashion. Because most versions of BASIC do not have recursion, to write the BASIC program I first "unrolled" the recursive C program into a nonrecursive form. I then wrote the BASIC program to adhere as closely as possible to that nonrecursive program.

In the nonrecursive program, the routine *build_denom* maintains a "stack." It pushes onto the stack, alternately, generated candidates and the value of the current flag. A variable named *tos* represents the index into the stack. The routine first generates the digits, returning to *top* for each new one. At each point, it checks those digits against the appropriate element of *used*. When it has built a five-digit denominator with no repeated digits, it checks the numerator with a call to *check_val*. Then the routine pops the saved values and flag values back, so that it can try the next appropriate candidate for *denominator*.

The rest of the program is the same as the recursive version.

Here is the nonrecursive C program. This program also runs in less than 3 seconds.

```
int used[10] = {0};
int denominator = 0;

main()
{
build_denom(0);
}

int stack[40];
int tos = 0;

build_denom(pos)
{
   int i, saved_val;

top :
   saved_val = denominator;
   denominator *= 10;
   for (i = 0; i <= 9; i++, denominator++) {
     if (used[i]) continue;
     used[i] = 1;
     if (pos < 4) {
       stack[tos++] = i;
       stack[tos++] = saved_val;
       pos++;
       goto top;
mid :
       saved_val = stack[_tos];
       i = stack[_tos];
       pos--;
       }
     else check_val();
     used[i] = 0;
     }
   denominator = saved_val;
   if (tos) goto mid;
```

```
}

check_val()
{
int i, n, loc[5];
long numerator;

if (denominator > 11111) exit(0);
numerator = denominator * 9L;

for (i = 0; i < 5; i++) {
  n = numerator % 10;
  if (used[n]) goto cleanup;
  used[n] = 1;
  loc[i] = n;
  numerator /= 10;
  }

printf ("%05ld / %05d = %ld\n", denominator * 9L,
  denominator, denominator * 9L / denominator);

cleanup: for(n = 0; n < i; n++) used[loc[n]] = 0;
}
```

In the BASIC version of the nonrecursive program, *PPP* is the same as *pos*, and *LLL* is the same as *loc*. *POS* and *LOC* are reserved words in GWBASIC and cannot be used in a program. Unlike the routines in the C program, the BASIC routines are not nicely separated visually into blocks, but, by comparing the two programs, you can see which group of BASIC statements corresponds to which C routine.

For example, the group of BASIC statements that corresponds to the C *build_denom* routine starts at statement 50 and ends at statement 280. The label *top* is statement 60, and *mid* is statement 180.

BASIC does not allow the execution of blocks based on certain conditions. To accomplish the same thing, a program must test for the opposite condition and then jump to another part of the program if it is true. In making this jump, it skips past the block to be executed if the opposite condition is false (that is, if the original condition is true). Therefore, where the C program has a statement like:

```
if (used[i]) continue;
```

the BASIC program has:

```
90 IF USED (I) <> 0 GOTO 240
```

This way of programming, necessitated by the sort of language BASIC is, sometimes produces spaghetti-like code, especially in the hands of beginners. It also precludes any kind of nice indented formatting. You can sometimes produce a better BASIC program by rewriting the equivalent algorithm from a structured language like C or Pascal.

The BASIC program runs in a little more than 1 minute 30 seconds.

```
10 DIM LLL (6)
20 DIM USED (11)
30 DENOM = 0
40 PPP = 0
50 TOS = 0
60 SAVED = DENOM
70 DENOM = DENOM * 10
80 I = 0
90 IF USED (I) <> 0 GOTO 240
100 USED (I) = 1
110 IF PPP >= 4 GOTO 290
120 STACK (TOS) = I
130 TOS = TOS + 1
140 STACK (TOS) = SAVED
150 TOS = TOS + 1
160 PPP = PPP + 1
170 GOTO 60
180 TOS = TOS - 1
190 SAVED = STACK (TOS)
200 TOS = TOS - 1
210 I = STACK (TOS)
220 PPP = PPP - 1
230 USED (I) = 0
240 DENOM = DENOM + 1
250 I = I + 1
260 IF I <= 9 GOTO 90
270 DENOM = SAVED
280 GOTO 180
290 IF DENOM > 11111 THEN END
300 NUMER = DENOM * 9
310 FOR III = 0 TO 4
320 N = NUMER - INT (NUMER / 10) * 10
```

```
330 IF USED (N) <> 0 GOTO 450
340 USED (N) = 1
350 LLL (III) = N
360 NUMER = INT (NUMER / 10)
370 NEXT III
380 PRINT DENOM * 9;"/";
390 IF DENOM > 9999 THEN 430
400 PRINT " 0";
410 PRINT USING "#### "; DENOM;
420 GOTO 440
430 PRINT DENOM;
440 PRINT "=";DENOM * 9 / DENOM
450 FOR N = 0 TO III - 1
460 USED (LLL (N)) = 0
470 NEXT N
480 GOTO 230
```

The Pascal program is similar to the recursive C program. The variable *ii* keeps track of the number of digits generated before a duplicate is found. If there are no duplicates, the program falls through this block. To guarantee that *ii* now has the value 5, the program explicitly assigns it, rather than relying on it to come out with that value.

The label *999* is equivalent to the C *cleanup* label.

Because the value of *denominator* × *9* can exceed single precision, *numerator,* a variable of type *real,* and hence capable of storing up to 11 significant digits, is first assigned the value of *denominator* and then multiplied by 9. That explains the following two lines:

```
numerator := denominator;
numerator := numerator * 9;
```

C can print numbers with as many leading zeros as you want; Pascal does not do this automatically, and so the program needs to handle the case of four-digit numbers. That is what this bit of code does:

```
if denominator < 10000 then begin
    write ('0');
    write (denominator:4)
  end
else
    write (denominator:5);
```

The Pascal program that follows runs in less than 7 seconds.

```
program alldigit(output);
var
  used : array [0 .. 9] of boolean;
  { flags to keep track of which digits are tied up }
  denominator, i : integer;
  finished : boolean;

procedure check_val; { see if (denominator * 9) contains
  any digits from 'denominator' }
label 999;
var
  i, n, ii : integer;
  loc : array [0 .. 4] of integer;
  t, numerator : real;

begin
  if (denominator > 11111) then begin
    finished := true;
    exit { because 11112 times 9 > 99999 }
  end;
  numerator := denominator;
  numerator := numerator * 9;

  for i := 0 to 4 do begin
    ii := i;
    t := numerator / 10;
    n := trunc (t);
    n := trunc (numerator - n * 10.0);
    if (used [n]) then goto 999;
    used [n] := True; { temporarily flag digit 'n'
      as used in the numerator }
    loc [i] := n;
    numerator := t
  end;

  ii := 5;
  { no duplicate digits, so we've found a match }
  write ((denominator * 9.0):5:0,' / ');
  if denominator < 10000 then begin
    write ('0');
    write (denominator:4)
  end
  else
    write (denominator:5);
  writeln (' =', (denominator * 9.0 / denominator):2:0);
```

```
  { clean up the digits we added in flags array while testing
    the numerator }
  999: for n := 0 to ii-1 do used [loc [n]] := False
end;

procedure build_denom (pos : integer);
      { recursively generate the sequence of 5 digit denominators }
  label 9;
var
  i, saved_val : integer;

begin
  if finished then exit;
  saved_val := denominator;
  denominator := denominator * 10;
  for i := 0 to 9 do begin
    if not used [i] then begin
      used [i] := True;
      if pos < 4 then build_denom (pos + 1)
      else check_val;
      used [i] := False
    end;
    denominator := denominator + 1
  end;
  denominator := saved_val
end;

begin
  finished := false;
  for i := 0 to 9 do used [i] := False;
  denominator := 0;
  build_denom(0)
end.
```

Each program produces the following result:

```
57429 / 06381 = 9
58239 / 06471 = 9
75249 / 08361 = 9
95742 / 10638 = 9
95823 / 10647 = 9
97524 / 10836 = 9
```

If you found only the last three and rejected the first three specifically because you do not consider a leading digit of 0 for a five-digit number a fulfillment of the original conditions, give yourself full credit.

PUZZLE 10

&

Problem: Find all the nine-digit numbers that are perfect squares and that use each of the digits 1 through 9 once each.

&

 With 123,456,789 as the lowest candidate and 987,654,321 as the highest, there are 864,197,532 numbers to check. You could generate all of them, one at a time, and check each first for no repeated digits and no zeros and then for whether it is a perfect square. That would certainly find all of the solutions, but it would take a very long time and is very inefficient.

 You can improve greatly on this. The square root of 123,456,789 is a bit over 11,111, and the square root of 987,654,321 is less than 31,427. If you work with the square roots rather than the squares, squaring and testing each of them, you will have only 31,427 − 11,111, or 20,316, numbers to test.

 You can do even better, however. The numbers 1 through 9 add up to 45. The digits of a perfect square containing one each of the numbers 1 through 9 must add up to 45. Mathematicians call the sum of the digits of a number its *digital root*. Any number whose digits add up to a multiple of 9 is itself evenly divisible by 9. If the square is divisible by 9, the square root must be divisible by 3. Therefore, you can generate the roots in increments of 3 rather than 1. Now you have only one-third as many numbers to test.

You can generate squares faster than by performing a multiplication each time. Multiplication is slower than addition. Once you know one square, you can find the next one to test by realizing the following:

$$(r + 3)^2 - r^2 = 6r + 9$$

because:

$$(r + 3)^2 = r^2 + 6r + 9$$

Thus, once you have established the first square, the next one to test is equal to 6 times the previous root plus 9.

Define a nine-element array. At the start of each test for different digits, fill the array with zeros. Each position represents, in order, one of the digits from 1 through 9. A 0 in a position means that the digit has not yet been used; a 1 means that it has.

Isolate the digits one at a time by dividing by 10, discarding the fractional part, multiplying the resulting number by 10, and subtracting it from the original number. Use that digit as the subscript into the array that indicates whether a digit has been used. If the array element for that digit has a value of 0, put a 1 into the element to indicate that the digit has been used. If you find a 1 there already, the digit has been used, and there is no need to test further. In such cases you exit the test, increment the root, and use it to generate another candidate for a square.

The test in each program loops from 1 to 9. To end the test, the program sets the loop variable to 9 whenever it finds a repeated digit.

The BASIC program defines those variables that will exceed single precision as doubles with the *DEFDBL* statement. The program sets *ROOT* first to 11109, so that the first *ROOT* to test is 11112. The highest value is 11109 + 20316 (31427), which is equal to 11109 + 3 × 6772; this explains the parameters of the controlling loop.

The BASIC program that follows runs in a bit less than 5 minutes.

```
10 DEFDBL S, R, X, Y
20 DIM USED(9)
30 ROOT = 11109: SQUARE = ROOT * ROOT: C = 0: USED(0) = 1
40 FOR I = 1 TO 6772
50   SQUARE = SQUARE + 6 * ROOT + 9
60   ROOT = ROOT + 3
70   FOR J = 1 TO 9
80    USED(J) = 0
90   NEXT J
100  X = SQUARE
110  FOUND = 0
120  FOR J = 1 TO 9
130   Y = X
140   X = INT ( X / 10 )
150   Y = Y - 10 * X
160   IF USED(Y) = 0 THEN 180
170    FOUND = 1: J = 9
180   USED(Y) = 1
190  NEXT J
200  IF FOUND <> 0 THEN 220
210   C = C + 1: PRINT USING " #########"; SQUARE;
220 NEXT I
230 PRINT : PRINT "There are";C;"squares with all nine digits."
```

The Pascal program uses reals for the variables that will exceed single precision. When it checks the *used* array, it converts the index generated from the earlier floating-point operations into an integer with the *trunc* transfer function.

The Pascal program executes in 63 seconds.

```
program ninedig;
var
  square, root, x, y : real;
  i, j, c : integer;
  used: array[0..9] of integer;
  found: boolean;

begin
  root := 11109.;
  square := root * root;
  c := 0;
  used[0] := 1;
  for i := 1 to 6772 do begin
    square := square + root * 6 + 9;
    root := root + 3;
```

```
      for j := 1 to 9 do
        used[j] := 0;
      x := square;
      found := true;
      for j := 1 to 9 do begin
        y := x;
        x := int ( x / 10 );
        y := y - 10 * x;
        if (used[trunc(y)] > 0) then begin
          found := false;
          j := 9
        end;
        used[trunc(y)] := 1
      end; { for j := 1 to 9 }
      if (found) then begin
        c := c + 1;
        write (square:10:0)
      end
    end; { for i := 1 to 6772 }
    writeln;
    writeln ('There are ', c, ' squares with all nine digits.')
  end.
```

The C program uses long integers for the variables that will exceed single precision. It is more C-like to jump outward one level than to change the value of the iteration counter, and so the C program uses *break* where the BASIC and Pascal set *j* to 9.

The C program executes in less than 7 seconds.

```
main()
{
  long square, root = 11109, x, y;
  int found, i, j, c, a[10];

  square = root * root;
  c = 0;
  a[0] = 1;
  for (i = 1; i < 6772; i++) {
    square += 6 * root + 9;
    root += 3;
    for (j = 1; j < 10; j++)
      a[j] = 0;
    x = square;
    found = 1;
```

```
      for (j = 1; j < 10; j++) {
        y = x;
        x /= 10;
        y -= 10 * x;
        if (a[y] > 0) {
          found = 0;
          break;
          }
        a[y] = 1;
        }
      if (found) {
        c++;
        printf ("%10ld", square);
        }
      }
    printf ("\nThere are %d squares with all nine digits.", c);
}
```

Each program produces the following solution:

```
139854276 152843769 157326849 215384976
245893761 254817369 326597184 361874529
375468129 382945761 385297641 412739856
523814769 529874361 537219684 549386721
587432169 589324176 597362481 615387249
627953481 653927184 672935481 697435281
714653289 735982641 743816529 842973156
847159236 923187456
There are 30 squares with all nine digits.
```

PUZZLE 11

‎❧

Problem: Find all whole numbers (with fewer than six digits) equal to the sum of the factorials of their digits.

‎❧

The program to solve this problem first fills a nine-element array with the values of the factorials of the numbers 0 through 8. Each position in the array represents the value of the factorial for that digit. Mathematicians have agreed that, by convention, zero factorial (0!) is 1, and this value is assigned to the first ("zeroth") element of the array. The others are calculated. The array has to use real numbers because 8! exceeds the single-precision storage. Nine factorial is 362,880, which has six digits and is therefore not needed.

Do not allow initial zeros for any solution, or you will get a lot more answers than you need.

This program is essentially five nested loops within one structure. The array *d* holds the digits of the number to be tested.

There is a very "nice" way of doing this puzzle, but to understand it, you should first look at a program that begins by finding one-digit solutions, then finds two-digit solutions, and continues on, through five-digit solutions.

In the one-digit case, the largest factorial to consider is 3, because 4! is a two-digit number. Loop from 1 to 3 and see if the number is equal to its factorial. If it is, print an answer.

For the two-digit case, assign two variables, *d1* and *d2*, to represent, respectively, the tens digit and the ones digit. The tens digit loops from 1 to 4 (because the initial digit cannot be 0), and the ones digit goes from 0 to 4. The maximum is 4 because 5! is a three-digit number. Assign $x1$ the value of $d1 \times 10$; it will be used in a moment in the test. Use $y1$ to hold the value of the factorial of the current digit represented by $d1$.

Form two nested loops. The inner loop cycles through the values for the ones digit ($d2$), and the outer loop cycles through the values for the tens digit ($d1$). Each trip through the inner loop, the number being tested is represented by $x1 + d2$, that is, 10 times the value of the outer loop counter plus the value of the inner loop counter. The sum of the factorials of the digits is represented by $y1 + f[d2]$; $f[d2]$ comes from the earlier array filled with the values of the factorials from 0 to 8. If the number is equal to the sum of the factorials of the digits, print an answer.

For the three-digit case, assign three variables, $d1$, $d2$, and $d3$, to represent, respectively, the hundreds, the tens, and the ones digit. The hundreds digit loops from 1 to 6 (because the initial digit cannot be 0), and the tens and ones loop from 0 to 6. The maximum is 6 because 7! is a four-digit number. Assign $x1$ the value of $d1 \times 100$, and assign $x2$ the value of $x1 + d2 \times 10$; both will be used for the test. These temporary variables are assigned values so as not to repeat calculations unnecessarily within inner loops. Whenever a value remains the same through the duration of a loop and is used several times within that loop, it should be calculated before the start of the loop. Use $y1$ to hold the value of the factorial of the current digit represented by $d1$, and use $y2$ to hold the value of $y1$ plus the factorial of $d2$.

Form three nested loops. The inner loop cycles through the values for the ones digit ($d3$); the next loop cycles through the values for the tens digit ($d2$), and the outer loop cycles through the values for the hundreds digit ($d1$). At each trip through the inner loop, the number being tested is represented by $x2 + d3$—that is, 100 times the value of the outer loop counter plus 10 times the value of the middle loop counter plus the value of the inner loop counter. The sum of the factorials of the digits is represented by $y2 + f[d3]$; $y2$ was calculated just before the start of the inner loop. If the number is equal to the sum of the factorials of the digits, print an answer.

The four-digit case is similar. Here, you multiply $x1$ by 1000, and the maximum digit can be a 7 (because 8! is a five-digit number). Use four nested loops, and perform the test in the inner loop.

Use five nested loops for the five-digit case.

If you understand the program that separates the calculations for each number of digits, you can also follow the far more elegant program that combines all the calculations into one routine, using new variables to determine the number of trips through each loop. This program is much more compact and uses the same routine repeatedly to do the task corresponding to each number of digits, rather than using separate routines that really do the same thing.

In this program the array x corresponds to the variables $x1$, $x2$, $x3$, $x4$, and $x5$, and the array y corresponds similarly to the y variables. A new array, t, keeps track of the power of *ten* that corresponds to the given digit, indicating the number by which it is to be multiplied. For the first digit, $t[1]$ is 1, indicating that $d[1]$ should be multiplied by 1; for the second digit, $t[2]$ is 10, indicating that $d[2]$ should be multiplied by 10; and so on, up to $t[5]$, which has the value 10000. The variable i represents the digit of the number, starting at the right.

The variable dm represents the maximum digit allowed for a given i. For example, when i is 1—you are dealing with a one-digit number—dm is 3. The value of dm is found through the use of $im1$ (that is, i minus 1). The value of p tells you how many elements of x and y to use.

The routine *nprint* formats the output properly. If there is more than one digit, all must be printed; if so, a plus sign must be printed after all but the last digit on the right of the equal sign.

The first Pascal program executes in just under 15 seconds, the second in just over 15 seconds.

```
program FactorialDigit(output);
var
  i, d1, d2, d3, d4, d5 : integer;
  x1, x2, x3, x4, y1, y2, y3, y4 : real;
  f : array[0..8] of real;

begin
  { fill array of factorials }
  f[0] := 1.0;
  for i := 1 to 8 do f[i] := i * f[i - 1];

  { the one-digit case }
  for d1 := 1 to 3 do begin
    if d1 = f[d1] then writeln (d1:1, ' = ', d1, '!')
  end;

  { the two-digit case }
  for d1 := 1 to 4 do begin
    x1 := d1 * 10;
    y1 := f[d1];
    for d2 := 0 to 4 do begin
      if x1 + d2 = y1 + f[d2] then writeln (d1:1, d2:1,
        ' = ', d1:1, '! + ', d2:1, '!')
    end
  end;

  { the three-digit case }
  for d1 := 1 to 6 do begin
    x1 := d1 * 100;
    y1 := f[d1];
    for d2 := 0 to 6 do begin
      x2 := x1 + d2 * 10;
      y2 := y1 + f[d2];
      for d3 := 0 to 6 do begin
        if x2 + d3 = y2 + f[d3] then begin
          writeln (d1:1, d2:1, d3:1, ' = ', d1:1, '! + ',
            d2:1, '! + ', d3:1, '!')
        end
      end
    end
  end;

  { the four-digit case }
  for d1 := 1 to 7 do begin
    x1 := d1 * 1000;
    y1 := f[d1];
    for d2 := 0 to 7 do begin
      x2 := x1 + d2 * 100;
      y2 := y1 + f[d2];
```

```
      for d3 := 0 to 7 do begin
        x3 := x2 + d3 * 10;
        y3 := y2 + f[d3];
        for d4 := 0 to 7 do begin
          if x3 + d4 = y3 + f[d4] then begin
            writeln (d1:1, d2:1, d3:1, d4:1, ' = ', d1:1, '! + ',
              d2:1, '! + ', d3:1, '! + ', d4:1, '!')
          end
        end
      end
    end
  end;

{ the five-digit case }
for d1 := 1 to 8 do begin
  x1 := d1 * 10000.;
  y1 := f[d1];
  for d2 := 0 to 8 do begin
    x2 := x1 + d2 * 1000;
    y2 := y1 + f[d2];
    for d3 := 0 to 8 do begin
      x3 := x2 + d3 * 100;
      y3 := y2 + f[d3];
      for d4 := 0 to 8 do begin
        x4 := x3 + d4 * 10;
        y4 := y3 + f[d4];
        for d5 := 0 to 8 do begin
          if x4 + d5 = y4 + f[d5] then begin
            writeln (d1:1, d2:1, d3:1, d4:1, d5:1, ' = ',
              d1:1, '! + ', d2:1, '! + ', d3:1, '! + ',
                d4:1, '! + ', d5:1, '!')
          end
        end
      end
    end
  end
end.
```

Here is the second, more "elegant" version:

```
program DigitFactorial(output);

var
  i,    { first a control variable; then number of digits  }
  im1,  { i minus 1: 1 less than number of digits           }
  dm,   { maximum digit for a given i                       }
```

```
    j,     { control variable                                  }
    di,    { the last, or i-th, digit                          }
    p : integer;
    d      { the largest through (i-1)th digit                 }
     : array [1..4] of integer;
    x,     { the value of the number so far                    }
    y      { sum of factorials so far                          }
     : array [0..4] of real;
    t      { power of ten by which to multiply current digit   }
     : array [1..5] of real;
    f      { factorial of this digit                           }
     : array [0..8] of real;

procedure nprint;
  var
    k : integer;
  begin
    if im1 > 0 then for k := 1 to im1 do write(d[k]:1);
    write(di:1, ' = ');
    if im1 > 0 then for k := 1 to im1 do write(d[k]:1, '! + ');
    writeln(di:1, '!')
  end; { nprint }


begin
  f[0] := 1.0;
  for i := 1 to 8 do f[i] := i * f[i - 1];
  x[0] := 0.0;
  y[0] := 0.0;
  for i := 1 to 5 do begin
    im1 := i - 1;
    dm := i + 3;
    if i < 3 then dm := i + 3;
    if i > 1 then begin
      for j := 1 to im1 do begin
        t[j] := 10 * t[j];
        d[j] := 0;
        x[j] := t[1];
        y[j] := j
      end
    end;
    t[i] := 1.0;
    d[1] := 1;
    repeat
      for di := 0 to dm do begin
        if x[im1] + di = y[im1] + f[di] then nprint
      end;
      p := im1;
      while d[p] = dm do p := p - 1;
```

```
     if p > 0 then begin
        d[p] := d[p] + 1;
        x[p] := x[p] + t[p];
        y[p] := y[p - 1] + f[d[p]];
        if p < im1 then begin
           for j := p + 1 to im1 do begin
              d[j] := 0;
              x[j] := x[p];
              y[j] := y[j - 1] + 1
           end
        end
     end
   until (p = 0)
 end
end.
```

The C programs use longs instead of the reals necessary in Pascal. The first C program is exactly the same as the first Pascal program.

The second C program is quite similar to the second Pascal program. Whereas the Pascal program has a procedure, *nprint*, at the start of the program to print out results, the C program performs the equivalent within the main program. The *do {...} while (p != 0);* block is similar to the *repeat ... until (p = 0)* of the Pascal program. Here is a difference between C and Pascal: Pascal uses *do while* for tests made at the start of a block, and it uses *repeat ... until* for tests made at the end of a block. C uses *do while* for both, the only difference being the placement of the *while*.

The first C program executes in less than 2 seconds, the second in less than 3 seconds. They are so much faster than the Pascal and BASIC programs because they do not use floating-point arithmetic.

Here is the first program:

```
main ()
{
   int  i, d1, d2, d3, d4, d5;
   long x1, x2, x3, x4, y1, y2, y3, y4, f[9];

   /* fill array of factorials */
   f[0] = 1;
   for (i = 1; i <= 8; i++)
      f[i] = i * f[i - 1];
```

```
/* the one-digit case */
for (d1 = 1; d1 <= 3; d1++)
  if (d1 == f[d1]) printf ("%d = %d!\n", d1, d1);

/* the two-digit case */
for (d1 = 1; d1 <= 4; d1++) {
  x1 = d1 * 10;
  y1 = f[d1];
  for (d2 = 1; d2 <= 4; d2++)
    if (x1 + d2 == y1 + f[d2])
      printf ("%d%d = %d! + %d!\n", d1, d2, d1, d2);
}

/* the three-digit case */
for (d1 = 1; d1 <= 6; d1++) {
  x1 = d1 * 100;
  y1 = f[d1];
  for (d2 = 1; d2 <= 6; d2++) {
    x2 = x1 + d2 * 10;
    y2 = y1 + f[d2];
    for (d3 = 1; d3 <= 6; d3++) {
      if (x2 + d3 == y2 + f[d3])
        printf ("%d%d%d = %d! + %d! + %d!\n", d1, d2,
          d3, d1, d2, d3);
    }
  }
}

/* the four-digit case */
for (d1 = 1; d1 <= 7; d1++) {
  x1 = d1 * 1000;
  y1 = f[d1];
  for (d2 = 0; d2 <= 7; d2++) {
    x2 = x1 + d2 * 100;
    y2 = y1 + f[d2];
    for (d3 = 0; d3 <= 7; d3++) {
      x3 = x2 + d3 * 10;
      y3 = y2 + f[d3];
      for (d4 = 0; d4 <= 7; d4++) {
        if (x3 + d4 == y3 + f[d4])
          printf ("%d%d%d%d = %d! + %d! + %d! + %d!\n", d1, d2,
            d3, d4, d1, d2, d3, d4);
      }
    }
  }
}

/* the five-digit case */
```

```
for (d1 = 1; d1 <= 8; d1++) {
  x1 = d1 * 10000L;
  y1 = f[d1];
  for (d2 = 0; d2 <= 8; d2++) {
    x2 = x1 + d2 * 1000;
    y2 = y1 + f[d2];
    for (d3 = 0; d3 <= 8; d3++) {
      x3 = x2 + d3 * 100;
      y3 = y2 + f[d3];
      for (d4 = 0; d4 <= 8; d4++) {
        x4 = x3 + d4 * 10;
        y4 = y3 + f[d4];
        for (d5 = 0; d5 <= 8; d5++) {
          if (x4 + d5 == y4 + f[d5])
            printf ("%d%d%d%d%d = %d! + %d! + %d! +
              %d!\n",
              d1, d2, d3, d4, d5, d1, d2, d3, d4, d5);
        }
      }
    }
  }
}
```

And here is the second:

```
main ()
{
  int   i, im1, dm, j, k, di, p, d[5];
  long x[5], y[5], t[6], f[9];

  f[0] = 1;
  for (i = 1; i <= 8; i++)
    f[i] = i * f[i - 1];
  d[0] = 0;
  x[0] = 0;
  y[0] = 0;
  for (i = 1; i <= 5; i++) {
    im1 = i - 1;
    dm = i + 3;
    if (i < 3) dm = i + 3;
    if (i > 1) {
      for (j = 1; j <= im1; j++) {
        t[j] *= 10;
        d[j] = 0;
        x[j] = t[1];
        y[j] = j;
        }
```

```
      }
      t[i] = 1;
      d[1] = 1;
      do {
        for (di = 0; di <= dm; di++) {
          if (x[im1] + di == y[im1] + f[di]) {
            if (im1 > 0) {
              for (k = 1; k <= im1; k++) printf ("%d", d[k]);
            }
            printf ("%d = ", di);
            if (im1 > 0) {
              for (k = 1; k <= im1; k++) printf ("%d! + ", d[k]);
            }
            printf ("%d!\n", di);
          }
        }

        p = im1;
        while (d[p] == dm) p--;
        if (p > 0) {
          d[p]++;
          x[p] += t[p];
          y[p] = y[p - 1] + f[d[p]];
          if (p < im1) {
            for (j = p + 1; j <= im1; j++) {
              d[j] = 0;
              x[j] = x[p];
              y[j] = y[j - 1] + 1;
            }
          }
        }
      } while (p != 0);
    } /* for (i = 1; i <= 5; i++) */
    return 0;
  }
```

The algorithms of the BASIC programs are the same as those of the Pascal programs. The underscores in the print statements cause the exclamation points to be printed literally.

The first BASIC program takes 3 minutes 56 seconds to produce its answers, and the second takes 3 minutes 43 seconds.

Here is the first:

```
10 DIM F(8)
20 F(0) = 1
30 FOR I = 1 TO 8
```

```
40  F(I) = I * F(I - 1)
50 NEXT I
59 REM The one-digit case
60 FOR D1 = 1 TO 3
70  IF D1 = F(D1) THEN PRINT USING "# = #_!"; D1, D1
80 NEXT D1
89 REM The two-digit case
90 FOR D1 = 1 TO 4
100   X1 = D1 * 10
110   Y1 = F(D1)
120   FOR D2 = 0 TO 4
130    IF X1 + D2 <> Y1 + F(D2) THEN 170
140      PRINT USING "#";D1, D2;
150      PRINT" = ";
160      PRINT USING "#_! + #";D1, D2
170   NEXT D2
180 NEXT D1
189 REM The three-digit case
190 FOR D1 = 1 TO 6
200   X1 = D1 * 100
210   Y1 = F(D1)
220   FOR D2 = 0 TO 6
230    X2 = X1 + D2 * 10
240    Y2 = Y1 + F(D2)
250    FOR D3 = 0 TO 6
260     IF X2 + D3 <> Y2 + F(D3) THEN 310
270       PRINT USING "#";D1, D2, D3;
280       PRINT" = ";
290       PRINT USING "#_!";D1;
300       PRINT USING " + #_!";D2, D3
310    NEXT D3
320   NEXT D2
330 NEXT D1
339 REM The four-digit case
340 FOR D1 = 1 TO 7
350   X1 = D1 * 1000
360   Y1 = F(D1)
370   FOR D2 = 0 TO 7
380    X2 = X1 + D2 * 100
390    Y2 = Y1 + F(D2)
400    FOR D3 = 0 TO 7
410     X3 = X2 + D3 * 10
420     Y3 = Y2 + F(D3)
430     FOR D4 = 0 TO 7
440      IF X3 + D4 <> Y3 + F(D4) THEN 490
450        PRINT USING "#";D1, D2, D3, D4;
460        PRINT" = ";
470        PRINT USING "#_!";D1;
480        PRINT USING " + #_!";D2, D3, D4
```

```
490     NEXT D4
500     NEXT D3
510    NEXT D2
520   NEXT D1
529   REM The five-digit case
530   FOR D1 = 1 TO 8
540     X1 = D1 * 10000
550     Y1 = F(D1)
560    FOR D2 = 0 TO 8
570      X2 = X1 + D2 * 1000
580      Y2 = Y1 + F(D2)
590     FOR D3 = 0 TO 8
600       X3 = X2 + D3 * 100
610       Y3 = Y2 + F(D3)
620      FOR D4 = 0 TO 8
630        X4 = X3 + D4 * 10
640        Y4 = Y3 + F(D4)
650       FOR D5 = 0 TO 8
660         IF X4 + D5 <> Y4 + F(D5) THEN 710
670           PRINT USING "#";D1, D2, D3, D4, D5;
680           PRINT" = ";
690           PRINT USING "#_!";D1;
700           PRINT USING " + #_!";D2, D3, D4, D5
710        NEXT D5
720       NEXT D4
730     NEXT D3
740    NEXT D2
750   NEXT D1
```

And here is the second:

```
10 DIM F(8), D(4), X(4), Y(4), T(5)
20 F(0) = 1
30 FOR I = 1 TO 8
40   F(I) = I * F(I - 1)
50 NEXT I
60 FOR I = 1 TO 5
70   IM1 = I - 1
80   DM = I + 3
90   IF I < 3 THEN DM = I + 2
100   IF I <= 1 THEN 160
110   FOR J = 1 TO IM1:T(J) = 10 * T(J)
120     D(J) = 0
130     X(J) = T(1)
140     Y(J) = J
150   NEXT J
160   T(I) = 1
170   D(1) = 1
```

```
180   FOR DI = 0 TO DM
190     IF X(IM1) + DI = Y(IM1) + F(DI) THEN GOSUB 1000
200   NEXT DI
210   P = IM1
220   IF D(P) <> DM THEN 250
230   P = P - 1
240   GOTO 220
250   IF P = 0 GOTO 360
260   D(P) = D(P) + 1
270   X(P) = X(P) + T(P)
280   Y(P) = Y(P - 1) + F(D(P))
290   IF P >= IM1 THEN 180
300   FOR J = P + 1 TO IM1
310     D(J) = 0
320     X(J) = X(P)
330     Y(J) = Y(J - 1) + 1
340   NEXT J
350   GOTO 180
360 NEXT I
370 END
1000 IF IM1 <= 0 THEN 1040
1010   FOR J = 1 TO IM1
1020     PRINT USING "#";D(J);
1030   NEXT J
1040 PRINT USING "# = "; DI;
1050 IF IM1 <= 0 THEN 1100
1060   FOR J = 1 TO IM1
1070     PRINT USING "#";D(J);
1080     PRINT "! + ";
1090   NEXT J
1100 PRINT USING "#_!"; DI
1110 RETURN
```

Each program shows the following four numbers less than 100,000, the factorials of whose digits add up to the number:

```
1 = 1!
2 = 2!
145 = 1! + 4! + 5!
40585 = 4! + 0! + 5! + 8! + 5!
```

PUZZLE 12

≥

Problem: Find all integers that satisfy the following condition: An integer is reduced to one-ninth its value when a certain one of its digits is removed; dividing the resulting integer by 9 results in the removal of another digit.

≥

Mathematically, you are trying to find some set of numbers such that the larger number, n, can be written:

$$n = a \times 10^{r+1} + b \times 10^r + q$$

where r depends on the number of digits that make up q. If q has one digit, r is 1; if q has two digits, r is 2; and so on. The single digit to remove is b, and q is the rest of the number. For example, in a number like 72,875, if b is 2, then, because q consists of three digits, r is 3. Thus, in this number, q is 875, $b \times 10^r$ is 2000, and $a \times 10^{r+1}$ is 70,000. When you add the three numbers, you get 72,875. Note also that q has to be less than 10^r. In 72,875, for example, 875 (q) is less than 1000 (10^r).

You now must find m, the number n with the digit b removed. The equation for m is:

$$m = a \times 10^r + q$$

such that:

$$n = 9m$$

This leads to:

$$a \times 10^{r+1} + b \times 10^r + q = 9(a \times 10^r + q)$$

and:

$$a \times 10^{r+1} + b \times 10^r + q = 9a \times 10^r + 9q$$

and:

$$a \times 10^{r+1} + b \times 10^r = 9a \times 10^r + 8q$$

and:

$$a \times 10^{r+1} + b \times 10^r - 9a \times 10^r = 8q$$

and:

$$8q = a \times 10^{r+1} + b \times 10^r - 9a \times 10^r$$

Because $a \times 10^{r+1}$ is the same as $10^r \times a \times 10$, this reduces to:

$$8q = a \times 10^r + b \times 10^r$$

or:

$$q = \frac{(a + b) \times 10^r}{8}$$

Because q is less than 10^r, $a + b$ must be less than 8, which means that a, too, is a single digit.

If n is a solution to the puzzle, $10 \times n$ must also be one, so your program need only find solutions for which q is not divisible by 10.

The program runs through all values of a and b in which $a + b \leq 7$. These are the nested loops in the BASIC program that start at lines 30 and 40 and end at 430 and 440.

In the BASIC program, q is represented by the variable *REST*. *A* and *B* are the first and second digits, and *REST* is the remaining digits.

In lines 100 through 160, the program finds the smallest R such that 8 divides evenly into $(A + B) \times 10^R$. It starts with R at 0—that is, with $(A + B) \times 10^0$, which equals $A + B$. If it passes the test at 110, that is, if $A + B$ (which is set equal to Z in line 60) is divisible by 8, the program leaves the loop by going to line 170. If not, it increases R by 1. The second time through the loop, then, it looks at $(A + B) \times 10^1$ which equals $(A + B) \times 10$. Line 120 adds 1 to R; 130 multiplies Z by 10; and 160 returns to 100 to start the test again.

If $10 \times (A + B)$ is divisible by 8, line 110 ends the process. If not, statement 120 increments R so that it now equals 2, and statement 130 produces $10 \times 10 \times (A + B)$, or $(A + B) \times 10^2$; then it goes back for another test.

When R is 3, 8 divides into 10^3 ($10^3 = 1000 = 8 \times 125$). Thus, the maximum number of trips through this loop is three. The test at line 110 causes a jump to line 170 when R is 3, regardless of the value of $(A + B)$.

Once the program finds a value for R that passes the test, it goes on, in lines 170 and 180, to calculate the resulting values for N and M. In line 190, the program checks to see whether M is evenly divisible by 9. If it is, in lines 200 to 360, it finds the digit to be deleted to perform the division.

If no digit can be deleted, which the program determines in the tests at lines 250 and 320, it announces this by printing "... found a counterexample."

If the program gets to line 310, it has determined that it could eliminate a digit; it prints this digit out and then starts the testing over again.

The BASIC program finds all the candidates in less than 2 seconds. Remember that you are only finding the lowest set, that is, those solutions that cannot be divided evenly by 10. You can generate an infinite number of solutions by adding zeros to each generated number.

```
10 CNTREX = 0
20 XMPL = 0
30 FOR A = 0 TO 7
```

```
40   FOR B = 0 TO 7 - A
50    IF A + B = 0 THEN 430
60    Z = A + B
70    U = 10 * A + B
80    V = A
90    R = 0
100   REST = Z/8
110   IF REST = INT(REST) THEN 170
120    R = R + 1
130    Z = 10 * Z
140    U = 10 * U
150    V = 10 * V
160    GOTO 100
170   N = U + REST
180   M = V + REST
190   IF M <> 9 * INT(M/9) THEN 430
200    Z = M/9
210    PRINT N; "= 9 x"; M ;
220    PRINT USING "(deleting the #"; B ;
230    PRINT ")"; and"; M; "= 9 x"; Z;
240    R = 0
250    IF M = 0 AND Z = 0 THEN ON R + 1 GOTO 370, 410
260    N = M - 10 * INT(M/10)
270    REST = Z - 10 * INT(Z/10)
280    IF N <> REST THEN 320
290     M = INT(M/10)
300     Z = INT(Z/10)
310     GOTO 250
320    IF R <> 0 THEN 370
330     R = 1
340     M = INT(M/10)
350     V = N
360     GOTO 250
370    PRINT
380    PRINT "... found a counterexample"
390    CNTREX = CNTREX + 1
400    GOTO 430
410     XMPL = XMPL + 1
420     PRINT USING "(deleting the #)."; V
430   NEXT B
440 NEXT A
450 PRINT "There are"; XMPL ;"examples";
460 IF CNTREX <= 0 THEN 490
470  PRINT "and"; CNTREX ;"counterexamples";
480  GOTO 500
490 PRINT " proving the result."
500 END
```

The reasoning behind the Pascal program is similar. The sections of the BASIC program that find M and identify the deleted digits are in separate procedures in the Pascal program. Also, extra variables are needed to handle the fact that Pascal cannot store all of the number to be found if it is larger than 32,767. The variable a, then, represents the first digit of N of the BASIC program, b represents the second digit, and u is the same as the BASIC program's *REST*.

The Pascal program generates its answers in less than 1 second.

```
program dropdigits;
  var
    j, k, a, b, m, u: integer;

  procedure findm;
    var
      z, v: integer;
    begin
      z := a + b;
      v := a;
      while z mod 8 > 0 do begin
        v := 10 * v;
        z := 10 * z
      end;
      u := z div 8;
      m := v + u
    end; { procedure findm }

  procedure checkdigit;
    var
      z, r, x, y, v: integer;
    begin
      z := m div 9;
      write ( a:1, b:1, u:1, ' = 9 x ', m:1,
        ' (deleting the ', b:1, ');');
      write (' and ', m:1, ' = 9 x ', z:1);
      r := 0;
      while (m > 0) or (z > 0) do begin
        y := m mod 10;
        x := z mod 10;
        if y = x then begin
          m := m div 10;
          z := z div 10
        end
```

```
              else if r = 0 then begin
                r := 1;
                m := m div 10;
                v := y
              end
              else begin
                r := 0;
                m := 0;
                z := 0
              end
          end; { while (m > 0) or (z > 0) }
          case r of
            0 :
              begin
                j := j + 1;
                writeln ('...a counterexample.')
              end;
            1 :
              begin
                k := k + 1;
                writeln (' (deleting the ', v:1, ').')
              end
          end { case r }
        end; { checkdigit }

begin
  j := 0;
  k := 0;
  for a := 0 to 7 do begin
    for b := 0 to 7 - a do begin
      if a + b > 0 then begin
        findm;
        if m mod 9 = 0 then checkdigit
      end { if a + b > 0 }
    end { for b := 0 to 7 - a }
  end; { for a := 0 to 7 }
  write ('there are ', k:1, ' examples ');
  if j > 0 then
      writeln ('and ', j:1, ' counterexamples.')
  else
      writeln ('proving the result.')
end.
```

The C program determines which digit is dropped in a somewhat different fashion. It has two character arrays, *large* and *small*, that represent, respectively, the digits of *n* and *m*. C easily assigns integer values to string arrays. This feature makes it easy to test digits as the elements of such strings.

The C program finds all the numbers in less than 1 second.

```
main()
{
char large[12], small[12];
int a, b, i, j;
long counter, xmpl, m, n, u, v, x, z;

for (counter = 0, xmpl = 0, a= 0; a <= 7; a++) {
  for (b = 0; b <= 7; b++) {
    if (a + b == 0) continue;
    z = a + b;
    u = 10 * a + b;
    v = a;
    for (; z != 8 * (x = z / 8);) {
      z *= 10;
      u *= 10;
      v *= 10;
      }
    n = u + x;
    m = v + x;
    if (m != 9 * (z = m / 9)) continue;
    printf
      (" %ld = 9 x %ld (deleting the %d); and %ld = 9 x %ld ",
      n, m, b, m, z);
    sprintf (large, "%d", m);
    sprintf (small, "%d", z);
    for (i = j = 0; large[i]; i++, j++) {
      if (large[i] != small[j]) printf ("(deleting the %c).\n",
        large[i]), j--;
      }
    if (j + 1 != i) counter++,
      printf ("... found a counterexample\n");
    else xmpl++;
    }
  }
printf ("There are %ld examples", xmpl);
if (counter) printf (" and %ld counterexamples\n", counter);
else printf (" proving the result.\n");
}
```

The programs show that the same digit is always dropped from the first number to produce a number that is one-ninth of the original.

That digit is a 0, and it is always in the second position. The digit dropped from the second number to reduce it to one-ninth of its value is always in the first position and is 1 larger each time. All of the programs give these results:

```
10125 = 9 × 1125 (deleting the 0); and 1125 = 9 × 125
  (deleting the 1).
2025 = 9 × 225 (deleting the 0); and 225 = 9 × 25
  (deleting the 2).
30375 = 9 × 3375 (deleting the 0); and 3375 = 9 × 375
  (deleting the 3).
405 = 9 × 45 (deleting the 0); and 45 = 9 × 5 (deleting the 4).
50625 = 9 × 5625 (deleting the 0); and 5625 = 9 × 625
  (deleting the 5).
6075 = 9 × 675 (deleting the 0); and 675 = 9 × 75
  (deleting the 6).
70875 = 9 × 7875 (deleting the 0); and 7875 = 9 × 875
  (deleting the 7).
There are 7 examples proving the result.
```

Notice that if you tack a 0 onto the end of each of the numbers (as, for example, 101250, 11250, 1250), you get another valid number group. The program asked for the lowest such set.

PUZZLE 13

ૐ

Problem: Determine the probability of turning up two cards that match if two people with two shuffled decks of cards simultaneously turn over one card at a time. Find the probabilities for decks of from 2 to 52 cards.

ૐ

This puzzle can be solved in two ways: by calculating the precise answer or by providing an approximation with a Monte Carlo-type simulation. It is also possible to fall into at least one trap that gives a close, but not exact, answer.

An incorrect algorithm that on the surface *seems* correct states that the probability of having at least one match in a deck of n cards is

$$1 - \left(\frac{(n-1)}{n} \right)^n$$

For 52 cards, that works out to the following:

$$1 - \left(\frac{(52-1)}{52} \right)^{52} \approx .6357$$

or approximately 0.6357. However, the probability of no matches is as follows:

$$\sum_{i=0}^{52} \frac{(-1)^i}{i!} = 1 - \frac{1}{1!} + \frac{1}{2!} - \frac{1}{3!} + \dots + \frac{(-1)^{52}}{52!}$$

(In standard mathematical notation, i is the summation index; it represents the sum of the series from $i = 0$ to 52.)

This is approximately as follows:

$$\frac{1}{e} = \frac{1}{2.71828182845904523536\ldots} \approx .6321205588285577$$

(where e is the base of natural logarithms), and the error is at most as follows:

$$\frac{1}{53!} \approx \frac{1}{4!} \times 10^{-69}$$

Thus, the error is at least beyond the seventieth decimal place. By the way, the probability of having exactly one match is $\frac{1}{e}$.

Although this answer is approximate, the chance of there being at least one match actually converges to $1 - \frac{1}{e}$. In fact, in any deck of more than six cards, the chance of a match is about the same, namely approximately 0.63212.

The programs here calculate the precise chances of turning up two identical cards. Such a solution is more accurate than a Monte Carlo approach (in which the situation is simulated and random selections are then made; the problem with that method is deciding how many trials are enough) and, at least in this case, is much faster.

The C program shows in a few seconds both the chances for any size of deck and that after eight cards the chances begin to converge to the correct value for any larger deck. This number eventually takes the value of an infinite series that is one of the definitions associated with the natural logarithm, in this case e^x, the inverse function of the natural logarithm. That is:

$$\sum_{n=0}^{\infty} \frac{x^n}{n!} = 1 + \frac{1}{1!} + \frac{1}{2!} + \frac{1}{3!} + \ldots$$

The heart of this program is the following piece of code:

```
for (m = 1; m <= n; m++)
    p[m] = 1 / (double) m;
```

This gives the probabilities for a match occurring on the first card with a deck of size n. That is, in a one-card deck, the probability is $\frac{1}{1} = 1$; in a two-card deck, it is $\frac{1}{2}$; in a three-card deck, it is $\frac{1}{3}$; and so on, up to $\frac{1}{n}$; for an n-card deck. Notice the cast operator in this fragment. If m were not specified as a double, integer division would take place, resulting in a value of either 1 or 0 for $p[m]$.

The following section of code is also important:

```
for (k = 2; k <= n; k++) {
    for (m = n; m >= k; m--)
        p[m] += (1 - p[m - 1]) / m;
}
```

When k is 2, this set of statements figures the probability of a match within the first two cards; when k is 3, it figures the probability of a match within the first three cards, and so on. When the loop ends, all of those figures added together determine the probability of a match when the entire deck has been turned over.

One of the decks is assumed to have the fixed distribution $(1 \ldots 52)$. You can see that fixing the composition of one deck and making the other random is exactly the same as making both random. As long as you do not change the order of the first deck, it can be in any order. There is, for example, a 1-in-52 chance that the second card will match the first *whether or not you know the value of the first*. The chance of the second card of the second deck matching the second card of the first deck is likewise unchanged, regardless of the value of the second card of the first, known or not.

You can easily see that in two decks of no cards, there is no chance of matching the cards. In two decks of one card each, there is a 100 percent chance of a match. (The program does not print this out, because the odds entry would cause a division-by-0 error.) In two decks of two cards each, the first card of each deck either matches the other or it doesn't. Those two possibilities are equally likely, and thus the chance of a match is 50 percent.

Assume that the first deck consists of the ace, two, and three of spades and that the second contains the same three cards. Arrange the first deck in ascending order. There are six possible sequences for the second deck: ace, two, three; ace, three, two; two, three, ace; two, ace, three; three, two, ace; and three, ace, two. Notice that in four of the six sequences at least one card (one or more, that is) is in the same position as its counterpart in the first deck. This represents a chance of 2 out of 3. You can also calculate the probability of a match in two decks of four cards by inspection, but by the time you get to five cards, there are 120 arrangements to consider, and it is too difficult to keep track of them all. At that point, you use the computer.

If you want to run the program for decks of more than 53 cards, change the initialization of p to a larger number.

The C program that follows prints out the probabilities for decks of between 2 and 52 cards in less than 7 seconds.

```c
#include "stdio.h"
main()
{
  double p[54], prob, odds;
  int k, m, n;

  printf("\nDeck size? ");
  scanf ("%d", &n);
  for (m = 1; m <= n; m++)
    p[m] = 1 / (double) m;
  for (k = 2; k <= n; k++) {
    for (m = n; m >= k; m--)
      p[m] += (1 - p[m - 1]) / m;
  }
  printf ( "\nDeck      Prob        Odds Favoring\n");
  printf ( "Size     of Match     a Match\n\n");
  for (k = 2; k <= n; k++) {
    prob = p[k];
    odds = prob/(1 - prob);
    printf (" %2d%24.16f%24.16f to 1\n", k, prob, odds);
  }
```

```
    return 0;
}
```

The Pascal program is the exact equivalent of the C program. It prints out the probabilities for all decks of between 2 and 52 cards in less than 3-1/2 seconds. The reason that this program executes in half the time required by the C program is that the Pascal program uses single precision, whereas the C program uses double precision.

Here is an aside about formatting Pascal source files for readability. Notice that one section of the code reads as follows:

```
for k := 2 to n do begin
 for m := n downto k do
  p[m] := p[m] + (1 - p[m - 1]) / m
end;
```

It could just as well have been one line as follows:

```
for k := 2 to n do for m := n downto k do p[m] := p[m] +
   (1 - p[m - 1]) / m;
```

That isn't nearly as easy to follow, however.

```
program deck(input, output);

var
  p : array [0..53] of real;
  prob, odds: real;
  k, m, n    : integer;

begin
    writeln;
    write('Deck size? ');
    readln(n);
    for m := 1 to n do
      p[m] := 1 / m;
    for k := 2 to n do begin
      for m := n downto k do
        p[m] := p[m] + (1 - p[m - 1]) / m
    end;
    writeln ( 'Deck    Prob      Odds Favoring');
    writeln ( 'Size    of Match      a Match');
```

```
      writeln;
       for k := 2 to n do begin
         prob := p[k];
         odds := prob / (1 - prob);
         writeln ( k:2, prob:18:11, odds:18:11, ' to 1')
       end
end.
```

The BASIC program is the same as the other two. It spreads the final printing over four statements because each is formatted differently to match the appearance of the output of the other two programs.

This program runs in about 8 seconds.

```
10 DEFDBL P, O
20 INPUT "Deck size";N
30 DIM P(N)
40 FOR M = 1 TO N: P(M) = 1/M: NEXT M
50 FOR K = 2 TO N
60  FOR M = N TO K STEP -1
70   P(M) = P(M) + (1 - P(M - 1))/M
80  NEXT M
90 NEXT K
100 PRINT : PRINT
110 PRINT "Deck      Prob         Odds Favoring"
120 PRINT "Size    of Match        a Match":PRINT
130 FOR K = 2 TO N
140  PROB = P(K): ODDS = PROB/(1 - PROB)
150  PRINT USING "##_ ";K;
160  PRINT USING "#.##############_ ";PROB;
170  PRINT USING "#.##############";ODDS;
180  PRINT " to 1"
190 NEXT K
```

For a maximum deck size of 52, the programs give these results:

```
Deck size?
Deck      Prob         Odds Favoring
Size    of Match        a Match

  2   0.5000000000000000   1.0000000000000000 to 1
  3   0.6666666666666666   1.9999999999999998 to 1
  4   0.6250000000000001   1.6666666666666674 to 1
  5   0.6333333333333333   1.7272727272727271 to 1
  6   0.6319444444444444   1.7169811320754715 to 1
  7   0.6321428571428572   1.7184466019417481 to 1
```

```
 6    0.6319444444444444    1.7169811320754715  to  1
 7    0.6321428571428572    1.7184466019417481  to  1
 8    0.6321180555555554    1.7182633317602636  to  1
 9    0.6321208112874780    1.7182836938934503  to  1
10    0.6321205357142857    1.7182816576664037  to  1
11    0.6321205607663941    1.718281842778275   to  1
12    0.6321205586787184    1.718281827351875   to  1
13    0.6321205588393088    1.718281828538486   to  1
14    0.6321205588278382    1.718281828453729   to  1
15    0.6321205588286029    1.718281828459379   to  1
16    0.6321205588285550    1.718281828459025   to  1
17    0.6321205588285578    1.718281828459046   to  1
18    0.6321205588285578    1.718281828459046   to  1
19    0.6321205588285577    1.718281828459045   to  1
20    0.6321205588285577    1.718281828459045   to  1
21    0.6321205588285576    1.718281828459044   to  1
22    0.6321205588285577    1.718281828459045   to  1
23    0.6321205588285578    1.718281828459046   to  1
24    0.6321205588285576    1.718281828459044   to  1
25    0.6321205588285578    1.718281828459046   to  1
26    0.6321205588285577    1.718281828459045   to  1
27    0.6321205588285579    1.718281828459046   to  1
28    0.6321205588285577    1.718281828459045   to  1
29    0.6321205588285577    1.718281828459045   to  1
30    0.6321205588285576    1.718281828459044   to  1
31    0.6321205588285577    1.718281828459045   to  1
32    0.6321205588285578    1.718281828459046   to  1
33    0.6321205588285577    1.718281828459045   to  1
34    0.6321205588285577    1.718281828459045   to  1
35    0.6321205588285578    1.718281828459046   to  1
36    0.6321205588285580    1.718281828459047   to  1
37    0.6321205588285577    1.718281828459045   to  1
38    0.6321205588285578    1.718281828459046   to  1
39    0.6321205588285578    1.718281828459046   to  1
40    0.6321205588285579    1.718281828459046   to  1
41    0.6321205588285578    1.718281828459046   to  1
42    0.6321205588285577    1.718281828459045   to  1
43    0.6321205588285581    1.718281828459048   to  1
44    0.6321205588285577    1.718281828459045   to  1
45    0.6321205588285577    1.718281828459045   to  1
46    0.6321205588285578    1.718281828459046   to  1
47    0.6321205588285581    1.718281828459048   to  1
48    0.6321205588285579    1.718281828459046   to  1
49    0.6321205588285578    1.718281828459046   to  1
50    0.6321205588285579    1.718281828459046   to  1
51    0.6321205588285578    1.718281828459046   to  1
52    0.6321205588285576    1.718281828459044   to  1
```

Actually, the last few digits are not the same for each program, but that depends on how much precision your compiler or interpreter has.

PUZZLE 14

২৯

Problem: Find the smallest square that begins with exactly sixteen 7s, and find its square root. Then find a square that begins with *any* specified set of digits.

২৯

To do this puzzle, you need to know how to compute square roots one digit at a time. This method used to be taught in the high schools, but I think that in this age of calculators it has been abandoned. Too bad.

This means of finding square roots, known as Horner's method, looks something like long division. Remember: $(a + b)^2 = a^2 + 2ab + b^2$.

The technique is best shown by an example. To find the square root of 3, you start by writing the following, adding enough zeros to find as many decimal places as you wish:

$$\sqrt{3.00\ \ 00\ \ 00\ \ 00\ \ \ldots}$$

You separate the digits into groups of two because, unlike long division, in this method two digits are "brought down" at a time.

Start with the first group to the left of the decimal point; here, that consists of the single digit 3. What is the largest number that could be its square root? Because 2 is too big, it must be 1. Put a 1 above the 3:

$$\overset{\displaystyle 1}{\sqrt{3.00\ \ 00\ \ 00\ \ 00\ \ \ldots}}$$

Place another 1 under the 3, just as you would in long division, subtract, and bring down the next two digits, which are zeros in this case:

$$
\begin{array}{r}
1 \\
\sqrt{3.00\ 00\ 00\ 00\ \dots} \\
1 \\
\hline
2\ 00
\end{array}
$$

Double the answer found so far, and place that number to the left of the digits you brought down:

$$
\begin{array}{r}
1 \\
\sqrt{3.00\ 00\ 00\ 00\ \dots} \\
1 \\
\hline
2\quad 2\ 00
\end{array}
$$

Now you are going to deal with the 200, that is, the number formed when you subtracted and brought down the zeros. Try placing a single digit to the right of the number being formed on the left, such that when the new number thus formed is multiplied by the new digit, it is the largest number less than 200. That is, if 5 is the digit to try, you will then multiply 5 by 25 to form 125. That is less than 200, but will a larger number work? Yes, 6 times 26 is 156; 7 times 27 is 189. What about 8 times 28? That's 224—too big. Therefore, you have the following:

$$
\begin{array}{r}
1.\ 7 \\
\sqrt{3.00\ 00\ 00\ 00\ \dots} \\
1 \\
\hline
27\quad 2\ 00
\end{array}
$$

The second digit of your answer is 7. Now multiply 7 by 27, subtract, and bring down two more zeros:

$$
\begin{array}{r}
1.\ 7 \\
\hline
\sqrt{3.00\ \ 00\ \ 00\ \ 00\ \ \ldots} \\
1 \\
\hline
\end{array}
$$

$$
27\quad
\begin{array}{r}
2\ 00 \\
1\ 89 \\
\hline
11\ \ 00
\end{array}
$$

As before, you now double the answer found so far and place the resulting number to the left of the digits brought down:

$$
\begin{array}{r}
1.\ 7\ \ \ ? \\
\hline
\sqrt{3.00\ \ 00\ \ 00\ \ 00\ \ \ldots} \\
1 \\
\hline
\end{array}
$$

$$
27\quad
\begin{array}{r}
2\ 00 \\
1\ 89 \\
\hline
\end{array}
$$

$$
34?\quad 11\ \ 00
$$

The question mark represents the next digit you will find.

What you are doing is narrowing the range within which the answer lies. That is, in the first step, you found that $1^2 < 3$ but $2^2 > 3$; in the second step, you found that $17^2 < 300$ but $18^2 > 300$. Now you will try to find what digit d must be added to 170 such that $17d^2 < 30,000$ but $(17d + 1)^2 > 30,000$.

You are asking for the term $170 + d$ on the top and $340 + d$ on the side. When you form a product, $2 \times 170 \times d + d^2$ is the term to add to 170^2 in the equation $(170 + d)^2 = 170^2 + (2 \times 170 \times d + d^2)$.

Remember this. It is one of the steps in the program that will be discussed presently.

Let us continue the example. After one more trial, you have:

```
        1. 7   3   ?
      √3.00  00  00  00 ...
        1
 27     2 00
        1 89
 343     11 00
         10 29
 346?        71 00
```

And, continuing:

```
        1. 7   3   2   0   5
      √3.00  00  00  00  00 ...
        1
 27     2 00
        1 89
 343     11 00
         10 29
 3462        71 00
             69 24
 346405       1 76 00 00
              1 73 20 25
                 2 79 75
```

As you can see, at one point you had to bring down two sets of zeros, because 0 was the largest digit for the last position. The decimal point has also been placed in the answer. You can see that this method is producing a good approximation of the square root of 3. If you multiply 1.73205 by 1.73205, you get 2.9999972.

Now for the BASIC program to solve the puzzle.

The program asks for a set of digits. It will find the smallest square that starts with those digits. It stores those digits as a string because any time that a number exceeds 16 digits during a computation, the extra digits are lost. Your program is supposed to handle any number of digits.

After you enter the number, the program checks to make sure that you have entered an integer. Most of the programs in this book do not check for good input, but this one does. It is not so critical in the BASIC program, because if it ever appears to be stuck in an infinite loop, you can interrupt it with a break. When a Pascal or C program "hangs," however, you often cannot get out without rebooting the computer. It is easy to enter a nondigit accidentally while you are testing the program, and so the program checks your input. When it finds a character that is not an integer, the program sets the loop counter equal to the number of digits that precede the noninteger. That number represents the upper limit for the loop counter, and it causes the remaining iterations of the loop to be skipped.

The program also checks whether your input starts with one or more zeros and asks you to reenter your number if it does.

BASIC is an interpreted language and can dimension arrays "on the fly." It calculates an upper limit for several arrays based on the length of the string entered by the user. This optimizes the speed and storage requirements of the program. Because it does this, the program starts with a *CLEAR* statement. If it traps inappropriate input, the program returns to this statement. If it did not do this, you would get the message "Duplicate Definition in 50."

In this program *L* represents the current length of the candidate for the square. The candidate grows one character at a time as it keeps trying new digits in the last position. The program also needs the original length of the string representing the group of numbers entered; that value is stored in the variable *ORIGLEN*.

In addition to checking for appropriate input, lines 80 through 130 store the digits of the string in the array *N*. *N(0,I)*, where *I* is the position of the digit being stored, represents each digit of the candidate for the square. For example, if you had entered 123 in response to the prompt "Enter initial digits:", the first four elements of $N(0,I)$ would be:

```
N(0,0)   0   (contains 0 until otherwise specified)
N(0,1)   1
N(0,2)   2
N(0,3)   3
N(0,4)   0   (contains 0 until otherwise specified)
```

This array represents 123, 1230, 12,300, 123,000, and so on as needed. The program is looking for a square that is as large as or larger than the number represented by the digits stored in $N(0,I)$.

The program then forms $N(1,I)$ by adding 1 to the last digit of $N(0,I)$, so that those elements then become the following:

```
N(1,0)   0   (contains 0 until otherwise specified)
N(1,1)   1
N(1,2)   2
N(1,3)   4
N(1,4)   0   (contains 0 until otherwise specified)
```

This is the upper bound for the square you are trying to find. That is, if you are finding the smallest square with initial digits 123, it must be less than a number that starts with the digits 124.

You are looking for an integer with either an odd number of digits or an even number. If that number is represented by x^2, and if it has an odd number of digits, it fits somewhere within one of these ranges:

$$123 <= x^2 < 124, 12300 <= x^2 < 12400, 1230000 <= x^2 < 1240000, \ldots$$

If the number has an even number of digits, it fits somewhere within one of these ranges:

$$1230 <= x^2 < 1240, 123000 <= x^2 < 124000, 12300000 <= x^2 < 12400000,$$
$$\ldots$$

K represents the number of digits in the square, and the program tries to find a K-digit square by working with $K = 1, K = 2, K = 3$, and so on. Two different square roots need to be calculated, because the square root is different depending on whether K is even or odd. For example, in the simple case of a square whose first digit is 1:

K is even:

$\sqrt{1} = 1$

$\sqrt{100} = 10$

$\sqrt{10000} = 100$

K is odd:

$\sqrt{10} = 3.16\ldots$

$\sqrt{1000} = 31.6\ldots$

$\sqrt{100000} = 316\ldots$

These numbers are maintained separately.

$SQ(0,I)$ stores the digits of the current candidate for the square with an odd number of digits (K is odd), while $SQ(1,I)$ stores the digits of the current candidate with the even number of digits (K is even).

$B(I)$ is a "working" array. For a given number of digits, it is the candidate for the digits in x^2.

$R(0,I)$, the root, stores the digits of the current odd-digit candidate (K is odd) for the number being squared (x), while $R(1,I)$ stores the digits of the current even-digit candidate (K is even) for the number being squared. This is always an L-digit number such that $L = INT((K + 1)/2)$, as set in line 200. This statement starts a loop that ends at line 530. Each time through this loop, J alternates in value between 1 and 0; J is the index into SQ and R and indicates whether the square of an odd or even number of digits is being examined. L changes in value as the root increases in length.

At each stage, the program tries to find the Lth digit of the current element of the R array being examined.

$DONE$ is a flag; when it is 0, an answer has not yet been found; it becomes 1 when the answer is found.

For input of 123, the $N(0,)$ elements are 0, 1, 2, 3, 0, 0, …, and the $N(1,)$ elements are 0, 1, 2, 4, 0, 0, …

$K = 1$ produces $R(0,)$ elements of 0 and 1 and $SQ(0,)$ elements of 0 and 1. $K = 2$ produces $R(1,)$ elements of 0 and 3 and $SQ(1,)$ elements of 0, 0, and 9. Those last two digits represent the square of 3; they must be two digits that form a square that is less than 12. $K = 3$ produces $R(0,\ )$ elements of 0, 1, and 1 and $SQ(0,\ )$ elements of 0, 1, 2, and 1. Those last three digits represent the square of 11; they must be three digits that form a square that is less than 123. $K = 4$ produces $R(1,\ )$ elements of 0, 3, and ? and $SQ(1,\ )$ elements of 0, ?, ?, ?, and ?. Those last four digits represent the square of 3?; they must be four digits that form a square that is less than 1240. The question marks represent some four-digit number from 30^2 to 39^2 such that it lies between 1230 and 1240.

Each iteration of the loop adds one more digit to R, squares it in the temporary array B, stores that number in the appropriate SQ, and tests against each element of $N(0,\ )$ and $N(1,\ )$ to see if it has found an answer.

The surrounding loop in lines 220 to 480 tests digits. M is both a loop counter and a flag. When the next digit becomes too large, M is set to 9 to bring the loop to an end.

The loop in lines 230 to 250 uses the formula $(x + 1)^2 = x^2 + 2x + 1$ (the one I said earlier to remember). If you know the value of x^2, you can find $(x + 1)^2$ by adding $2 \times x$ and 1. This is done starting at the last digit of the square and working forward digit by digit. To each digit the program adds twice the value of the corresponding R digit. The 1 is added to the last digit of the square by the operation $+ ABS(I = 0)$. In Microsoft BASIC, *true* is $- 1$; in some other versions of BASIC, *true* is $+ 1$. In all versions, *false* is 0. Using the ABS function guarantees that the expression is either 0 or $+ 1$. This is equivalent to saying, if I is 0, then add an extra 1.

In the process of adding to the digits, some become larger than 9. Lines 260 to 310 take care of this by "rippling" through the digits. For example, if the digits were 1, 8, and 5, and to them were added 0, 2, and 6, you would have "digits" of 1, 10, and 11. The 11 is reduced to 1 (lines 280 and 290). X is the amount to carry; line 300 performs the carry. So 1, 10, 11 produces 1, 11, 1, which produces 2, 1, 1.

Line 320 sets X to 0 and jumps to a subroutine at line 1000, where X is used for a different purpose. There it indicates that the elements of $N(0,\ )$ should be checked to determine whether it has found the answer.

The subroutine does this by comparing each element of B with the corresponding element of N.

At the end of this routine, EQ is -1, 0, or 1, depending on whether B is less than, equal to, or greater than N, respectively. The routine keeps comparing one element of B to the corresponding element of N until it finds a difference, and then it returns. If it does not find a difference, EQ is 0. When the test is against $N(0,)$ elements, this means that the square is too small. Against $N(1,)$ elements, this result means the square is too big.

After the test, if B is less than the $N(0,)$ elements, the program adds 1 to the root, stores B in SQ, and tries again (by going through the loop). (B is acting like $INT(SQR(N))$; it is an integer whose square is less than the goal. If that number ever equals $SQR(N)$, you have an answer.)

If B is larger than $N(0,)$, you have gone too far.

The program next performs the same test on the $N(1,)$ elements. If B is smaller than $N(1,)$, it is the square you want—that is, B now lies between the $N(0,)$ and $N(1,)$ elements. The last element for the root is 1 too small, so the program adds 1 and prints the answer. Whatever J is at this point, that holds the answer.

Lines 510 to 530 compensate for those times when the series of starting digits forms a perfect square followed by one or more zeros. Without these lines the program would find the correct answer but would not print out enough of it. In line 540 K determines the number of digits of the square to print, and in line 590 L determines how many digits of the square root to print. If K is less than the length of the original input string, it is because the test in the subroutine at line 1000 causes the program to leave the M loop (lines 220 to 480) whenever all that remains is a string of zeros. Thus, K and L must be adjusted.

The test at line 570 simply makes sure that there is room enough for the message on the same line as the output. If there is not room, it goes on the next line.

For input of sixteen 7s, the BASIC program that follows finds an answer in 34 seconds. For shorter input, it runs considerably faster. Also, it gives an answer for a 1 followed by fifteen 0s in less than 1 second.

```
10 CLEAR
20 PRINT "Enter initial digits:"
30 LINE INPUT " ";A$
40 ORIGLEN = LEN (A$): MAX = 2 * ORIGLEN + 5
50 DIM N(1,MAX), B(MAX), R (1,MAX), SQ(1,MAX)
60 NONINTEGER = 0
70 FOR I = 1 TO ORIGLEN
80   DIGIT = ASC (MID$ (A$,I,1))
90   IF DIGIT < ABS(I = 1) + 48 OR DIGIT > 57 THEN
NONINTEGER = 1: I = ORIGLEN
100  N(0,I) = DIGIT - 48
110  N(1,I) = N (0,I) + ABS(I = ORIGLEN)
120 NEXT I
130 IF NONINTEGER > 0 THEN PRINT "A positive integer,
please." : GOTO 10
140 FOR I = ORIGLEN TO 1 STEP -1
150  IF N(1,I) < 10 THEN I = 1: GOTO 180
160  N(1,I) = N(1,I) - 10
170  N(1,I - 1) = N(1,I - 1) + 1
180 NEXT I
190 K = 0: J = 1: DONE = 0
200 K = K + 1: J = 1 - J: L = INT ((K + 1 ) / 2)
210 FOR I = 0 TO K: B(I) = SQ(J,I): NEXT I
220 FOR M = 1 TO 9
230  FOR I = 0 TO L
240   B(K - I) = B(K - I) + 2 * R(J, L - I) + ABS(I = 0)
250  NEXT I
260  FOR I = K TO 1 STEP - 1
270   IF B(I) < 10 THEN 310
280    X = INT (B(I) / 10)
290    B(I) = B(I) - 10 * X
300    B(I - 1) = B(I - 1) + X
310  NEXT I
320  X = 0
330  GOSUB 1000
340  IF EQ <> -1 THEN 400
350   R(J,L) = R(J,L) + 1
360   FOR I = 0 TO K
370    SQ(J,I) = B(I)
380   NEXT I
390   GOTO 480
400  IF EQ <> 0 THEN 440
410   DONE = 1
420   M = 9
430   GOTO 480
440  X = 1
450  GOSUB 1000
460  M = 9
470  IF EQ = -1 THEN DONE = 1
```

```
480 NEXT M
490 IF DONE < 1 THEN 200
500 R(J,L) = R(J,L) + 1
510 IF NOT (EQ = 0 AND K < ORIGLEN) THEN 540
520   K = K + 2 * INT ((ORIGLEN + 1 - K) / 2)
530   L = INT ((K + 1) / 2)
540 FOR I = 1 TO K
550   PRINT USING "#";B(I);
560 NEXT I
570 IF K > 30 AND K < 81 THEN PRINT
580 PRINT " is the smallest square starting with those digits."
590 FOR I = 1 TO L
600   PRINT USING "#";R(J,I);
610 NEXT I
620 PRINT " is its square root."
630 END
1000 EQ = 0
1010 FOR I = 0 TO MAX
1020  IF B(I) = N(X,I) THEN 1050
1030   EQ = SGN (B(I) - N(X,I))
1040   I = MAX
1050 NEXT I
1060 RETURN
```

If your version of BASIC does not have the *PRINT USING* con-struct, you can replace lines 550 and 600 with the following:

```
550   PRINT CHR$(B(I));
600   PRINT CHR$(R(J,I));
```

The Pascal program is essentially the same as the one in BASIC. The comparison of the *b* array with the appropriate elements of the *n* array is done in a procedure before the start of the main part of the pro-gram, as is the usual Pascal custom, instead of in a subroutine at the end of the program, as is generally done in BASIC.

Some Pascal programmers like to write their programs entirely in lowercase letters; that is what I have done so far. This program is writ-ten in a style that other programmers prefer: The keywords are in up-percase, and procedure and label names are in mixed case. Because case does not matter in Pascal, there is no compelling reason for either, and I prefer all lowercase. C is case sensitive, and the preferred C style is all lowercase except for elements set up with a *define* statement.

Because a Pascal program cannot assign storage space "on the fly," as BASIC can, the program arbitrarily assigns values to *max* and *long* of 105 and 50, respectively. If you want to look for squares that begin with more than 50 digits, just change *max* and *long* appropriately. Except for memory constraints, there is no limit on the sizes of the numbers this program can handle.

For input of sixteen 7s, the Pascal program finds an answer in less than 1 second.

```
PROGRAM LongSquare;
  LABEL Top;
  CONST
    max = 105;
    long = 50;
  VAR
    n, r, sq : ARRAY[0..1, 0..max] OF integer;
    b : ARRAY[0..max] OF integer;
    ask : STRING[long];
    i, j, k, l, m, orig_len, x, done, eq : integer;

  PROCEDURE Compare;
  BEGIN
    eq := 0;
    i := 0;
    WHILE (eq = 0) AND (i <= max) DO BEGIN
      IF b[i] < n[x, i] THEN
        eq := -1;
      IF b[i] > n[x, i] THEN
        eq := 1;
      i := i + 1
    END { WHILE (eq = 0) AND (i <= max) }
  END; { PROCEDURE Compare }

  BEGIN
    FOR i := 0 TO max DO BEGIN
      b[i] := 0;
      FOR j := 0 to 1 DO BEGIN
        r[j, i] := 0;
        n[j, i] := 0;
        sq[j, i] := 0
      END
    END; { FOR i := 0 TO max }
  Top:
    writeln ('Enter initial digits:');
    readln (ask);
```

```
orig_len := length(ask);
FOR i := 1 TO orig_len DO BEGIN
  IF ((ask[1] = '0') OR (ask[i] < '0') OR
      (ask[i] > '9')) THEN BEGIN
    writeln ('A positive integer please.');
    GOTO Top
  END;
  n[0, i] := ord(ask[i]) - ord('0');
  n[1, i] := n[0, i]
END; { FOR i := 1 TO 1 }
n[1, orig_len] := n[1, orig_len] + 1;
FOR i := orig_len DOWNTO 1 DO BEGIN
  IF n[1, i] >= 10 THEN BEGIN
    n[1, i] := n[1, i] - 10;
    n[1, i - 1] := n[1, i - 1] + 1
  END
END; { FOR i := orig_len DOWNTO 1 }
k := 0;
j := 1;
done := 0;
WHILE done < 1 DO BEGIN
  k := k + 1;
  j := 1 - j;
  l := (k + 1) DIV 2;
  FOR i := 0 TO k DO
    b[i] := sq[j, i];
  REPEAT
    m := m + 1;
    FOR i := 0 TO l DO
      b[k - i] := b[k - i] + 2 * r[j, l - i];
    b[k] := b[k] + 1;
    FOR i := k DOWNTO 1 DO BEGIN
      IF b[i] >= 10 THEN BEGIN
        b[i - 1] := b[i - 1] + b[i] DIV 10;
        b[i] := b[i] MOD 10
      END
    END; { FOR i := k DOWNTO 1 }
    x := 0;
    Compare;
    IF (eq = -1) THEN BEGIN
      r[j, l] := r[j, l] + 1;
      FOR i := 0 TO k DO
        sq[j, i] := b[i]
    END;
    IF eq = 0 THEN BEGIN
      done := 1;
      m := 9
    END;
```

```
    IF eq = 1 THEN BEGIN
       x := 1;
       Compare;
       m := 9;
        IF eq = -1 THEN
           done := 1
      END; { IF eq = 1 }
   UNTIL m = 9
 END; { WHILE done < 1 }
 r[j, 1] := r[j,1] + 1;
 IF (eq = 0) AND (k < orig_len) THEN BEGIN
   k := k + 2 * ((orig_len + 1 - k) DIV 2);
   1 := (k + 1) DIV 2
 END;
 FOR i := 1 TO k DO
   write(b[i] : 1);
 if (k > 30) and (k < 81) THEN writeln;
 writeln(' is the smallest square starting
   with those digits.');
 FOR i := 1 TO 1 DO
   write(r[j, i] : 1);
 writeln(' is its square root.')
END.
```

The C program also uses the same algorithm, although it attempts to do so in concordance with C idioms.

As in the Pascal program, the comparison of the *b* array with the appropriate elements of the *n* array is done in a separate routine, this time at the end of the program. It could also fall before it, but most C programmers like to start a self-contained program with *main*. And, as is the C practice, *compare* is actually a function. (It is equivalent to Pascal's procedure, but C doesn't have procedures.) The *for* loop of the function simply "walks through" both arrays either until it reaches *MAX* or until the *b* element is not equal to the equivalent *n* element. It then sets the value of *eq*, to be used in other parts of the program, in the same way as in the BASIC and Pascal programs. Notice also that the comparison stops at $MAX - 1$. This is because the arrays have *MAX* dimensions, which means that the largest element in each is $MAX - 1$.

The carry routine that ripples through the digits is performed in the function *ripple_inc*. That function also increments the last element of the array.

As in the Pascal program, you should change the values of *MAX*
and *MAXLEN* to handle larger numbers.

For input of sixteen 7s, the C program that follows finds an answer
in less than 1 second.

```
#include "stdio.h"
#define MAX 105
#define MAXLEN 50

char ask[MAXLEN];
int n[2][MAX], r[2][MAX], sq[2][MAX], b[MAX];
int i, j, k, l, m, orig_len, done, eq;

main()
{

Top:
printf ("Enter initial digits:\n");
gets(ask);
orig_len = strlen(ask);
for (i = 0; i < orig_len; i++) {
  if (ask[i] < ('0' + (i == 0)) || ask[i] > '9') {
    printf ("A positive integer, please.\n");
    goto Top;
    }
  n[0][i + 1] = n[1][i + 1] = ask[i] - '0';
  }
ripple_inc(n[1], orig_len);
k = 0;
j = 1;
done = 0;
while (!done) {
  k++;
  j = 1 - j;
  l = (k + 1) / 2;
  for (i = 0; i <= k; i++)
    b[i] = sq[j][i];
      for (m = 0; m < 9; m++) {
        for (i = 0; i <= l; i++)
          b[k - i] += r[j][l - i] << 1;
        ripple_inc(b, k);
        compare(0);
        if (eq == -1) {
          r[j][l]++;
          for (i = 0; i <= k; i++)
            sq[j][i] = b[i];
          }
```

```
              if (eq == 0) {
                done = 1;
                m = 9;
                }
              if (eq == 1) {
                compare(1);
                m = 9;
                if (eq == -1) done = 1;
                }
              }
          }

  r[j][l]++;
  if (eq == 0 && k < orig_len) {
    k += 2 * ((orig_len + 1 - k) / 2);
    l = (k + 1) / 2;
    }
  for (i = 1; i <= k; i++)
    putchar(b[i]+'0');
  if (k > 30 && k < 81) printf("\n");
  printf(" is the smallest square starting with those digits.\n");
  for (i = 1; i <= l; i++)
    putchar(r[j][i]+'0');
  printf(" is its square root.\n");
  }


  compare(x)
  {
  for (i = eq = 0; i < MAX - 1 && b[i] == n[x][i]; i++)
    {}
  if (b[i] < n[x][i]) eq = -1;
  else if (b[i] > n[x][i]) eq = 1;
  }


  ripple_inc(num, len) int *num;
  {
  int i;

  num[len]++;
  for (i = len; i >= 1; i--) {
    if (num[i] >= 10) {
      num[i - 1] += num[i] / 10;
      num[i] %= 10;
      }
    }
  }
```

Starting with input of sixteen 7s, all of the programs produce the following result:

```
Enter initial digits:
7777777777777777
777777777777777744351960257494201
 is the smallest square starting with those digits.
27888667551135851 is its square root.
```

PUZZLE 15

જ

Problem: For totals less than $10, find all sets of four numbers whose sum is the same as their product.

જ

That is, find $i, j, k,$ and l such that:

$i + j + k + l = n$

and:

$i \times j \times k \times l = n \times 1,000,000$

You will recall from Puzzle 8 that the prime factors of 1,000,000 are:

$5 \times 5 \times 5 \times 5 \times 5 \times 5 \times 2 \times 2 \times 2 \times 2 \times 2 \times 2$

The solutions to this problem fall into two categories:

- Two of the terms are divisible by 25 (that is, at least two terms have two 5s as factors).
- One of the terms is 625 ($6.25 in dollars), and two of them are divisible by 5 and *not* 25 (that is, one term has four 5s, and two 5s are spread among the other three).

To support the second contention, consider this: You know that $i \times j \times k \times l$ is divisible by 5^6. If $j, k,$ and l are not divisible by 25, then i must be divisible by 125. Now, if i is not divisible by 625, then all three of $j, k,$ and l

228

must be divisible by 5 (to account for the remaining three 5s as factors). Because each term is thus divisible by 5, the sum of the four must also be divisible by 5. But if $n = i + j + k + l$ is divisible by 5, then $n \times 1,000,000 = i \times j \times k \times l$ must be divisible by 5^7, not just 5^6, which is an impossibility.

Thus, because the condition of i being properly divisible by 625 is not possible, i must equal 625, and two of j, k, and l must have 5 as a factor.

You then write a program that accounts for both cases.

Let's follow the logic in the BASIC program.

For the first condition, the four prices are $25 \times I$, $25 \times J$, K, and L. To get $25 \times (I + J) < 1000$, $(I + J) \leq 39$; $I \leq J$ gives $I \leq 19$. This gives the loop parameters of statements 120 and 130.

Now, $1 \leq K \leq L$, and $K + L \leq 999 - 25 \times I - 25 \times J$. This sets an upper bound for K (given as UP) of $INT((999 - 25 \times (I + J))/2)$. Assuming that you know I, J, and K, you can solve $625 \times I \times J \times K \times L = (25 \times I + 25 \times J + K + L) \times 1,000,000$ for L by writing:

$$(625 \times I \times J \times K - 1,000,000) \times L = (25 \times I + 25 \times J + K) \times 1,000,000$$

Divide both sides by 625 to get:

$$(I \times J \times K - 1600) \times L = (25 \times I + 25 \times J + K) \times 1600$$

In the program, $(I \times J \times K - 1600)$ is A, and $(25 \times I + 25 \times J + K)$ is B. A must be greater than 0 for this to be solvable. This means that:

$$K \geq \frac{1600}{I \times J}$$

This gives K a lower bound (LO) of the lowest integer that is greater than or equal to $1600/(I \times J)$. Line 140 finds that bound. The two minus signs in this statement cause INT to find the lowest integer that is greater than or equal to a given number (as opposed to its usual result of finding the closest integer that is lower than that number).

You want L to be an integer that is greater than or equal to K (as was shown earlier); hence, the test in statement 220. You haven't given L an upper bound, and so you check that the total sum (given as Z) is less than 1000. If it is, you go to the routine that eliminates duplicates for the case in which two of the terms are divisible by 25.

If three of the items are divisible by 25, there would be three duplicates; if all four prices are divisible by 25, there would be six. The one the test keeps is the one in which the two smallest multiples of 25 occur as I and J. That is, if either K or L is evenly divisible by 25 and is less than 25 $\times$ J, it is a duplicate and is thus not to be used. If you have not found a duplicate, then go to the routine that sorts the four prices into ascending order.

Once you have found all totals that fit the first category of solutions, you find those that fit the second, that is, those in which one of the terms is 625 and two are divisible by 5 and not 25.

Given that one price is 625, the others are specified as $5 \times I$, $5 \times J$, and L. Lines 310 and 370 enforce the condition that I and J must not be divisible by 5 (so that $5 \times I$ cannot be divisible by 25). T and S are iteration counters that cause the program to jump to the next iteration every fifth time, that is, when I or J is divisible by 5. Like before, you have $625 \times 5 \times I \times 5 \times J \times L = (625 \times 5 \times I + 5 \times J + L) \times 1{,}000{,}000$. You solve for L by writing:

$$(625 \times 5 \times I \times 5 \times J - 1{,}000{,}000) \times L = (625 + 5 \times I + 5 \times J) \times 1{,}000{,}000$$

Divide both sides by 5^6 to get:

$$A \times L = B$$

Thus:

$$L = B / A$$

At this point, if L is an integer (statement 440), you now test, just as you did in the 25/25 routine, whether the total price (given as Z) is less than 1000. If it is, you go to the routine that eliminates duplicates for the case in which one term equals 625 and two others are each divisible by 5.

Here, if three items are divisible by 5 and the third is not divisible by 25, there would be three duplicates; if three items are divisible by 5 and the third *is* divisible by 25, there would be two duplicates. The one the test keeps is the one in which only the two smallest multiples of 5 occur. That is, if L is evenly divisible by 5 and if it is less than $5 \times J$, it is one of the duplicates and is not to be used. If you have not found a duplicate, then go to the routine that sorts the four prices into ascending order.

The sorting routine for each total starts at 980; it is a simple bubble sort. It also assigns the total to $P(0,C)$, where C is the number of the total under consideration, and it assigns the individual prices to $P(1,C)$ through $P(4,C)$.

After all the totals are assigned to the P array, the program creates, in lines 490 to 700, an index table to print the prices in ascending order. To speed execution, it does not actually manipulate the data. Instead, it uses the Q array as indexing into the P array. This is known as an insertion sort. The routine first compares two totals, the $P(0,)$ elements. If the first total is larger, its value in the Q array is switched with that of the second. If the first is smaller, nothing is done. If the two are the same, the first price of the two totals is compared (the $(P1,)$ elements), and a switch is made if necessary. If these prices are the same, the process is repeated through the other prices until two that differ are found. At the end of the routine, the Q array stores a list of the order in which to print the P array. $Q(1)$ points to the element of P to be printed first, $Q(2)$ points to the second, and so on. The totals are arranged in order from lowest to highest; if two totals are the same, they are arranged in ascending order based on the first price, and so on. The four prices were sorted earlier so that they are in ascending order from left to right. This routine permits checking all the way to the fourth price, in case the first three are all the same; in practice, however, it never gets past the second price, because no set of prices has more than two terms that are the same.

Next, in lines 710 to 780, the program prints out all the results. It divides each total and each individual price by 100 to convert them to dollars and cents. The routine prints each total only once. It does this by checking whether the previous total was the same (line 720).

Finally, the program prints the number of totals it has found, and then it ends.

The majority of the work of the program is in generating the totals and individual prices. Because it stores these in an array and then sorts the array, doing no output until this point, it spends some time calculating. The actual printing of all the totals and prices does not take long. So that you don't start to worry that the program isn't working, two print statements monitor its progress (lines 831 and 911). They are not necessary to the program.

The BASIC program runs in 7 minutes 4 seconds.

```
100 DIM P(4,200), Q(200), W(4)
109 REM Two prices divisible by 25
110 C = 0
120 FOR I = 1 TO 19
130   FOR J = I TO 39 - I
140     LO = -INT((-1600)/(I * J))
150     UP = INT((999 - 25 * (I + J))/2)
160     IF LO > UP THEN 260
170     FOR K = LO TO UP
180       A = K * I * J - 1600
190       IF A = 0 THEN 250
200         B = (K + 25 * (I + J)) * 1600
210         L = B / A
220       IF L < K OR L <> INT(L) THEN 250
230         Z = K + L + 25 * (I + J)
240         IF Z < 1000 THEN GOSUB 810
250     NEXT K
260   NEXT J
270 NEXT I
279 REM One price is 625
280 T = 0
290 FOR I = 1 TO 37
300   T = T + 1
310   IF T <> 5 THEN 340
320   T = 0
330   GOTO 480
```

```
340  S = T - 1
350  FOR J = I TO 74 - I
360   S = S + 1
370   IF S <> 5 THEN 400
380    S = 0
390    GOTO 470
400    A = I * J - 64
410    IF A < 1 THEN 470
420    B = (625 + 5 * (I + J)) * 64
430    L = B / A
440    IF L <> INT(L) THEN 470
450    Z = 625 + 5 * (I + J) + L
460     IF Z < 1000 THEN GOSUB 900
470  NEXT J
480 NEXT I
489 REM Creates index table to put prices in order
490 Q(1) = 1
500 FOR I = 2 TO C
510   M = P(0, I)
520   Q(I) = I
530   FOR J = 1 TO I - 1
540    IF P(0,Q(J)) < M THEN 680
550    IF P(0,Q(J)) > M THEN 630
560    T = 0
570    FOR K = 1 TO 4
580     IF P(K,Q(J)) = P(K,I) THEN 610
590      IF P(K,Q(J)) > P(K,I) THEN T = 1
600      K = 4
610    NEXT K
620    IF T = 0 THEN 680
630    FOR K = I - 1 TO J STEP -1
640     Q(K + 1) = Q(K)
650    NEXT K
660    Q(J) = I
670    J = I - 1
680   NEXT J
690 NEXT I
700 PRINT
709 REM Print the table of prices
710 FOR I = 1 TO C
720   IF P(0,Q(I)) = P(0,Q(I - 1)) THEN PRINT "    :";: GOTO 740
730   PRINT USING "_$#.##_ _:"; P(0,Q(I))/100;
740   FOR J = 1 TO 3
750    PRINT USING "##.##_,"; P(J,Q(I))/100;
760   NEXT J
770   PRINT USING "##.##"; P(4,Q(I))/100
780 NEXT I
790 PRINT C; "solutions"
800 END
```

```
809 REM Eliminate duplicates for 25/25 case
810 IF K = 25 * INT(K / 25) AND K < 25 * J THEN 890
820 IF L = 25 * INT(L / 25) AND L < 25 * J THEN 890
830  C = C + 1
831  PRINT C;
840  W(1) = 25 * I
850  W(2) = 25 * J
860  W(3) = K
870  W(4) = L
880  GOSUB 980
890 RETURN
899 REM Eliminate duplicates for 625 case
900 IF L = 5 * INT(L / 5) AND L < 5 * J THEN 970
910  C = C + 1
911  PRINT C;
920  W(1) = 5 * I
930  W(2) = 5 * J
940  W(3) = L
950  W(4) = 625
960  GOSUB 980
970 RETURN
979 REM Sort four individual prices for a single solution
980 FOR M = 1 TO 3
990  FOR N = M + 1 TO 4
1000   IF W(N) >= W(M) THEN 1040
1010    SW = W(M)
1020    W(M) = W(N)
1030    W(N) = SW
1040  NEXT N
1050 NEXT M
1060 P(0,C) = Z
1070 FOR M = 1 TO 4
1080  P(M,C) = W(M)
1090 NEXT M
1100 RETURN
```

The Pascal program is almost the same as the one in BASIC. However, it has two instructions that appear to have no counterparts in the BASIC program. These are in the portion of the program that finds totals when one price is 625:

```
if i mod 5 <> 0 then ...
```

and:

```
if j mod 5 <> 0 then ...
```

In fact, they *are* actually in the BASIC program, but they are hidden. What is happening here makes what is happening in the BASIC program clearer. In lines 280 through 390 in the BASIC program, you are finding $T = I \ MOD \ 5$ and $S = J \ MOD \ 5$ without having a BASIC *MOD* routine.

In the Pascal program, ll temporarily stores the value of l as a real so that you can see whether b divides evenly into a by comparing ll with its integer representation.

The Pascal program, like the BASIC program, prints out where it is so that you don't think it has gone off into space. It runs in 61 seconds.

```
program smeqprod;
  var
    i, j, k, l, lo, up, c, z: integer;
    a, b, ll: real;
    w: array[1..4] of integer;
    q: array[1..200] of integer;
    p: array[0..4, 1..200] of integer;

  { Sort individual prices for a single solution }
  procedure reorder;
    var
      m, n, sw: integer;
    begin
      for m := 1 to 3 do begin
        for n := m + 1 to 4 do begin
          if w[n] < w[m] then begin
            sw := w[m];
            w[m] := w[n];
            w[n] := sw
          end { if w[n] < w[m] }
        end { for n := m + 1 to 4 }
      end; { for m := 1 to 3 }
      p[0,c] := z;
      for m := 1 to 4 do p[m,c] := w[m];
      write(c:4)
    end; { reorder }

  { Eliminate duplicates for solutions with two factors
    divisible by 25 }
  procedure test1;
    var
      test : integer;
```

```
    begin
      test := 0;
      if (k mod 25 = 0) and (k < 25 * j) then test := 1;
      if (l mod 25 = 0) and (l < 25 * j) then test := 1;
      if test = 0 then begin
        c := c + 1;
        w[1] := 25 * i;
        w[2] := 25 * j;
        w[3] := k;
        w[4] := l;
        reorder
      end
    end; { procedure test1 }

  { Eliminate duplicates for solutions with one factor equal
  to 625 }
  procedure test2;
    var
      test : integer;
    begin
      test := 0;
      if (l mod 5 = 0) and (l < 5 * j) then test := 1;
      if test = 0 then begin
        c := c + 1;
        w[1] := 5 * i;
        w[2] := 5 * j;
        w[3] := l;
        w[4] := 625;
        reorder
      end
    end; { procedure test2 }

{ main program }
begin
  c := 0;
  { two prices divisible by 25 }
  for i := 1 to 19 do begin
    for j := i to 39 - i do begin
      lo := (1600 div (i * j)) + 1;
      up := (999 - 25 * (i + j)) div 2;
      if lo < up + 1 then begin
        for k := lo to up do begin
          a := k * i * j - 1600.0;
          b := (k + 25 * (i + j)) * 1600.0;
          l1 := b / a;
          if l1 < 1000.0 then begin
            l := trunc(l1);
            if (l1 = l) and (l >= k) then begin
```

```
            z := k + 1 + 25 * (i + j);
            if z < 1000 then test1
          end { if (l1 = l) and (l >= k) }
        end { if abs(l1) < 1000.0 }
      end { for k := lo to up }
    end { if lo < up + 1 }
  end { for j := i to 39 - i }
end; { for i := 1 to 19 }

{ one price is 625 }
for i := 1 to 37 do begin
  if i mod 5 <> 0 then begin
    for j := i to 74 - i do begin
      if j mod 5 <> 0 then begin
        a := i * j - 64.0;
        if a > 0.0 then begin
          b := (625.0 + 5 * (i + j)) * 64.0;
          l1 := b / a;
          if l1 < 1000.0 then begin
            l := trunc(l1);
            if (l1 = l) then begin
                z := 625 + 5 * (i + j) + l;
                if z < 1000 then test2
            end { if (l1 = l) }
          end { if abs(l1) < 1000.0 }
        end { if a > 0.0 }
      end { if j mod 5 <> 0 }
    end { for j := i to 74 - i }
  end { if i mod 5 <> 0 }
end; { for i := 1 to 37 }
{ create index table to order output }
q[1] := 1;
for i := 2 to c do begin
  q[i] := i;
  j := 1;
  repeat
    k := 0;
    while p[k,q[j]] = p[k,i] do k := k + 1;
    if p[k,q[j]] > p[k,i] then begin
      for k := i - 1 downto j do q[k + 1] := q[k];
      q[j] := i;
      j := i - 1
    end; { if p[k,q[j]] > p[k,i] }
    j := j + 1;
  until ( j = i )
end; { for i := 2 to c }

{ print table of prices }
writeln;
for i := 1 to c do begin
```

```
  if p[0,q[i]] = p[0,q[i - 1]] then write ('   : ')
   else                 write ('$', (p[0,q[i]]/100):4:2, ' : ');
   for j := 1 to 3 do write ((p[j,q[i]]/100):4:2, ', ');
   writeln((p[4,q[i]]/100):4:2)
  end; { for i := 1 to c }
  writeln(c:3, ' solutions.')
end.
```

The C program is virtually the same as the one in Pascal. It tests whether *ll* is an integer in this way:

```
if (ll * a == b) {
```

This is because *ll* is not a floating-point number, and the division of *a* by *b* leaves no fractional part.

Notice the left shift to accomplish multiplication by 64:

```
b <<= 6;
```

Numbers are manipulated in the computer in binary format. The higher-level-language instructions are transformed into assembly language. Bit shifts are very fast in machine language, and multiplication and division by multiples of 2 is much faster with bit shifts than with the corresponding arithmetic operations. If you consider an integer in its binary representation, you can see that to multiply the number by 2, you move all the bits one position to the left, and to divide by 2, you move them one position to the right. To multiply or divide by 4, you move all the bits two positions; to multiply or divide by 8, you move them three positions; and so on. The C idiom for multiplication by 64 is a bit shift six positions to the left. Thus, $b <<= 6$ is the same as $b *= 64$.

Turbo Pascal does not have long integers, so it has to do some of its work in floating point, which slows things down considerably. The C program uses only integer arithmetic and thus does a lot of work in a short time.

The C program's *do ... while* construct:

```
do {
    .
    .
    .
} while ( j != i );
```

is the same as the following in Pascal:

```
repeat
    .
    .
    .
until ( j = i )
```

The only actual use of floating-point arithmetic in the C program
is in the final printing out of totals and prices, and a cast operator ensures that when each element is divided by 100, it prints properly.

The C program executes in a zippy 17 seconds.

```
      int i, j, k, l, lo, up, c, z, w[5], q[201], p[5][201];
      int reorder(), test1(), test2();
      long a, b, ll;


main ()
{
  c = 0;
  /* two prices divisible by 25 */
  for (i = 1; i <= 19 ; i++) {
    for (j = i; j <= 39 - i ; j++) {
      lo = (1600 / (i * j)) + 1;
      up = (999 - 25 * (i + j)) >> 1;
      if (lo < up + 1) {
        for (k = lo; k <= up ; k++) {
          a = k * i * j - 1600;
          b = ( k + 25 * (i + j));
          b *= 1600;
          ll = b / a;
          l = ll;
          if (ll < 1000L) {
            if (ll * a == b && ll >= k) {
              z = k + l + 25 * (i + j);
```

239

```
                    if (z < 1000) test1();
                    }
                }
            }
        }
    }
}

/* one price is 625 */
for (i = 1; i <= 37 ; i++) {
  if (i % 5 != 0) {
    for (j = i; j <= 74 - i ; j++) {
      if (j % 5 != 0) {
        a = i * j - 64;
        if (a > 0) {
          b = (625 + 5 * (i + j));
          b <<= 6;
          l1 = b / a;
          l = l1;
          if (l1 < 1000L) {
            if (l1 * a == b) {
              z = 625 + 5 * (i + j) + l ;
              if (z < 1000) test2();
            }
          }
        }
      }
    }
  }
}

/* create index table to order output */
q[1] = 1;
for (i = 2; i <= c ; i++) {
  q[i] = i;
  j = 1;
  do {
    k = 0;
    while (p[k][q[j]] == p[k][i]) k++;
    if (p[k][q[j]] > p[k][i]) {
      for (k = i - 1; k >= j; k--) q[k + 1] = q[k];
      q[j] = i;
      j = i - 1;
      }
    j++;
  } while ( j != i );
}

/* print table of prices */
printf("\n");
```

```
for (i = 1; i <= c ; i++) {
  if (p[0][q[i]] == p[0][q[i - 1]]) printf ("    : ");
  else                printf ("$%4.2f : ", (float)
    p[0][q[i]]/100);
  for (j = 1; j <= 3; j++)
    printf ("%4.2f, ", (float) p[j][q[i]]/100);
    printf("%4.2f\n", (float) p[4][q[i]]/100);
  }
printf("%d solutions.\n", c);
}
/* sort individual prices for a single solution */
reorder()
  {
      int m, n, sw;
      for (m = 1; m <= 3 ; m++) {
        for (n = m + 1; n <= 4 ; n++) {
          if (w[n] < w[m]) {
            sw = w[m];
            w[m] = w[n];
            w[n] = sw;
          }
        }
      }
    p[0][c] = z;
    for (m = 1; m <= 4; m++) p[m][c] = w[m];
    printf("%d ", c);
  }

/* Eliminate duplicates for solutions with two factors
divisible by 25 */
test1()
{
  int test = 0;
  if ((k % 25 == 0) && (k < 25 * j)) test = 1;
  if ((l % 25 == 0) && (l < 25 * j)) test = 1;
  if (test == 0) {
    c++;
    w[1] = 25 * i;
    w[2] = 25 * j;
    w[3] = k;
    w[4] = l;
    reorder();
  }
}

/* Eliminate duplicates for solutions with one factor
equal to 625 */
```

```
test2()
{
  int test = 0;
  if (((1 % 5 == 0) && (1 < 5 * j)) test = 1;
  if (test == 0) {
    c = c + 1;
    w[1] = 5 * i;
    w[2] = 5 * j;
    w[3] = 1;
    w[4] = 625;
    reorder();
  }
}
```

All of the programs produce this output:

```
$6.44 : 1.25, 1.60, 1.75, 1.84
$6.51 : 1.25, 1.40, 1.86, 2.00
$6.60 : 1.10, 1.50, 2.00, 2.00
$6.63 : 1.25, 1.25, 1.92, 2.21
$6.65 : 1.00, 1.75, 1.90, 2.00
$6.72 : 1.12, 1.50, 1.60, 2.50
$6.75 : 1.00, 1.50, 2.00, 2.25
      : 1.20, 1.25, 1.80, 2.50
$6.78 : 1.13, 1.25, 2.00, 2.40
$6.80 : 1.00, 1.60, 1.70, 2.50
$6.84 : 1.00, 1.44, 1.90, 2.50
      : 1.14, 1.20, 2.00, 2.50
$6.86 : 1.00, 1.40, 1.96, 2.50
$6.89 : 1.06, 1.25, 2.08, 2.50
$6.93 : 0.88, 1.75, 1.80, 2.50
      : 1.00, 1.50, 1.68, 2.75
$7.02 : 1.17, 1.25, 1.60, 3.00
$7.05 : 1.00, 1.20, 2.35, 2.50
$7.07 : 0.80, 1.75, 2.02, 2.50
      : 1.00, 1.25, 2.02, 2.80
$7.08 : 1.00, 1.18, 2.40, 2.50
$7.11 : 1.20, 1.25, 1.50, 3.16
$7.13 : 1.00, 1.15, 2.48, 2.50
$7.14 : 1.02, 1.12, 2.50, 2.50
      : 1.19, 1.25, 1.50, 3.20
$7.20 : 0.80, 1.50, 2.40, 2.50
      : 1.00, 1.20, 2.00, 3.00
      : 1.00, 1.50, 1.50, 3.20
$7.25 : 0.80, 1.45, 2.50, 2.50
$7.26 : 0.75, 1.76, 2.00, 2.75
$7.28 : 0.70, 2.00, 2.08, 2.50
      : 1.00, 1.28, 1.75, 3.25
```

```
$7.29 : 1.00, 1.25, 1.80, 3.24
$7.35 : 0.70, 1.75, 2.40, 2.50
      : 1.00, 1.05, 2.50, 2.80
      : 1.20, 1.25, 1.40, 3.50
$7.37 : 0.67, 2.00, 2.20, 2.50
$7.47 : 0.90, 1.25, 2.00, 3.32
$7.50 : 1.00, 1.00, 2.50, 3.00
$7.52 : 0.64, 1.88, 2.50, 2.50
$7.56 : 0.80, 1.26, 2.50, 3.00
      : 0.96, 1.25, 1.75, 3.60
      : 1.12, 1.25, 1.44, 3.75
      : 1.25, 1.25, 1.28, 3.78
$7.62 : 1.00, 1.27, 1.60, 3.75
$7.65 : 0.60, 2.00, 2.50, 2.55
      : 0.75, 1.50, 2.00, 3.40
      : 1.00, 1.00, 2.25, 3.40
      : 1.00, 1.20, 1.70, 3.75
$7.67 : 0.59, 2.08, 2.50, 2.50
$7.70 : 1.00, 1.00, 2.20, 3.50
      : 1.00, 1.25, 1.60, 3.85
$7.74 : 0.75, 1.29, 2.50, 3.20
      : 0.80, 1.25, 2.25, 3.44
      : 1.20, 1.25, 1.29, 4.00
$7.77 : 0.80, 1.25, 2.22, 3.50
$7.79 : 0.76, 1.25, 2.50, 3.28
$7.80 : 0.75, 1.25, 2.60, 3.20
      : 1.00, 1.30, 1.50, 4.00
$7.82 : 0.92, 1.00, 2.50, 3.40
$7.83 : 0.58, 2.00, 2.25, 3.00
$7.86 : 0.80, 1.31, 2.00, 3.75
$7.92 : 0.72, 1.25, 2.75, 3.20
      : 0.75, 1.25, 2.40, 3.52
      : 0.90, 1.00, 2.50, 3.52
$8.00 : 1.00, 1.00, 2.00, 4.00
$8.01 : 0.75, 1.20, 2.50, 3.56
$8.03 : 0.88, 1.00, 2.50, 3.65
$8.10 : 0.50, 2.40, 2.50, 2.70
      : 0.60, 1.50, 3.00, 3.00
      : 0.75, 1.20, 2.40, 3.75
      : 0.75, 1.35, 2.00, 4.00
      : 0.80, 1.25, 2.00, 4.05
$8.12 : 0.50, 2.32, 2.50, 2.80
$8.16 : 0.85, 1.00, 2.56, 3.75
$8.19 : 0.84, 1.00, 2.60, 3.75
      : 1.04, 1.25, 1.40, 4.50
$8.22 : 0.48, 2.50, 2.50, 2.74
$8.25 : 0.50, 2.00, 2.75, 3.00
```

```
$8.28 : 0.48, 2.30, 2.50, 3.00
      : 0.60, 1.50, 2.50, 3.68
      : 0.69, 1.25, 2.50, 3.84
$8.33 : 0.70, 1.25, 2.38, 4.00
      : 0.85, 0.98, 2.50, 4.00
      : 0.85, 1.25, 1.75, 4.48
$8.36 : 0.76, 1.10, 2.50, 4.00
$8.37 : 0.62, 1.50, 2.25, 4.00
$8.40 : 0.50, 2.00, 2.40, 3.50
      : 0.70, 1.20, 2.50, 4.00
$8.45 : 0.65, 1.30, 2.50, 4.00
$8.46 : 0.64, 1.25, 2.82, 3.75
      : 1.00, 1.25, 1.41, 4.80
$8.52 : 0.60, 1.42, 2.50, 4.00
$8.55 : 0.50, 1.90, 2.40, 3.75
      : 0.50, 2.00, 2.25, 3.80
      : 0.75, 1.00, 3.00, 3.80
      : 0.80, 1.50, 1.50, 4.75
      : 1.00, 1.00, 1.80, 4.75
$8.60 : 0.80, 1.00, 2.50, 4.30
$8.64 : 0.50, 1.80, 2.50, 3.84
      : 0.54, 1.60, 2.50, 4.00
      : 0.64, 1.50, 2.00, 4.50
      : 1.00, 1.20, 1.44, 5.00
$8.67 : 0.50, 1.70, 2.72, 3.75
$8.69 : 0.79, 1.00, 2.50, 4.40
$8.73 : 0.60, 1.25, 3.00, 3.88
$8.75 : 0.50, 1.75, 2.50, 4.00
      : 1.00, 1.00, 1.75, 5.00
$8.76 : 0.80, 1.46, 1.50, 5.00
$8.78 : 0.64, 1.25, 2.50, 4.39
$8.82 : 0.42, 2.40, 2.50, 3.50
      : 0.70, 1.12, 2.50, 4.50
      : 0.75, 1.25, 1.92, 4.90
      : 0.75, 1.47, 1.60, 5.00
      : 1.12, 1.20, 1.25, 5.25
$8.85 : 0.40, 2.50, 2.95, 3.00
$8.88 : 0.75, 1.28, 1.85, 5.00
$8.91 : 0.45, 2.00, 2.50, 3.96
      : 0.81, 1.10, 2.00, 5.00
$8.94 : 0.50, 1.49, 3.20, 3.75
$8.96 : 0.40, 2.50, 2.56, 3.50
$9.00 : 0.40, 2.50, 2.50, 3.60
      : 0.50, 1.50, 3.00, 4.00
      : 0.50, 2.00, 2.00, 4.50
$9.02 : 0.82, 1.00, 2.20, 5.00
$9.03 : 0.43, 2.10, 2.50, 4.00
      : 0.48, 1.75, 2.50, 4.30
```

```
$9.12 : 0.60, 1.52, 2.00, 5.00
$9.18 : 0.48, 1.70, 2.50, 4.50
      : 0.68, 1.00, 3.00, 4.50
$9.20 : 0.40, 2.30, 2.50, 4.00
      : 0.50, 1.60, 2.50, 4.60
$9.23 : 1.00, 1.25, 1.30, 5.68
$9.24 : 0.64, 1.00, 3.75, 3.85
$9.27 : 0.40, 2.25, 2.50, 4.12
$9.35 : 0.40, 2.20, 2.50, 4.25
      : 0.85, 1.00, 2.00, 5.50
$9.36 : 0.50, 1.56, 2.50, 4.80
      : 0.52, 1.25, 3.75, 3.84
      : 0.65, 0.96, 3.75, 4.00
$9.38 : 0.70, 1.00, 2.68, 5.00
$9.45 : 0.35, 2.50, 3.00, 3.60
      : 0.40, 1.80, 3.50, 3.75
      : 0.45, 1.50, 3.50, 4.00
      : 0.75, 0.90, 2.80, 5.00
      : 0.80, 0.90, 2.50, 5.25
$9.48 : 0.50, 1.28, 3.75, 3.95
      : 0.50, 1.58, 2.40, 5.00
$9.54 : 0.75, 0.80, 3.75, 4.24
$9.57 : 0.75, 1.00, 2.32, 5.50
$9.59 : 0.35, 2.50, 2.74, 4.00
$9.60 : 0.60, 1.00, 4.00, 4.00
      : 0.80, 0.80, 3.00, 5.00
      : 1.00, 1.00, 1.60, 6.00
$9.62 : 0.37, 2.00, 3.25, 4.00
$9.63 : 0.50, 1.25, 3.60, 4.28
      : 0.60, 1.00, 3.75, 4.28
$9.66 : 0.50, 1.40, 2.76, 5.00
      : 0.80, 1.25, 1.61, 6.00
$9.68 : 0.80, 0.88, 2.50, 5.50
$9.69 : 0.34, 2.50, 2.85, 4.00
      : 0.40, 2.04, 2.50, 4.75
$9.72 : 0.72, 1.50, 1.50, 6.00
$9.75 : 1.00, 1.20, 1.30, 6.25
$9.78 : 0.40, 1.63, 3.75, 4.00
$9.80 : 0.40, 2.00, 2.50, 4.90
      : 0.70, 1.00, 2.50, 5.60
$9.81 : 0.50, 1.20, 3.75, 4.36
$9.86 : 0.80, 1.36, 1.45, 6.25
      : 0.85, 1.16, 1.60, 6.25
$9.87 : 0.47, 1.40, 3.00, 5.00
      : 0.94, 1.00, 1.68, 6.25
$9.89 : 0.92, 1.00, 1.72, 6.25
$9.90 : 0.50, 1.25, 3.20, 4.95
      : 0.50, 1.50, 2.40, 5.50
      : 0.60, 1.00, 3.30, 5.00
```

```
        : 0.75, 0.75, 4.00, 4.40
        : 0.80, 1.20, 1.65, 6.25
$9.92 : 0.32, 2.50, 3.10, 4.00
$9.99 : 0.50, 1.44, 2.50, 5.55
        : 0.74, 0.75, 4.00, 4.50
        : 0.74, 1.00, 2.25, 6.00
        : 0.74, 1.20, 1.80, 6.25
183 solutions.
```

The printing out of the counter *c* is not shown.

When you look at these results, you can answer the questions about them. The most sets of answers for one total is five, and five totals have this many sets of answers: $8.10, $8.55, $8.82, $9.45, and $9.90. One of the sets of answers that total $9.90 has two prices that are the same: 0.75, 0.75, 4.00, 4.40; so does one of the sets of answers for $8.55: 1.00, 1.00, 1.80, 4.75. There are others. The total having the same price in three different sets of answers is $9.99; the recurring price is 0.74.

APPENDIX:

CONVERTING PROGRAMS TO APPLESOFT BASIC

The program modifications presented in this appendix allow you to convert all of the BASIC programs in this book to Applesoft BASIC so that you can run them on an Apple II. In general, the following five points need to be addressed:

- Applesoft BASIC does not have the *PRINT USING* construct.
- Applesoft BASIC does not have double-precision variables.
- Due to floating-point errors, exponentiation produces a different answer than multiplication would.
- Applesoft BASIC does not permit variable names containing embedded reserved words.
- Applesoft BASIC "sees" only the first two letters of a variable name.

The run time for each program on an Apple IIc is included with each program.

PUZZLE 1

In converting the first BASIC program, you need to change the variable *TOP* to *TP*. As mentioned, Applesoft does not permit variable names with embedded reserved words and changes *TOP* to *TO P*.

Also, Applesoft BASIC does not print extra spaces around numbers, as does GWBASIC. So change line 70 to:

```
70  IF SUM = 10000 THEN PRINT "Found a sequence from ";I;" to ";
TOP - 1;" inclusive."
```

The program runs in 11 minutes, 25 seconds.
In the second BASIC program, change the spacing in line 50 to:

```
50  IF SUM = 10000 THEN PRINT "Found a sequence from "; FIRST;
" to "; I; " inclusive."
```

The program runs in 2 minutes, 30 seconds.

PUZZLE 2

Because Applesoft BASIC does not have double-precision variables, line 20 is not present, and all of the double-precision symbols (#) become simple variables. However, it has sufficient accuracy for 9999^2, which is enough to prove the condition, as explained in the solution to this puzzle.

Applesoft BASIC cannot handle numbers as large as $I*I*I$ and $I*I*I*I$ would become, so only I and $I*I$ are printed.

This program runs in 5 minutes, 30 seconds.

```
10 FOR I = 1000 TO 9999
30 LASTIDIGIT = i - 10 * INT (i / 10)
40 IF LASTIDIGIT = 1 OR LASTIDIGIT = 5 OR LASTIDIGIT = 6 THEN 60
50 GOTO 100
60 SQUARE = I * I
70 SQMOD = SQUARE - INT(SQUARE / 10000) * 10000
80 IF ABS(I - SQMOD) > .00001 THEN 100
90 PRINT " i = "; I; "; i^2 = "; I * I
100 NEXT I
```

PUZZLE 3

Omit line 10 (Applesoft BASIC does not have the *DEFINT* statement) and all the pound signs.

Because of the lack of significance beyond the first two characters of variable names and the restriction against embedded keywords, finding descriptive names is more difficult in Applesoft BASIC. Both the variables *NUMERATORS* and *ITERATIONS* contain reserved words (two instances each of *AT*, *TO*, and *ON*), so change the names of these variables to *N* and *I*, respectively.

Because of floating-point arithmetic inaccuracies, X^3 does not produce the same answer as $X*X*X$. Replace X^3 with $X*X*X$ in line 50, and Y^3 with $Y*Y*Y$ in line 80. In line 130, replace $6*A^3$ with $A*A*A*6$. Be aware that $6*A*A*A$ *THEN* parses incorrectly.

The program runs in 2 minutes, 40 seconds.

PUZZLE 4

SUMAB and *SUMSQ* are the same to Applesoft BASIC, so change the latter to *SSQ*.

Applesoft BASIC does not have the *MOD* operator, so change line 1030 to this:

```
1030 PRINT CHR$ (PASSVAL - INT(PASSVAL/10) * 10 + 48);
```

The program runs in 4 minutes, 30 seconds.

PUZZLE 5

PARTSUM and *PART4THS* both are *PA* to Applesoft BASIC, so change these names to *PSUM* and *P4THS*.

Applesoft BASIC has no *PRINT USING* construct, so change lines 170 and 180 to:

```
170     PRINT H; "^4 + "; I; "^4 + "; J; "^4 + ";
180     PRINT K; "^4"
```

The program runs in 2 minutes, 20 seconds.

PUZZLE 6

Change X^3 and Y^3 to $X*X*X$ and $Y*Y*Y$. Rename the variable *SECOND* to *SECND* (because it contains the reserved word *ON*), and remove the *PRINT USING*.

The program runs in 18 minutes, 10 seconds.

PUZZLE 7

Line 20 needs extra spaces so that it does not print, for example, "... of3elements:"

Because only the first two characters of a variable name are significant in Applesoft BASIC, the variable names *SUM1* and *SUM2* are seen as the same. So change these to *S1UM* and *S2UM* (or two other names with a difference in the first two characters).

Because of floating-point arithmetic inaccuracies, X^2 does not produce the same answer as $X*X$. You need to use multiplication in lines 60 and 90 instead of exponentiation so that *S1UM* and *S2UM* become equal. Using an improper comparison has the potential for problems. If the test at line 110 fails, the loop essentially becomes infinite.

Remove the *PRINT USING* construct from lines 160, 180, 200, and 220. Line 160, for example, becomes:

```
160   PRINT X; "^2 + ";
```

Applesoft BASIC always executes a loop at least once, so add a test to skip over lines 190 to 210 when $(SERIES + 1)/2 + 1$ is greater than $SERIES - 1$ (which happens when *SERIES* is 3).

This program runs in 13 seconds.

```
10 FOR SERIES = 3 TO 11 STEP 2
20   PRINT "For a series of "; SERIES; " elements:"
30   TRYNUM = 0
40   S1UM = 0 : S2UM = 0
50   FOR X = TRYNUM + 1 TO TRYNUM + (SERIES+1)/2
```

```
60    S1UM = S1UM + X * X
70   NEXT X
80   FOR X = TRYNUM + (SERIES + 1) / 2 + 1 TO TRYNUM + SERIES
90    S2UM = S2UM + X * X
100   NEXT X
110   IF S1UM = S2UM THEN 140
120    TRYNUM = TRYNUM + 1
130    GOTO 40
140   PRINT
150   FOR X = TRYNUM + 1 TO TRYNUM + (SERIES + 1) / 2 - 1
160    PRINT X; "^2 + ";
170   NEXT X
180   PRINT X; "^2 = ";
185   IF (SERIES + 1) / 2 + 1 > SERIES - 1 THEN X
= TRYNUM + SERIES : GOTO 220
190   FOR X = TRYNUM + (SERIES + 1) / 2 + 1 TO TRYNUM + SERIES - 1
200    PRINT X; "^2 + ";
210   NEXT X
220   PRINT X; "^2";
230   PRINT "(Total = "; S1UM; ")";
240  NEXT SERIES
```

PUZZLE 8

Use only the second version, the one preceded by the sentence, "If your version of BASIC does not have the *PRINT USING* construct, you can substitute this:"

The program runs in 39 seconds.

PUZZLE 9

Because of embedded reserved words, *TOS* would become *TO S* and *SAVED* would become *SAVE D*. I suggest changing *TOS* to *J* and *SAVED* to *SVD*.

In line 400, I dropped the space in front of the zero so that everything would line up nicely.

Since Applesoft BASIC does not have *PRINT USING*, lines 410 and 420 are not necessary.

The program runs in 7 minutes, 35 seconds.

PUZZLE 10

Remove statement 10 and the *PRINT USING* construct of line 210 so that it reads:

```
210   C = C + 1 : PRINT SQUARE;
```

No other changes are needed.
The program runs in 20 minutes, 30 seconds.

PUZZLE 11

Remove the *PRINT USING* constructs. No other changes are needed for this program.

The first BASIC program runs in 11 minutes, 10 seconds and the second in 16 minutes, 40 seconds.

PUZZLE 12

Remove the *PRINT USING* constructs. No other changes are needed for this program.

The program runs in 7 seconds.

PUZZLE 13

Remove statement 10 and the *PRINT USING* constructs. No other changes are needed. The results do not print with as much accuracy as is shown in the solution to the puzzle.

The program takes 25 seconds for a deck of 52.

PUZZLE 14

The variables *ORIGLEN*, *NONINTEGER*, and *DONE* contain embedded reserved words. So change these variables to *OL*, *NN*, and *DN*, respectively.

Change line 30 to read:

```
30 INPUT "";A$
```

Line 570 formats the numbers so that they don't break across the line on an 80-column screen. You can remove that statement.

The program takes 40 seconds with input of seven 7s, and 3 seconds with input of the number 22.

PUZZLE 15

Remove the *PRINT USING* constructs. No other changes are needed for this program.

The program runs in 38 minutes, 45 seconds.

Michael Wiesenberg

Michael Wiesenberg is the creator of *Computer Calisthenics*, the popular column in *A+* magazine. He has written articles on a variety of computer-related topics for *Dr. Dobb's Journal*, *MicroTimes*, *Compute!*, *inCider*, and *Desktop Publishing*, as well as for *The San Francisco Chronicle* and *The San Jose Mercury-News*. He is co-author (with Frederic Davis and John Barry) of *Desktop Publishing*, published in 1986 by Dow Jones-Irwin. Michael Wiesenberg lives in Palo Alto, California.

The manuscript for this book was prepared and submitted to
Microsoft Press in electronic form. Text files were processed
and formatted using Microsoft Word.
Cover design by Becker Design Associates
Interior text design by Microsoft Press
Principal typographer: Russell H. Steele
Text composition by Microsoft Press in Baskerville
with display in Helvetica Bold Condensed,
using the Magna composition system and the
Mergenthaler Linotron 202 digital phototypesetter.